BISON
BOOKS

LAW
WEST OF
FORT SMITH

A History of Frontier Justice in
the Indian Territory, 1834-1896

by Glenn Shirley

Illustrated with Photographs

UNIVERSITY OF NEBRASKA PRESS
LINCOLN/LONDON

FOR THE PEOPLE, LIVING AND DEAD,
WHO SAW THE LAW COME WEST OF FORT SMITH

PREFACE

Most works of Western American history and lore tell of the acts of men performed within the law, detailing their lives that made ours better by their living. We like to exult in our American greatness, particularly the resounding booms of the Southwest. This is good. But too often we fail to make sober investigation into how these things came about and the reason for our being here in a state of opulence and good repute. We shy from the fact that all history is crowded with deeds of lawlessness; but without recording these, the complete history of an era or the subject dealt with cannot be written.

Crime is sordid; dragging it from the grave doesn't better its reputation. It is not done here to perpetuate the infamy of men who transgressed the law. In *Law West of Fort Smith* I have written a full account of the lawless conditions on our last and wildest frontier, and how a lone federal judge became a potent influence in the regulation of affairs that brought order out of chaos in a vast section of country. By the same token, I have preserved the gallant acts of the quiet men with rifles and six-shooters who aided him in the legal side of the controversy.

Ignoring the efforts of such officials and portraying criminals as picturesque figures, unfortunately, is an old and shameful practice. Robin Hood slants have been given atrocious careers. Homicidal exhibitionists like Jesse James and Billy the Kid have been painted as good men who got their thinking twisted because they were victims of passion and mistaken loyalty, or were sinned against by society, and an industrious school of fiction has embroidered this theme with lariats and rattlesnakes and lies. In the same way, or simply out of thin air, illusions have been built around the gangster of the Oklahoma frontier; but a little serious consideration of the facts shows that here, too, he prevailed only through illegal acts, continuous cruelty, and brutality.

The land on which he thrived was all that territory west of Fort Smith, Arkansas, from Texas and Kansas to Colorado and no man's land, called "Indian country." Over it roamed the native red man, and to it in the 1830's came the Five Civilized Tribes, who brought their own laws and tribal courts.

But the Indian courts took no cognizance of the white man. Tribal laws had no application. The white intruder fell directly under the laws of the United States—then a vague and distant thing in this land now called Oklahoma.

What really happened?

Soldiers of fortune rode the plains. The cattle and horse thief, the prostitute, the desperado, the whisky peddler—all sought refuge where there was no "white man's court" and no law under which they could be extradited to the state or territory where they had committed their crimes.

The Civil War wrecked the peace of the Five Tribes. Its aftermath was a maelstrom of racial hatred and unbridled vice. Rape, robbery, and pillage became common offenses. Killers traveled in gangs.

Some of these outlaws, like the Daltons, Bill Powers, Dick Broadwell, and Henry Starr, were hard livers who turned to a life of outlawry with little effort. A few, like Jim Reed and Belle Starr, were products of the war.

Others were like Ned Christie, Smoker Mankiller, John Billee, Blue Duck, and Cherokee Bill, whose wanton whim was shedding blood.

Martin Joseph and Jason Labreu were rapists. And many were simply renegades and looters, like Bob Rogers, Jim French, the Cook gang, and the Rufus Buck outlaws.

Their savagery flaunted itself. It seemed that every white man, Negro, and half-breed who entered the country was a criminal in the state from which he had come; that the last thing on his mind at night was thievery and murder, and it was his first thought in the morning. No American frontier ever saw leagues of robbers so desperate, any hands so red with blood. By 1875 this civilization was in the balance. Decent men, red and white alike, cried to the government for protection.

The only court with jurisdiction over the Indian country was the United States Court for the Western District of Arkansas at Fort Smith. To it came Judge Isaac Charles Parker. It fell upon him to rout these gangs of criminals. He was given only two hundred marshals to police nearly seventy-four thousand square miles and sixty thousand people; but he issued warrants for the gangs and number-one bad men and ordered the deputies to bring them in alive—or dead. Sixty-five of these marshals gave their lives in the field in line of duty before they were able to hold the outlaws in check and, in a gratifyingly large number of cases, extinguished them.

A brutally picturesque drama it was—with amazing interludes punctuated by the dull thud of the gallows trap as men, singly, in pairs, or six at a time, were plunged to oblivion. The death penalty was prescribed more often and for more flagrant violations of law than anywhere on the American continent. That Judge Parker's administration was stern to the extreme is attested by the fact that he sentenced 160 men to die and hanged 79 of them.

His court was the most remarkable tribunal in the annals of jurisprudence, the greatest distinctive criminal court in the world; none ever existed with jurisdiction over so great an area, and it was the only trial court in history from the decisions of which there was, for more than fourteen years, no right of appeal. He helped to build, and loved, an empire. He lived only a short time after it crumbled before the march of white aggression.

Certainly no man of his time exerted a greater civilizing influence on this section of the West, and it may almost be said that no other one man could have accomplished the great work that his intellect, strength, and unswerving administration of justice enabled him to do. If it appears that his efforts were fanatical or bloodthirsty, it is well to remember that the times produced this hero. The people owe him a debt of gratitude they should not forget. Even in the town in which he lived and presided with distinction he deserves more than a meager marker in the National Cemetery.

From authentic sources, an accumulation of material resulting from extensive correspondence and research over a ten-year period, this volume is designed to throw light on the real story of why he hanged men, the kind of society he served, and the law that created and destroyed his jurisdiction. As a faithful record of fact, it is offered with the hope that his great service will be better understood by a generation that knows little of our indebtedness to him, and that his example will not only interest but strengthen our faith in and admiration for human courage and unselfish purpose.

GLENN SHIRLEY

Stillwater, Oklahoma

CONTENTS

LAW WEST OF FORT SMITH

I

'JOHN CHILDERS' SOUL HAS GONE TO HELL—'

Deputy United States Marshal James Messler adjusted the noose about the prisoner's neck. He placed the big knot under the left ear in the hollow just back of the jawbone and took up the slack. Then, mopping huge drops of perspiration from his forehead with a soiled bandanna, he stared down the thirteen steps at the two thousand sweating sight-seers who packed the jail yard inside the grim stone walls of abandoned Fort Smith.

Outside, the walls of the fort were lined with hacks, spring wagons, and saddle horses. Many had come on foot. Others had traveled hundreds of miles and had been in town as much as two days, camping on the ground and sleeping at the foot of the scaffold the night before to have ringside places. The whole population, it seemed, along the Arkansas River on the Arkansas border—all colors and sexes, from babes in arms to the halt and graybeard—had turned out to watch, with eager, morbid curiosity, the spectacle of the first human being to die on the newly erected gallows.

It was the afternoon of August 15, 1873. The sun boiled down. There was not even a tiny stir of breeze. The sky was clear except for a small black cloud coming up in the southwest. It crossed the Arkansas, and as Messler adjusted the noose, seemed to pause and hover over the scene.

The crowd waited.

The prisoner was John Childers. He was strong, of muscular build, five feet eleven inches in height, and one hundred sixty pounds in weight. Twenty-four years before this, his last day of life on earth, he had been born on Cowskin Creek in the Cherokee Nation, the son of John Childers, a white man, and Katy Vann, his Cherokee wife. He had spent his childhood in wickedness, and at the time of his arrest was a member of one of the worst bands of brigands and plunderers to infest the widespread "Indian country." His crime was murder, and it had been committed with such cold-blooded viciousness that scarcely one among the many assembled could not recite the revolting details.

Reyburn Wedding was an old man who made his living traveling through the Indian country trading flour and bacon for hides and produce. On the morning of October 14, 1870, Childers met him near Caney Creek below the Kansas line in the Cherokee Nation. A fine black horse that Wedding was driving caught the outlaw's fancy, and he began dickering for a trade. Wedding declined, saying he was not interested in parting with the animal, and drove on.

Childers' face darkened. Deciding to have the horse at any cost, he spurred his pony ahead, overtaking the peddler. Hitching his mount to the tail gate of the wagon, he climbed into the seat beside him.

Together he and Wedding rode on toward Caney Creek, while Childers, according to testimony developed later at his trial, bargained for the horse twenty-seven times, and twenty-seven times Wedding refused. Finally Childers seized the surprised trader by the head, whipped a long knife from his belt, and before Wedding could move to defend himself, stretched the old man across the back of the seat and slashed his throat from ear to ear. Then the outlaw dumped the body in the water, stripped the harness from the horse he coveted, and rode away.

Deputy Marshal Vennoy traced the well-known animal to Childers' home near Klo Kotchka (now Broken Arrow) in the Creek Nation and placed the killer under arrest. He was taken to Van Buren, at that time the location of the federal court, and arraigned before the United States Commissioner on December 2, 1870.

There being no court in session at the time, Childers was ordered held for action of the next grand jury. A few weeks later, he and six other prisoners tunneled their way from the jail and fled to the woods.

The others were soon captured. But Childers returned to his old haunts, joined a renegade gang that was terrorizing the Cherokee and Creek Nations, and succeeded in eluding officers for months.

He might never have been rearrested nor Wedding's death avenged had he not become enamored of a Fort Smith prostitute whom he visited frequently. For $10 the woman confessed the affair to Vennoy and agreed to aid in his capture. One evening, while the fugitive was "reveling in her charms," Vennoy and Deputy Sheriff Joe Peevy entered the room and snapped on the handcuffs.

During the period intervening his escape and capture, Congress had passed an act removing the United States Court for the Western District of Arkansas from Van Buren to Fort Smith.[1] In its new location, on May 15, 1871, a grand jury brought in eleven indictments charging sixteen persons with major offenses and John Childers with murder. He was found guilty on November 11, 1872, and on May 19, 1873, was sentenced to die on the scaffold, the execution date being August 15.[2]

Behind Childers now stood a guard of six deputies headed by

Marshal John Sarber and, at his side, Deputy Messler. As yet no regular hangman had been appointed to carry out the decrees of this court, and Messler, for this occasion, had volunteered his services.

Marshal Sarber faced the prisoner and the mumbling of the crowd quieted down. Slowly he read the death warrant, while Childers puffed a cigar with an air of indifference that had been with him throughout his trial. Witnesses had furnished an alibi. Even after his conviction he had felt confident that he would receive a pardon or commutation. For the criminal class was a power in the Indian country, and strong petitions for executive clemency had been sent to Washington. Perhaps it was the influence brought to bear on the case from southern Kansas, where Wedding had resided, that had caused the attorney general, only a few days before the date of execution, to refuse to interfere. On the trap of the gallows, Childers still exhibited such nonchalance that the hanging might not have been his own, and the crowd stirred restlessly as if impatient at the delay.

Marshal Sarber spoke again, and anxious faces looked in his direction.

"Are there any last words you wish to say, Childers?" asked Sarber.

The killer tossed away his cigar. For the first time since his capture he appeared disturbed.

Finally he broke his silence, and for sixteen minutes he talked. He quibbled at first, then admitted that he had murdered Wedding, but claimed that he should not have been convicted because the prosecution had erred as to the time and date of the offense. It was the only murder he had ever committed alone, he said, and he regretted it and hoped that he would be forgiven. He admitted that the witnesses who had testified that he was sixty miles away when the crime was committed had lied, and he hoped God would forgive them too. Then, looking out over the crowd that was eagerly drinking in his every word, he added:

"My pals and me once swore to help each other, no matter what the circumstances. But they don't seem to be doing anything for me now."

The marshal's voice rose: "If you will give me their names, Childers, I pledge not to hang you now. What is your answer?"

It grew so quiet in the jail yard that the drone of insects in the elms was the only sound. Dust and tobacco smoke hung motionless in the air. The heat was stifling.

The condemned man's gaze, jerking away from Sarber, again flicked over the crowd. Among them he recognized many of his boon companions in crime, but to have turned informer would have violated the morbid code that bound them each to the other.

Instead, he waved them farewell with a general sweep of his hand. To the marshal's offer he replied in a firm, clear voice that all could hear:

"Didn't you say you were going to hang me?"

"Yes," Sarber replied.

"Then," Childers responded coolly, "why in hell don't you!"

Deputy Messler buckled his hands to his sides, while the prisoner offered a short prayer. The black hood was adjusted. Then the marshal gave the signal. The deputy released the bolt, and John Childers' neck tilted curiously to one side as he shot down to the end of the rope.

And at exactly the same moment a remarkable thing happened.

As the door fell from under Childers' feet, a tremendous clap of thunder shook the earth of the enclosure, drowning completely the thudding noise of the cumbrous trap. The black cloud hanging above the fort had seemed innocent enough. From it now shot a bolt of lightning. It struck the frame of the gibbet, shooting a thousand tiny sparks into the air.

"John Childers' soul has gone to hell—I done heerd de chains a-clankin'!" screamed an ashen-faced Negro woman as she hysterically waved her arms and swooned in the center of the throng. Then the cloud burst open and for several minutes rain poured down, soaking the bewildered crowd.

The disposition of Childers' soul, as described by this frantic Negro woman, might be questioned; none present, however, could ever deny the startling phenomenon that attended its violent liberation from his body. The entire proceedings—the grim ritual on the scaffold, the celestial detonation, pyrotechnics, and sudden drenching—filled the spectators with awe.

Those who believed in the supernatural shuddered with fear, fools who had come to mock and jeer at the law never attempted an explanation. Some believed that the fall did not kill Childers; that after being cut down he regained consciousness, climbed over the wall near the gallows, and fled. This story gained such credence that for several years after his execution there were persons who claimed they had seen him in the Indian nations, alive and well.[3]

The facts are that at 2:00 P.M. on that fatal day Deputy Messler pulled the bolt that released the trap; a moment later the ghastly work was done, the cloud had vanished, and all that was left of John Childers hung limp and quivering.

Perhaps the accompanying thunder, lightning, and rain should be interpreted as God's wrathful condemnation of the swelling battle between right and wrong in Oklahoma—the Armageddon of the West. For John Childers was to be the first of more than fourscore convicted felons to die on this gallows for crimes committed in what is now that state.

Nor was the fight to be easily won. It was to rage for more than twenty-one years. For Childers himself, as he stood on the scaffold with the noose around his neck, had revealed the temper of the men who composed the forces of evil when he refused to name his companions in crime and said:

"Didn't you say you were going to hang me? Then why in hell don't you!"

II

LAND OF THE SIX-SHOOTER

The battle to wrest Oklahoma from the host of evil will best be understood if, before entering upon a recital of the same, an explanation is given of the origin of the Fort Smith court and the conditions of the crude period that brought on the circumstances surrounding the execution of John Childers.

The first shadow of the court fell across the Indian country when the Twenty-third Congress, on its last day in session, June 30, 1834, passed the Intercourse Law, placing many restrictions on the relations of the whites and Indians. It was entitled "An Act to Regulate Trade and Intercourse with the Indian Tribes and Preserve Peace on the Frontiers." [1] It described the Indian country as "all that part of the United States west of the Mississippi and not within the States of Missouri or Louisiana or the Territory of Arkansas, also that part of the United States east of the Mississippi and not within any state, to which the Indian title has not been extinguished," [2] and provided "that for the sole purpose of carrying this act into effect, all of that part of the Indian country west of the Mississippi River that is bounded north by the north line of the lands assigned to the Osage Indians, produced (or continued) east to the State of Missouri; west by the Mexican possessions; south by the Red River; and east by the west line of the Territory of Arkansas and the State of Missouri, shall be and hereby is, annexed to the Territory of Arkansas; and that for the purpose aforesaid, the residue of the Indian Country west of the Mississippi River shall be and hereby is annexed to the judicial district of Missouri; and for the purpose aforesaid, the several portions of the Indian Country east of said river shall be, and are hereby severally annexed to the Territory in which they are situated." [3] Thus the section of Indian country that is now Oklahoma and a strip of country fifty miles wide across southern Kansas was made subject to the Western District of Arkansas for judicial purposes, and "so much of the laws of the United States as provides for punishment of crimes committed within any place within the sole or exclusive jurisdiction of the United States shall be in force in the Indian country. PROVIDED, that the same shall not extend to crimes committed by one Indian against the person or property of another Indian." [4]

On June 15, 1836, the Territory of Arkansas was admitted to the Union and the new state made one federal judicial district.[5] A district court was created to consist of one judge, holding at the seat of government of the state at Little Rock two sessions annually, "and he shall, in all things, have and exercise the same jurisdiction and powers which were by law given to the judge of the Kentucky District under an act of September 24, 1789, entitled, 'An Act to Establish the Judicial Courts of the United States.' " The salary of the judge was fixed at $2000 per year, payable quarterly; he was empowered to appoint a clerk who should receive the same fees as the clerk for the Kentucky District; provision was made for the appointment of a district attorney to be paid, in addition to his stated fees, $200 yearly, and the appointment of a marshal "to perform the same duties, be subject to the same regulations and penalties and be entitled to the same fees as are prescribed to the marshal in other districts, and he shall be entitled to $200 annually as compensation for extra services." [6]

On March 1, 1837, Congress approved an act giving the Court of the United States for the District of Arkansas "the same jurisdiction and power in all respects, whatever, that was given to the several district courts of the United States, by an act of Congress entitled, 'An Act to Regulate Trade and Intercourse With the Indian Tribes and Preserve Peace on the Frontiers'," and provided that "the courts of the United States in and for the District of Arkansas be and hereby are vested with the same power and jurisdiction to hear, try, determine and punish all crimes committed within that Indian country designated in the twenty-fourth section of the act to which this is a supplement, and therein and thereby annexed to the Territory of Arkansas as were vested in the courts of the United States for said territory before the same became a state. And for the sole purpose of carrying this act into effect all that Indian country hereunto annexed by the said twenty-fourth section of the act aforesaid to the Territory of Arkansas be, and the same is, annexed to the State of Arkansas." [7]

A military post had been established on the Arkansas near Fort Smith as early as 1817 to preserve order among the Indian tribes. Western Arkansas and eastern Oklahoma were the choice hunting grounds of the Quapaws, Comanches, and Cherokees. The Osages, a proud and insolent people, ranged the country from eastern Missouri south to the Red River and west to the Rocky Mountains. They drove the native tribes from the region, perpetrated outrageous offenses against their people and property, and defied the authority of their own chiefs until the War Department directed General Andrew Jackson, then head of the Southern Division of the United States Army, to establish a fort on the Arkansas near the Osage line and erect, as quickly as possible, a stockade adequate to accommodate a company. [8]

General Jackson communicated his orders to General Thomas A. Smith, commander of the Ninth Military Department of the United States Army at St. Louis, who in turn directed Major S. H. Long to select a suitable spot on the Arkansas border and there erect a military post. The site chosen by Major Long was Belle Point, a sandstone bluff in the forest overlooking the juncture of the Poteau and Arkansas rivers.[9] Here the new fort was constructed,[10] named Cantonment Smith in honor of Thomas A. Smith, renamed Fort Smith; and the first company of troops under the command of Major William Bradford arrived on December 25. Indian hostilities were soon brought under control, and by September, 1819, the warring tribes sat in the first council at Fort Smith and smoked the pipe of peace.

But peace did not last. When Congress organized Arkansas Territory, the Indian country was made one country, and the Indians within the tract were placed under the supervision of the territorial governor. Hostilities again broke out, and the Seventh Infantry was ordered from St. Louis to Fort Smith in February, 1822.[11]

Despite these re-enforcements, the Osages continued their war for control of the territory to the west. White settlers and traders farther up the Arkansas demanded protection, and in April, 1824, with the establishment of Forts Gibson and Towson in the Indian country, the troops were removed to these points. It was not until March 22, 1833, that troops were again stationed at Fort Smith to assist in carrying out Indian treaties and the government's fixed policy of moving the Indian population from east of the Mississippi into their western homes. The following June these troops were ordered to Fort Coffee, farther up the river, and later to Fort Wayne to the north, so that Fort Smith was again unoccupied until 1838.

During this period many people had settled in this section of the Southwest. The Arkansas being navigable for boats of light draught and the only outlet for staple products, the little frontier town became the center of activity. A month before the admission of the Territory as a state, so much pressure had been brought to bear for the erection of a post that would more adequately defend its western border that Congress, by an act approved May 14, 1836, authorized the removal of the garrison at Fort Gibson "to some feasible point that would better accommodate the troops" and "for better defense of the Arkansas frontier," and appropriated $50,000 for a fort to be built at the new point selected.[12] On April 4, 1838, a resolution was passed authorizing the Secretary of War "to take not to exceed $15,000 from the sum appropriated" and purchase a site for a fort at or near the western border of Arkansas.[13] The new site purchased was on the east bank of the river at the head of what is now Garrison Avenue. Here a new and more substantial fort was constructed and the modern city of Fort Smith developed.

The new fort was in the shape of a pentagon enclosed by heavy walls of stone blasted from the bluff at Belle Point. Loopholes four feet apart were provided for musketry. Cannon bastions were built on the northeast and southeast corners and on the south face, the latter being used as a powder magazine. Inside were two large two-story brick buildings to quarter officers and a barracks building for enlisted personnel. A small building was erected near the northeast wall for a guardhouse, and four blockhouses of stone, to be mounted with heavy artillery, were under construction when General Zachary Taylor, in command of the military forces of the United States in the Southwest, arrived in 1842.[14]

By this year most of the Indians composing the Five Civilized Tribes had been settled in Oklahoma and the warring Osages routed. General Taylor thought the government was wasting money. He believed he could protect the Arkansas frontier from the tricks of the half-civilized Indians and allay the fears of the white citizens without an expensive fortification, and opposed an appropriation for further construction.

Two of the blockhouses were abandoned at their foundation. The others were so near completion that they were finished, not to accommodate heavy ordnance as originally intended, but as ordinary stone buildings. One was used by the quartermaster, the other as a commissary.[15] The annexation of Texas to the United States in 1845 was highly displeasing to the Mexican government, which still entertained hope of reconquering the country despite the ten years of independence; and with the outbreak of hostilities in the Mexican War, General Taylor was relieved of command at Fort Smith and ordered to take possession of the country to the Rio Grande.[16]

Meanwhile the town itself had boomed as a commercial point. Extensive trade with the Indians attracted the attention of the entire Southwest.[17] In 1849 Fort Smith became the jumping-off place for numerous companies en route to the California gold fields; and later, when John Butterfield launched his project to unite the East and the West by means of an overland mail line, Fort Smith became an important center on the stage routes,[18] and began demanding railroad connection with the settled areas west of the Mississippi River.

This increase of population on the border of the Indian country increased the business of the federal court. By an act approved March 3, 1851, Congress divided Arkansas into two districts, the Western District embracing Benton, Washington, Crawford, Franklin, Johnson, Madison, Carroll, Scott, and Polk counties, and "all that part of the Indian country within the present judicial district of Arkansas."[19] The court seat was at Van Buren, five miles down the river, and by virtue of the same act, the new court was presided over by Judge Daniel Ringo, who was also judge of the Eastern District of Arkansas. By an amendment approved March 27, 1854, "offenders convicted in the Western District of Arkansas and punishable by confinement at hard labor in the penitentiary" could be sentenced by the court "to the Penitentiary House in the Eastern District of Arkansas the same as if the Penitentiary House was in the Western District of Arkansas"; and by the same amendment the counties of Sevier and Sebastian, of which Fort Smith was the county seat, were added to the Western District.[20]

The court had tremendous power, but Judge Ringo made little use of it. Already the echoes of civil war rolled close to the border. In the Indian country the Five Tribes split into factions, most of them joining the South.[21] The Federal troops at Fort Smith found themselves sandwiched between a handful of Northern sympathizers and a large majority of Southern advocates. A thousand regulars of the United States Army were ordered dispatched to Fort Smith immediately to augment the garrison.[22] On the same day, April 24, 1861, three thousand state troops under the command of Colonel Solon Borland seized and occupied the United States post,[23] and on May 6 Arkansas seceded from the Union. On September 3, 1863, the fort was recaptured for the North by Brigadier General James C. Blount and used as one of the centers from which Federal troops were sent to ravage the Indian country until the end of hostilities.[24] In September, 1871, Fort Smith was again abandoned, the soldiers removed to Fort Gibson, and the property transferred from the War Department to control of the Department of the Interior and placed in charge of the Marshal for the Western District of Arkansas.

To what extent the United States court functioned during the war is not known. Judge Ringo remained on the bench until 1860, when, because of his sympathy with the South, he resigned and turned over all court records to his clerk, John B. Ogden. He was then appointed by President Davis of the Confederacy as judge of the Confederate court established at Helena, Arkansas.[25] In February, 1863, a company of Federal soldiers raided Van Buren. The courthouse was burned and the records destroyed.

The court continued to function at Van Buren from 1865 to 1871, but most of the cases filed were for treason and confiscation of enemy's property, and the majority of these were "nolle prosequi" because of the general pardon issued by the President. On March 3, 1871, Congress approved an act moving the offices of the judge, marshal, district attorney, and clerk of the court to Fort Smith.[26] By the same act "so much of the act of March 3, 1851, as gives the judge of the Eastern District of Arkansas jurisdiction over the Western District of said state, be and hereby is repealed." Henry J. Caldwell, then judge of the Eastern District of Arkansas at Little Rock, was appointed by President Grant as the first judge of the Western District court for its exclusive use.

Judge Caldwell opened the first session of court in Fort Smith in the second story of an old brick building at the corner of Second and A streets in May, 1871. John Childers was indicted for murder. His trial was begun, and was continued to the November term as one of the first cases on the November docket. On the night of November 13 this building burned. An adjournment was taken to November 14 at the Sebastian County Circuit Court room, where a two-day session was held. Marshal Logan H. Roots then received permission from the Department of the Interior to open the large brick building within the garrison enclosure that had been used as a soldiers' barracks. In this building Childers' trial continued to its successful conclusion, and he was sentenced as the first man to die inside the walls of the abandoned military post.[27]

In 1872 Caldwell was succeeded by an officious young lawyer named William Story. Story was a product of the "carpetbag" rule of the Reconstruction Period, and a man of little character, who somehow wangled the appointment from President Grant. He served less than fourteen months, and his tenure was attended by incompetency and corruption. Although court costs for the period ran into the fabulous sum of $400,000, few cases were ever tried. Marshal Roots was removed from office. Marshal John Sarber, who succeeded Roots, made little effort to improve conditions. Few arrests were made. Certificates issued witnesses and jurors for services went unpaid, and many who were subpoenaed from distant points on the frontier were forced to sell their personal effects to pay their expenses and walk home. Often important witnesses who became disgusted with the situation and left Fort Smith before their funds were depleted were sent after by the court and thrown in jail. District Attorney Newton J. Temple was summoned to Washington as a witness before the Judiciary Committee, and although no charges were made against him he was requested to resign. A strong case of bribery, however, was made against Judge Story, and in June, 1874, he resigned to avoid impeachment proceedings.[28] The vacancy caused by the resignation of Temple was filled by President Grant appointing Judge William H. H. Clayton of the Arkansas First Judicial Circuit; and upon instructions from Washington,[29] Judge Caldwell, from the Eastern District of Arkansas, was ordered to come to Fort Smith and preside over the court during the November term and until the vacancy could be filled.

There was strong sentiment in Washington in favor of abolishing the court at that time, but a new threat had thrust itself into the Oklahoma situation.

The Five Tribes had been given the area for their exclusive use at the time of their removal from east of the Mississippi, and the Intercourse Law had been passed to insure them federal protection. In 1866, as penalty for their alliance with the Confederacy, they were compelled to cede the western half of their lands to the Plains tribes.[30] On these scattered reservations were settled the roving, half-savage Cheyenne and Arapaho, Wichita-Caddo, Kaw, Tonkawa, Ponca, Otoe-Missouria, Pawnee, Iowa, Kickapoo, Sac and Fox, Potawatomie-Shawnee, Osage, Kiowa, Comanche, and Apache.

Into this section also came the cattlemen. Already Texas drovers had trailed more than a million longhorns across the Indian country to railhead shipping points in Kansas.[31] The Intercourse Law prohibited the grazing of livestock in the Indian country under penalty of a one-dollar fine per head of stock so grazed; but the law was difficult to enforce, and the Five Tribes had permitted this transient invasion when paid for the right to graze these herds while getting them ready for market. Many cattlemen had moved onto the free range in the central part of the territory—an area still held by the government and not given to any tribe, called the "Unassigned Lands."

In the eastern half of the country steel rails were fingering south and west. The Atlantic and Pacific Railroad had crossed the Missouri border and built as far as Vinita, Cherokee Nation, in 1871. The Missouri, Kansas and Texas, with evident expectation that large herds would be trailed through from Texas rather than taken on the longer drives to shipping points in central and western Kansas, had built to a point south of Muskogee in the Creek Nation and constructed large cattle-loading yards. Muskogee was a terminus settlement of tents, shacks, and shanties where the vicious element of the country congregated, as it did in the new towns that sprang up overnight along the lines of the western railways built across the Great Plains in Kansas and Nebraska during this same period.

J. H. Beadle,[32] a Cincinnati newspaper correspondent, who visited the "end of the track" of the Missouri-Kansas-Texas Railway at Muskogee, reported the following conditions:

Of the town proper, the majority of the citizens were negroes, with them a few whites of doubtful "rep" and perhaps a dozen Indians. The negroes were formerly slaves to the Indians, but slavery here was never severe, and they are little more their own masters than they were before. They earned a precarious subsistence, the women by washing and the men by teaming and chopping, and all were sunk deep, deep in poverty and ignorance.

Here, as in Vinita, I saw no farms, no signs of cultivation. The Indians live off the railroads, in the timber and along the streams. Around the town, far as the eye can reach, extend fertile prairies of rich green rivaling Ohio meadows in May, while five miles northeast a heavy line of timber marks the course of the Arkansas. Muscogee, or, if spelled as pronounced, Mooskokee, is the aboriginal name for the tribe we call the Creeks, and, having decided to thoroughly inspect these Indian sovereignties, and their relations with the General Government, we begin with these:

"Brad Collins is on a big spree, ain't he?"

"You bet he's chargin'!"

"Killed anybody yet?"

"No, only had one fuss. Him and two other Cherokees went into the car last night with cocked six-shooters and scared some eastern fellers darned near to death."

"Mind the time he shot that ar marshal?"

"I reckon! Killed him right in front of this car. Shot him twice afore. Fetched him dead that time. Then came in next day and give himself up. Tuck him down to Fort Smith and turned him loose in a little while. Lord, that court don't amount to nothin'."

"Marshal's got a good thing, though."

"I see you; best place to make money in the United States. These deputies are the biggest rascals in the country. That court is a disgrace to the American people. 'Ll ruin us here yet."

Such was the conversation we heard our second morning at the table of the dining-car in Muscogee. It was anything but encouraging to a man of peaceful proclivities. A few days after, I had my first view of this somewhat notorious Brad Collins. I was sitting in the tent of an old Cherokee woman, listening to her account of the expulsion from the "old Nation in Geawgey" when shots were heard not far off and an athletic, rosy-featured young man came running by the tent with a pistol in his hand. The old woman merely said, "Brad's got his shooter; there's a fuss some'ers," and went out for a look. It proved to be nothing but some freedmen practicing on a stray hog, a wanderer from the Creek farms, which they brought down after a dozen shots! Collins walked back with a marked air of disappointment, muttering, "If I couldn't hit a hog first shot, I'd throw away my pistol." And the old lady entertained me by his story which has since been verified by others. He is nearly white, an outcast from the Cherokee Nation, a smuggler of whiskey, a desperado and a dead shot. It is said that he has been known to throw a pistol in the air, causing it to make a half dozen turns, catch it as it fell, bring it instantly to level and hit an apple at thirty paces. He is reported to be "quick on the trigger" and that all the other "shootists" in the country have an awe of him. He is known to have killed three men and was then under bond of one thousand dollars to appear in the May term of the Federal Court in Fort Smith for shooting at a United States marshal with intent to kill. Many excuse him in the case where he actually killed a marshal, as it was a private quarrel in which both had sworn to "shoot on sight." Associated with him were a dozen or more young "White Cherokees," who were suspected of being robbers, and known to be drunkards and gamblers. A dozen such men can do the cause of Cherokee independence and nationality more harm than all the Rosses and Downings and their able compeers can do it good. . . .

The records are simply horrible. During the few weeks that the terminus and stage offices were at Muscogee and Gibson, sixteen murders were committed at those two places, and, in a very short time, five more were killed at the next terminus. One man was shot all to pieces just in front of the dining-car at Muscogee, and another had his throat cut at night, almost in the middle of the town. . . . A few days after our arrival, a Texan reached Canadian Station with the proceeds of a cattle sale. . . . He was seen that night at 10 o'clock, drunk and generous with his money; a few days after his body was washed ashore some miles down the Canadian. . . .

Other terminus towns were Pryor Creek, Gibson Station, and Perryville. While the records of all were bloody, Muskogee and Gibson Station were the worst. A half-dozen other railroad-building projects had been launched by the government under Indian opposition, and other terminus towns were in the making.

A great flood of whites connected with railroad-building were entered under the classification of "traders."[33] Even hotel-keepers, livery-stable operators, and barbers were permitted to carry on business in the country so long as they obtained a federal license and paid a tax to the tribal treasuries, and their presence was protected by the government. The United States Indian Office held that legal white residents of railroad towns could sell or bequeath the right of occupancy to business or resident lots to other white men, and merchants obtained business locations and opened stores supplying everything from saddles, carbines, and wagon tongues to kitchen knives, calico dresses, sunbonnets, tobacco, and snuff.

On the other hand any attempt to settle on Indian land, to mark out boundaries, or make surveys was punishable by a fine of $1000. No purchase of land from an Indian was valid, and in addition a fine of $1000 was provided for such offenses. Many avoided this law by leasing land from the Indian year after year until they virtually possessed it. Others married Indian women. Thus they became members of the tribes and entitled to all rights to hold land and engage in business as though they themselves were of Indian blood.

This march of civilization and primitive condition of the country attracted a horde of riffraff, the refuse of humanity.[34] There were no extradition laws effective by which a criminal entering the area could be removed to answer for his offense elsewhere, and the country became infested with hundreds of fugitives from justice. Many of this type married among the Indians, and the half-breed was reputed to be a product "inheriting the bad traits of both races and the good ones of neither." There was also a large infusion of Negro blood emanating from the slaves brought in by the Cherokees and freed following the Civil War, and these mixed-bloods seemed little disposed toward law and order.

Each tribe had its own sovereign government, modeled after the government in Washington, with a legislative, an executive, and a judicial branch. Their statute laws, courts, and tribal procedure were much like the white man's courts. They had Indian lawyers and judges. There were few intricacies and technicalities, and they dispensed a grim but highly efficient brand of aboriginal punishment. Each tribe had its groups of Light Horse (Indian police), but their authority extended only over Indian citizens. There was little safety for the whites who were in the country legally. Every man protected his own property and right to do business under tribal sanction. Sordid crimes were committed upon lone travelers and against women and children. Many of the outlaws banded together and terrified the settlements, robbed the railroads and freight caravans and stage lines, and made wild forays into the border states of Texas, Kansas, and Missouri. And the situation had grown doubly worse under Judge Story.

The Fort Smith *New Era* observed in 1872: "The Indian country is beginning to be a rough region." And the Denison *Journal* stated: "A great many horses have disappeared from northern Texas during the past six months and there is a rendezvous for horse thieves in the Indian nations." [35] The Atoka *Vindicator* told of three men killed on a cattle trail through the Chickasaw Nation when rustlers attempted to stampede a herd of cattle,[36] and in a later issue of December 22 stated: "Two men and two women were murdered on the prairie near the coal mines; the prairie was set on fire and the bodies severely burned." When the *Oklahoma Star* declared that "reports of crime in the Indian territory are being greatly exaggerated," the *Indian Progress* published a "calendar of operations of the knife and pistol," listing fifteen murders, most of them unsolved, some not even investigated, committed within a thirty-mile radius of the "peaceful precincts" of Caddo in 1873 and 1874.[37] "Add to the above sickening list the innumerable minor crimes which harass, vex and disrupt society, for which there is no law, no punishment, on the one side and no safety or salvation on the other, and then talk about exaggeration." [38]

The editor of Fort Smith's *Western Independent* summed up the conditions as follows:

> It is sickening to the heart to contemplate the increase of crime in the Indian country. . . . It is time Congress took this matter in hand and organized a territory, for if crime continues to increase there so fast, a regiment of deputy marshals cannot arrest all the murderers.[39]

In a later issue he added:

We have lived in and around the Indian country since the spring of 1834, but have never known such a state of terror. Now it is murder throughout the length and breadth of the Indian country. It has been the rendezvous of the vile and wicked from everywhere, an inviting field for murder and robbery because it is the highway between Texas, Missouri, Kansas and Arkansas. . . . Stealing horses is an everyday occurrence, and murder and robbery seem to equal that sin. It is dangerous to travel alone where villains from four quarters of the United States congregate to murder, rob and steal. . . .[40]

There was plenty of law to enforce. In fact the Intercourse Law was so laden with tedious provisions for the protection of the Indian that anything near perfect enforcement was impossible. Death by hanging was the fixed punishment in capital offenses. Arson carried a term of two to twenty-one years at hard labor. Assault with a deadly weapon with intent to kill or maim was punishable by imprisonment at hard labor for not less than one and not more than five years. Horse-stealing carried a maximum thousand-dollar fine and fifteen years' imprisonment. Obstructing railroads was punishable at hard labor not to exceed twenty years, and if a person killed another as the result of such obstruction, he could be prosecuted for murder. Selling, bartering, or giving any ardent spirits or wines to an Indian brought a five-hundred-dollar fine; a three-hundred-dollar fine could be assessed for introducing or attempting to introduce the same into the Indian country; and for operating any distillery for the manufacture of any ardent spirits the fine was $1000. Indian agents and other government officers were authorized to search any suspects, persons, boats, or carriers of any kind in order to prevent liquors being carried or manufactured in the Indian country; and to enlist the aid of the population in apprehending violators, the law provided that confiscated goods be divided equally between the informer and the

United States government. Notwithstanding this provision, intoxicants flowed freely.

There were various other statutes. But for all the enforcement given them during the tenure of William Story, they might as well have applied to the jungles of Africa. It is estimated that over half a hundred killings for which no arrests were made were committed in the Indian country during his fourteen months on the bench. People called the area "Robbers' Roost" and "The Land of the Six-Shooter." At the time of the hanging of John Childers, crime was so rampant that the condition gave rise to the phrase: "There is no Sunday west of St. Louis—no God west of Fort Smith."

III

JUDGE PARKER

THESE CURRENT STATEMENTS WERE NOT EXAG-gerated. By 1875, the year Isaac Charles Parker came to the Fort Smith bench, there was no worse spawning place for Satan's own on the western frontier.

Parker came from English ancestry. His father, Joseph Parker, was a native of Maryland, though the family had orig-inally settled in Massachusetts. In his early life he had mi-grated to a farm in Ohio and there married Jane Shannon, a native of Belmont County, where Parker was born in a log cabin October 15, 1838.

Isaac was evidently destined to become a public officer. Six of his grandfather's brothers had held official positions. One great-uncle, Wilson L. Shannon, was twice governor of Ohio, minister to Mexico, member of Congress, and finally governor of Kansas. His father and mother were both respected for their industry, strong domestic discipline, intellectual strength, but mild and kindly dispositions. Both were "firm-believin'" Meth-odists in a community where people had exceedingly strong ideas and stood by them, and their ideals and strong traits of character they passed along, in his formative years, to their son Isaac.[1]

When a lad, Parker could attend school only as work on his father's farm permitted, but he managed to acquire a knowledge of common school subjects, and through private study became well versed in English literature. At seventeen he decided upon becoming a lawyer and began teaching school as a means of promoting this study. For four years he alternately taught school and attended Barnesville Academy. The Kansas-Nebraska question was the absorbing topic of the day, and young Parker, fond of debate, took active part in its discussion. In 1859, when he was twenty-one, he was admitted to the Ohio bar.[2]

Everyone in this year had the fever to go West, and that is what Isaac did. He went down the Ohio River by packet, caught a boat up the Missouri, and landed at St. Joseph. St. Joseph was the gateway to the great western frontier. Trappers, traders, scouts, gamblers, and the nondescript were assembled here on the border. Ben Holladay was running a freight line to the West. The first pony express riders were to start to California from St. Joseph the next year. Later, the notorious outlaw Jesse James was to be slain here by a member of his own gang. It was a wild town on a wild frontier. A man with a little legal knowledge was needed, and welcome. Parker liked the place and hung up his shingle.

In this same year, after beginning the practice of law, he met laughing, dark-eyed Mary O'Toole. She was born in St. Joseph and graduated from the Convent of the Sacred Heart. She was a Catholic and Parker a Protestant, which delayed but did not prevent their marriage.[3] To them were born two sons, Charles and James. Mary was devoted to Isaac and the children, and Isaac was an affectionate and indulgent husband and father. For fourteen years he practiced law in St. Joseph and made friends and a professional reputation that soon led him into a career of public service.

From April, 1861, to April, 1864, he held two public positions. He served two terms as city attorney and was a corporal in the state militia as assistant provost marshal at St. Joseph.[4] His early training and political convictions to some extent fitted Parker for service in the South. He was a firm believer in the dignity of the law and the idea that the wicked should suffer, and until the outbreak of the Civil War he was an ardent Democrat like his Uncle Bill Shannon. He was president of the first Stephen A. Douglas club organized in Missouri and strongly supported the "Little Giant" in his bid for the Presidency against his fellow Illinoisan, Abraham Lincoln.[5] After Lincoln was elected and the South seceded, Parker, a Northerner and nonslaveholder, threw his support to Lincoln and used all his political skill in keeping Missouri on the Northern side. He also espoused the Republican principles and remained a strong adherent to the party thereafter.

His reputation grew. In 1864, as Presidential elector, he helped cast Missouri's vote for Lincoln for his second term. In this same year Parker was elected state's attorney for the Twelfth Judicial Circuit of Missouri. In November, 1868, he was elected judge of the Twelfth Judicial Circuit for a term of six years. He served in this position until 1870 when he was elected representative to Congress from the Sixth Missouri District, a position he was to fill until he accepted the appointment to the judgeship for the Western District of Arkansas.[6] At the time of his appointment, despite the redistricting of his congressional area so that it contained a Democratic majority of three thousand, Parker had been re-elected by a majority of more than 143 votes and was serving his second term in the Forty-third Congress.[7]

Purposely or not, Parker laid the foundation here for becoming a federal judge. During his first term in Congress he served as chairman of the Committee on Expenditures of the Navy Department and was a member of the Committee on Territories. He became deeply interested in the problem of the American Indians and was sympathetic to their cause. His second term afforded him even richer opportunities. He was appointed to the Committee on Appropriations, a committee of which every member was later to receive higher honors.[8] He engineered the Indian Appropriation Bill of 1872, and sponsored a measure to organize a territorial government for the Indian country in the Western District of Arkansas, which he was unable to pass.[9] Little by little he became the champion of the Indian and became known in Congress as "the Indian's best friend."

That Parker's work pleased President Grant is evidenced in the latter's last annual message in 1872, in which he stated:

> The policy which was adopted at the beginning of this Administration with regard to the management of the Indians has been as successful as its most ardent friends anticipated within so short a time. It has reduced the expense of their management, decreased their forays upon the white settlements, tended to give the largest opportunity to the extension of the great railways through the public domain, and the pushing of settlements into more remote districts of the country, and at the same time improved the condition of the Indians.[10]

The President was concerned with conditions in the Indian country, for he also said:

> The subject of converting the so-called Indian Territory, south of Kansas, into a home for the Indian, and erecting therein a territorial form of government, is one of great importance, as a complement of the existing Indian policy. . . . A territorial government should protect the Indians from the inroad of whites for a term of years until they have become sufficiently advanced in the arts and civilizations to guard their own rights, and from the disposal of lands held by them for the same period.[11]

In 1874, when Parker aspired for election to the United States Senate, Missouri had gone Democratic and he could not hope to win. Neither had he a chance, despite his own popularity, of being re-elected to the House. However the Republicans were in control at Washington, and Parker was entitled to party favors. When he retired from Congress in March, 1875, President Grant appointed him Chief Justice of the Territory of Utah.

Before the appointment could be confirmed, however, Parker wrote the President a letter. Utah was all right with him, but it was far away. Furthermore, the job would be only temporary. As soon as Utah became a state, territorial officers would cease to function. On the other hand, there was a vacancy at Fort Smith, closer to Parker's home. He had lived and served as judge in a region not unlike Arkansas, and he knew better the needs of the Indian country. He had done much for the Indians; look at his record in Congress in handling Indian affairs.

The Republican senators from Arkansas also requested that he be appointed to the vacancy existing at Fort Smith. The Republican party was in a decrepit condition in this section of the Southwest. Arkansas was passing through the throes of reconstruction. It had witnessed, only a short time before, the split in the Republican ranks in the state that had resulted in the so-called Brooks-Baxter War. The tenure of William Story had added scandal. What that bench needed was a fighting, honest, incorruptible outsider who could regain respect for the party, and who could not be identified with either side of the factional split.[12]

Upon receiving these requests, the President withdrew the previous nomination and appointed Parker judge of the court for the Western District of Arkansas at a salary of $3500 per annum. This second appointment was promptly confirmed. Parker became the youngest judge on the federal bench, he then being only thirty-six years of age.[13]

The judge and his wife and two children arrived at Fort Smith by steamboat up the shallow, winding Arkansas on Sunday morning, May 2, 1875. Although its population numbered less than twenty-five hundred, the town was listed as the chief center of commerce and trade. River navigation then afforded a low-cost means of transportation; wholesale warehouses had been established, and the town was the distribution center for a large region of the eastern Indian country and much of western Arkansas. So the Parkers expected something in the way of comfort and progress.

They found little of this. It was a town of the second class. There were no paved streets, no sidewalks, no street lights, no factories, no decent hotels or public schools; and the chief means of travel were river craft and horse-drawn carriages.[14] The Little Rock and Fort Smith Railroad extended through to the Indian country at a point across the river, but no bridge spanned the river to connect town and depot. Ferryboats and skiffs were the only means of conveying merchandise and passengers from the depot to the city, until Jay Gould promoted the construction of a combination railroad and wagon bridge in 1891.[15] It already boasted of four newspapers [16] serving its vast area, and thirty saloons which did a thriving business with steamboat and railroad men, cowboys returning from long Texas drives, and transient traffic to the great Southwest. One bank, the First National, had been established in 1872 at 600 Garrison Avenue, where it stands today. Garrison Avenue, the main street that ran from the central part of town to the garrison of the old fort, was a wide, rutted roadway, a mass of mud when it rained and a fog of dust that baffled animal and pedestrian on days when the wind blew and the sun shone hot, as it did the day the Parkers arrived.

Many had gathered at the docks, not especially to welcome the newcomers but to get a good look at this new judge. They saw a broad-shouldered man over six feet tall, weighing two hundred pounds, with piercing blue eyes and tawny mustache and goatee. They saw more than that. They noted his quick, firm step and square-set jaw, and they guessed he was no weakling. Beyond this, he was another appointment of President Grant, to be looked upon with considerable misgiving, and all the more so because he was an out-of-state man and had been endorsed by the Republican senators who had been placed in power by the carpetbagger regime that for years had denied Arkansas its state government by force of arms. The term "carpetbagger" was anathema in the ears and hearts of the majority of these people present, and thinking men looked at the judge and wondered if another mere carpetbagger had been foisted upon them. In Mrs. Parker they saw a pleasant woman, larger than average, and the two children were remarkably handsome.

After Parker got his family settled, he took a look about town and the garrison court and sized up the situation. Only then did he realize that he had accepted one of the most difficult offices in the country.

Story's weakness had allowed the court to slide into disrepute. People on the streets still openly criticized his regime and the wasteful and inefficient methods of his court. Witnesses were difficult to secure, and the good citizens of the court's jurisdiction had become strongly antagonistic toward its officers. The bar itself was sullen and even openly rebellious, and the old stockade of hewed logs standing on the Poteau bluffs that was being used as a jail was jammed with prisoners who had not been tried.[17]

In addition, there was considerable distrust of Parker by triumphant and righteously indignant Democrats because of his switch to the Republican party. Local newspapers had expressed their disgust at Parker's congressional votes on bills affecting sectional issues.[18] Despite the acknowledged success of President Grant's Indian policy, in the Indian country they felt that it had been a complete failure.[19] Parker also had been a member of the Forty-third Congress that had attempted to abolish the court for the Western District of Arkansas in a revision session held in 1873 and 1874. The upshot of the matter had been the passage of a redistricting act [20] that made the jurisdiction consist of thirteen counties [21] in the western and northwestern part of Arkansas, seventeen counties [22] in the eastern and northeastern part of the state, and the Indian country—leaving Clay County in the extreme northeastern corner, and Lee County in the central east on the Mississippi, in the Eastern District: a gerrymander to aid carpetbag control of state government at the expense of costly and difficult functioning of an already corrupt and inefficient bench.

> The spectacle of counties away in the east being made to constitute a portion of the *western* district while other counties in the western part of the state, one of them actually bordering the Indian Territory, were retained in the *eastern* district, was a fraud so palpable it smelled to Heaven and was the cause of much deserved censure being heaped upon the heads of the statesmen who secured the passage of the act by means best known to themselves and their tools.[23]

The newspapers gave the judge only guarded publicity.

"We have made a great mistake, Isaac," said Mary.

"No, Mary," the judge replied, "We are faced with a great task. These people need us. We must not fail them."

Failure would have meant bloodshed and fierce domination by the criminal class. Parker had lived through the bloody warfare of William Clarke Quantrill, Bloody Bill Anderson, and the Jameses and Youngers of western Missouri. He knew the type of ruthless refugees into whose hands the Indian country had been abandoned for years. He saw from the beginning that politics must be set aside. Politics could play no hand in bringing law and order to this frontier. The country's salvation, the fate of this great jurisdiction, lay in the hands of these Arkansas people. Only if he could have their help and cooperation in tackling this "vast problem of crime" could he achieve his ideal, "a great government, where liberty, regulated by law, would be guaranteed to all, even the humblest."

For clerk of the court he chose Stephen Wheeler,[24] a favorite of these people and at that time clerk of the Federal Circuit

Court at Fort Smith, a division of the Eighth Judicial Circuit. Wheeler accepted the appointment and never left this position until June, 1897, nearly a year after Parker's death. In the twenty-two years he held the office he was to issue 18,877 writs for the arrest of persons charged with violations of every federal statute written on the books.[25] As private bailiff, Parker retained George S. Winston, private bailiff under both Caldwell and Story. Winston always gave close attention to court affairs, and he came to Parker with the unanimous recommendation of the other court officers. Parker appointed J. A. Hammersly court crier. A stern disciplinarian, Hammersly was of such genial nature that everyone who had dealings with the court liked him. He too remained in office until after Parker's death, then retired to private life.

James F. Fagan was United States Marshal. He had been appointed by Grant to succeed John Sarber during the clean sweep begun with the resignation of Story in 1874.[26] Charley Burns, head jailer under both Roots and Sarber, was retained in that capacity, and George Maledon, a former Fort Smith policeman and Sebastian County deputy sheriff, was placed in charge of execution of condemned prisoners. Burns was to hold his position, with the exception of one period of four years, until February, 1882, and Maledon was to achieve national notoriety comparable to Parker's.

Parker also got acquainted with his working partner and chief prosecutor for the court, William H. H. Clayton. Behind Clayton lay a brief but brilliant record as a soldier. He had served as a lieutenant in Company H, 124th Pennsylvania Infantry, under Colonel Hawley, and fought in the battles of South Mountain, Antietam, Burnside's Defeat at Fredericksburg, and Hooker's Battle of the Wilderness. Retiring from service, he took a position as teacher of military tactics in Village Green Seminary until the autumn of 1864, when he resigned to join his brothers, Powell and John M. Clayton, on their two-thousand-acre plantation below Pine Bluff on the Arkansas, and to study law. He was admitted to the Arkansas bar in 1871, and in March of the same year was appointed prosecutor for the First Judicial Circuit of Arkansas. Two years later he was appointed judge of the First Judicial Circuit, which office he resigned in July, 1874, to accept the appointment from Grant as United States Attorney for the Western District at Fort Smith. He was reappointed by President Hayes in 1879, and except for four years, 1885 to 1890, when he was succeeded by M. H. Sandel, an appointee of President Cleveland, he was district attorney until 1893. In that year, James H. Read was appointed his successor by Grover Cleveland, in his second term as President, and Read served in that capacity until 1897. During his fourteen years of service Clayton was to prosecute over ten thousand cases, convict eighty men of murder, and see forty of them hanged.[27]

Clayton's chief assistant was James Brizzolara, former city attorney and mayor of Fort Smith for several years after the town was incorporated. A prosecutor in his own right, Brizzolara fought beside Clayton for three terms. On June 12, 1878, he resigned to accept an appointment as United States Commissioner for the Western District, which position he held until it was abolished by an act of Congress in 1897.

The physical setting of the court was as grim as the work it was to perform for the next twenty-one years. The two-story brick building where John Childers had been convicted and sentenced to death was partitioned for a court room, jury rooms, and offices for clerks, attorneys, and the marshal. The basement beneath the building, eight feet deep and partitioned by a solid stone wall into two compartments each twenty-nine by fifty-five feet, was converted into a jail, and the old log prison on the Poteau abandoned. The small basement windows provided the chief source of light and ventilation. Buckets placed in the old basement chimneys answered the purpose of toilets, while kerosene barrels cut in half were used for bath tubs. Entrances to the two basements were made from the outside on either side of the porch facing southeast. Inside each basement entrance was constructed a small vestibule, eight by ten feet square, where prisoners could come from the depths of the damp, foul-smelling dungeons to consult with their attorneys during court sessions.[28]

Judge Parker took up quarters in the stone commissary building. Three hundred feet away, on the site formerly occupied by the fort's powder magazine and within clear view of his window, stood the gallows that already had launched John Childers' soul into eternity. It was a strong structure of heavy timbers. The I beam was a twelve-by-twelve supported by similar timbers. The four traps were thirty inches wide and twenty feet long, furnishing room for twelve men to stand side by side and drop to their deaths simultaneously. Later the structure was roofed and the back walled, so that executions could proceed even in inclement weather.

The people wanted proof that Judge Parker wasn't a corruptionist, and they quickly got it. On May 10, only eight days after his arrival at Fort Smith, he opened his first term of court. Eighteen persons came before him charged with murder and fifteen were convicted. Eight of these he sentenced to die on the gallows on September 3. Before the date arrived, however, one tried to escape and was brought down by the rifle fire of George Maledon; and another, because of his youth, had his sentence commuted to life imprisonment by the President and was later pardoned.

The hanging of the remaining six called the attention of the world to the court and its judge. Newspapermen came from Little Rock, St. Louis, and Kansas City; many of the great Eastern and Northern daily newspapers sent representatives to cover the event. Even strangers from abroad, reading the announcement of the unusual "attraction," began filtering into the city a week before the execution. Men and their families living within forty to fifty miles of Fort Smith began pouring into the city at daybreak. More than five thousand packed the jail yard and clung from the tops of the old fort's stone walls to view the major event.

At 9:30 A.M. they saw the six condemned felons, unshackled in their cells, led by four local clergymen and surrounded by a dozen well-armed guards, march from the grimy dungeon jail onto the gallows. Three were white men, two Indians, and one a Negro.

One of the white men, Daniel Evans, had murdered a nineteen-year-old boy named William Seabolt and robbed him of a fine horse and saddle. The youth's body had been found beside a stream in the Creek Nation with a bullet in the head and the feet without boots or shoes. Evans was convicted on the fact that at the time of his trial he was wearing a pair of fancy, high-heeled boots taken from the young man's body.[29]

William Whittington had murdered an elderly man named John Turner with whom he had associated and drunk whisky on a Sunday. While riding back to the Chickasaw Nation from across the Texas border, Whittington clubbed him from the saddle, cut his throat with a bowie, and robbed him of $100. He had been apprehended with the money in his pocket and his knife still red with his victim's blood. In pronouncing judgment on him, Judge Parker said:

> The man you murdered was your friend. You spent most of the Sabbath in his company. In an unsuspecting hour when he no doubt was treating you as a trusted companion, you set upon him unperceived and aimed a deadly weapon at his head and with the fateful knife you brutally hacked his throat to pieces and with these fatal instruments of death you mangled, you murdered your victim.
>
> But your guilt and your depravity did not stop there. Scarcely had you committed the bloody deed before you entered upon the commission of another crime. You converted to your person as spoils of the murder your victim's money.

James Moore, the third white man, was a member of an organized band of horse thieves raiding from the Missouri and

Kansas borders to the western counties of Texas. He had killed his eighth victim, Deputy Marshal William Spivey, in a desperate flight from the posse that had captured him near Red River.[30]

One of the Indians, Smoker Mankiller, borrowed a Winchester of William Short, a neighbor, used the weapon to assassinate him, then rode about the country openly boasting of his treachery. Because he spoke and understood only Cherokee, his trial had consumed most of three days. When the jury brought in its verdict of guilty, he commented gloomily:

"The law has come upon me."

"Yes," said Judge Parker sharply, "the sword of human justice is about to fall upon your guilty head."

The other Indian, Samuel Fooy, had slain and robbed a young white man named John Emmit Neff, known as "The Barefooted School Teacher." Neff had been carrying $250 earned from teaching in the Cherokee Nation, and Fooy had shot him to secure the money. He hid the body near Tahlequah on the Illinois River, and no trace of the victim was found until the bones of his skeleton and a teacher's manual with the flyleaf still bearing his name and other memoranda were discovered nearly a year later.

To Fooy, Parker said: "You have taken human life, you have sent a soul unprepared to its Maker. You have set at defiance God's law."

The crime of Edmund Campbell, the Negro, had been the most senseless of all. He had gone to the farm of Lawson Ross in the Choctaw Nation and slain both Ross and his mistress in cold blood in revenge for a fancied insult. The apparent lack of motive and the sheer brutality of the offense obviously convinced Parker that the prisoner had no chance for commutation.

"Your fate is inevitable," he said. "Let me, therefore, beg of you to fly to your Maker for that mercy and that pardon which you cannot expect from mortals . . . and endeavor to seize upon the salvation of His Cross."

To all of them, after commenting separately on their cases, the judge said: "Farewell forever until the court and you and all here today shall meet together in the general resurrection."

The six felons were seated on the rough plank bench along the back of the gallows and their death warrants read to them by Marshal Fagan, Mankiller's both in English and Cherokee.

Die brave; show no emotion; do not falter in the shadow of the gallows. This was the code of the doomed men, the example set them by John Childers.

Asked if he had any last words to say, handsome, blue-eyed Daniel Evans stared defiantly at the marshal and shook his curly brown head.

Tall, broad-shouldered James Moore, staring out over the crowd, spoke in a loud, clear voice: "I have lived like a man, and I will die like a man. . . . I see men in this crowd who are worse than I have ever been. I hope you make peace with God before brought to my condition."

"I am as anxious to get out of this world as you are to see me go," said Sam Fooy.

"I didn't shoot anybody," denied the short, stocky Campbell, cool and calm. "I am innocent and ready to die."

Smoker Mankiller, glum-faced and dull-eyed, addressed the crowd through his interpreter, and they leaned forward eagerly to drink in every word. "I did not kill Short; I would admit it if I did. I stand before you convicted by prejudice and false testimony."

Lean, sallow-faced William Whittington had a wife and three children in the Chickasaw Nation. He had become ill while in jail awaiting execution, and this, coupled with his concern for his family, had made him doubtful that he would be up to making a speech on the scaffold. Accordingly, he had written his message under the caption "How I Came to the Gallows," and it was read to the crowd by Reverend H. M. Granade, his spiritual adviser:

My father taught me to be honest and avoid those great sins that disgrace the world, but he did not teach me to be religious. If he had, I would have been a Christian from my boyhood. I was *just what my father taught me to be.* He showed me how to drink whiskey, and set me the example of getting drunk. I took to his practice and this is what has brought me to the gallows. When I got drunk I knew not what I was doing and so killed my best friend. If it had been my brother it would have been the same. If I had been blessed with the good instruction I have had since I have been in prison I would be a good and happy man today with my family. Oh! what will become of my poor wife and two dear little boys, who are away out on Red River? I fear that people will slight them, and compel them to go into low, bad company, on account of the disgrace that I have brought upon them. But I leave them in the hands of that gracious God in whom I have learned to trust. . . . Oh! that men would leave off drinking altogether. And, O, parents, I send forth this dying warning to you today, standing on the gallows: *Train up your children the way they should go.* My father's example brought me to ruin. God save us all! Farewell! Farewell!

The preliminaries over, there were prayers, the singing of hymns, and farewells. Then the six felons were lined up on the scaffold with their feet across the crack where the planks forming the death trap came together. Their arms were bound securely, the black hoods pulled over their faces shut out the light forever, and George Maledon adjusted the nooses about their necks.

"Jesus save me!" cried William Whittington.

The trap door fell, and the six men died at the end of ropes with broken necks.

Reports in the press of the event shocked people throughout the nation. "Cool Destruction of Six Human Lives by Legal Process!" screamed the headlines. In the minds of those who read their pleas on the gallows and were unfamiliar with the details of their atrocities, human sympathy naturally went to the victims and caused the belief that "none but a heartless judge could be so lacking in compassion as to decree such whole-sale killing."

But what about the people of the Indian country who had seen vicious bands running roughshod over lives and property? J. W. Weaver, a reporter for the *Western Independent* and valued correspondent of the New York *Herald* and other big Eastern dailies, knew the frontier outlaw better than any man of his day. He aptly expressed their sentiments in closing his report of the execution.

"These terrible scenes have made a lasting impression." While "these men were young and in the full prime of strength, and should have been active and useful members of society, the pride of their friends, the staff of their aged parents . . . so-ciety, through the stern mandates of the law, has thus consigned them to death and exterminated them from the face of the earth." Why? "Because they are preying wolves upon the lives and property of their fellow beings, unfit to live and unsafe to remain at large." This fact "should not be lost in the ex-citement and glare of the terrible exhibition, nor forgotten in the morbid curiosity which absorbs the mind in witnessing an event so rare and tragical."

To those prone to criticize Parker's first session on the bench, he replied: "If criticism is due, it should be the system, not the man whose duty lies under it. . . ."

Those active in their arrest and prosecution were relieved that the desperadoes were gone. In his appointments Judge Parker had showed from the start that he did not intend to use his new office as a steppingstone to something else. In ordering these executions, he gave evidence of his unbounded energy and fearlessness in enforcing the laws and his determination to bring order and decency to this "Godless" frontier.

IV

'BRING THEM IN ALIVE—OR DEAD!'

ONE OF JUDGE PARKER'S EARLY MOVES WAS TO AP-
point two hundred deputy marshals to police the area over
which he had jurisdiction and bring in the lawbreakers. He
reopened investigations into many old, unsolved murders and
other felonies, issued warrants for the arrests of the most
notorious brigands and their gangs, and told these marshals:
"Bring them in alive—or dead!"

Thus began, in the language of the judge, "a fight between
the court and the lawless element of that country" that continued unabated for twenty-one years.[1]

It was a big order. Two hundred men were a mere handful
to cover an area of 74,000 square miles, where the outlaws
knew every trail and hideout and the deputies had little protection other than their own discretion and skill in serving these
processes of law. A year's imprisonment was the only penalty
attached to resisting a federal officer. "To a man who will risk
his life to avoid arrest," commented the attorney general, "a
year's confinement is a small matter."[2]

In the north of the Territory were the Boston Mountains, and to the south were the Winding Stair and the Kiamichi, while scattered between were many hills and canebrakes which gave ready refuge to those 'on scout.' Game was still plentiful and water and firewood could be found in every hollow. There was a border class of confederates who gave assistance and warning to the criminals, even though they were not active members of the gang.[3]

The problem was made even more difficult by the practice of some of the settlements to furnish known criminals "a sort of asylum in exchange for immunity"; often whole gangs of outlaws "bore themselves so quietly among the citizens of the town while their lurid escapades filled the border press." [4] Here also was a large class of citizens who "hated marshals and hampered them in every possible turn." [5] Decent citizens were afraid to let a marshal stay overnight or otherwise accommodate him for fear of reprisals the next day. "Many a wanton, unprovoked and unpunished murder had shown that there was a real basis for that fear." [6]

Add to this the fact that the marshals often had to transport desperate prisoners to Fort Smith from distances of two and three hundred miles; that, traveling by wagon and horseback, with no bridges crossing the streams and no open paths or roads, their progress was slow; that frequently they were ambushed by criminal gangs in attempts to deliver a fellow criminal, and fierce gun fights sometimes resulted in death to the officer and the escape of prisoners—and it is not hard to appreciate the dangers these men faced.

For these outlaws had committed themselves to crime and fled to the Indian country for the protection and opportunity it afforded to further satiate their keen appetites. Marshals were "intruders" in their criminal empire, and they connived and banded together to prevent them from performing their duty. From the prairies in the wild country to the west rose high knobs or hills, which they used as lookout points. Lights at night or flashing signals in the daytime, relayed from one knob to another, often warned fugitives miles away that officers were in a certain locality, told the size of their force, and even gave their identity.[7] Many a deputy had to conceal his identity and sometimes associate with his quarry for weeks to obtain enough evidence to insure a conviction and to await an opportunity to make a successful capture.

Take the case of Deputy Marshal H. D. Fannin, who went after Jason Labreu. Labreu was a Creole cowboy wanted for killings in Texas and New Orleans. With his carefree smile and flashing eyes, he captivated pretty Leona Devere, the daughter of a prominent western Arkansas farmer. The two went for a walk in the meadow in search of wild flowers, and the girl was not seen again until her body was found face down in a small brook, badly decomposed and brutally ravished.

Fannin traced Labreu to the Chickasaw Nation, where he located him working for a wealthy farmer named Jack Crow. The next day Fannin, dressed as a farm hand, appeared at Crow's farm and hired out to assist with the spring planting. He was put to work in the fields beside Labreu.

The killer's dark eyes hardened when he saw the new hand. He did not even appear relieved by the fact that Fannin was unarmed. Fannin had concealed his revolver and handcuffs at the house in his saddlebags. Labreu was a dead shot; he carried his Winchester strapped to his back while he worked, and Fannin realized his only chance lay in catching him at a disadvantage.

For weeks they worked and ate together and slept in the same bed at night, but still Labreu did not trust him and remained tense and watchful. One night as they lay in the lean-to where the farm hands slept, Fannin had an idea.

"I had to kill him," he muttered, as though talking in his sleep. "He caught me stealin' his cattle. I can't ever go back to Texas!"

The next day in the field Fannin noted that, although Labreu continued to study him through slitted eyes, the fugitive had relaxed and was more friendly. Late in the evening Labreu confided to him: "I've killed a dozen men myself, but I was never bothered in my sleep until I killed a girl."

"I shot a woman once in Dallas," Fannin lied, "but she didn't die."

Labreu grew moody. "I drowned the one I killed," he said.

Then followed the revolting details of how he had lured Leona Devere into the meadow, crammed a handkerchief into her mouth to muffle her cries, and raped her; and how, afterward, as she sat on the grass sobbing, covering her face with her hands in shame and begging him to marry her, he had dragged her into the brook and held her face beneath the water until she had ceased to struggle.

The confession was half the battle, but Fannin still had to arrest Labreu. During the next several days he thought of a dozen plans and discarded all of them. Labreu kept his Winchester ready while he worked, ate, and slept, and in all his waking moments continued to keep Fannin under close scrutiny. The marshal could think of no way to throw him off guard.

One morning they went to the field as usual. The day was sultry hot. The killer washed his face and hands for the noon meal, but this time, instead of leaning his rifle against his thigh as he did usually, Labreu leaned it against the door casing.

Fannin waited his turn in line behind him. Labreu emptied the basin, took the towel from a nail, and lifted it to his bearded face. Fannin acted in a split second, and the cowboy found himself covered with his own rifle. Looking into the muzzle of the weapon and the grim face of the man who held it, he knew he had been outwitted. He lifted his hands and calmly allowed Crow, whom Fannin directed to get the cuffs from his saddlebags, to clamp the irons about his wrists.

The deputy and his prisoner had been in the saddle several days and were within a few hours ride of Fort Smith when they were forced to stop at a railroad crossing for an approaching train. Labreu was still handcuffed, and a lead rope from Fannin's saddle was fastened to his horse's bridle. The deputy dismounted to tighten a cinch, and Labreu saw his chance. The horses, restless and frightened by the train, responded to the outlaw's savage kicks. His mount reared and snapped the lead rope, and Fannin's horse plunged away, leaving him on foot. His rifle was in the saddle boot, but he quickly drew his six-shooter and fired. Labreu rolled from the saddle. When Fannin reached his side, the outlaw was dead.

It took quick thinking and quick shooting to stop these killers. Fannin had avenged the death of Leona Devere, but he had forfeited all fees and expenses he might have collected. A deputy had to arrest his man and deliver him safely to the court—or serve the papers in lesser cases—or he could collect no fees or mileage. Nor could he leave the corpse unattended. If the man he was forced to kill had no friends or relatives to dispose of the body, the deputy had to bury it at his own expense. It cost Fannin sixty dollars to bury Jason Labreu.

An incredible feature of the heroic work done by these deputy marshals is the pecuniary compensation they received at the hands of the government. There were no fixed salaries for deputies. A deputy depended on fees, mileage, and such rewards as came his way. He received six cents a mile when out on official business—all expenses of transportation and board to be paid by him out of these six cents—if proper receipts were obtained, and obtaining receipts was practically an impossibility in the majority of localities in the Indian country.

For arresting a suspected or guilty party at the risk of his own life and becoming the marked victim of the arrested outlaw's friends, he received the munificent sum of *two dollars!* And this was the same whether he was arresting a whisky peddler, or horse thief, or a desperado like Jason Labreu, even when it meant pursuing the murderer hundreds of miles, hiring a posse or buying information from his own pocket, and then having to take him in a bloody fight.

If he returned with his two-dollar prisoner in charge, he was allowed ten cents to feed and transport himself, pay the assistants he might need, and meet the expense of the prisoner himself. If he was sent out to subpoena witnesses, he received six cents a mile only one way, fifty cents for contacting the first witness, and thirty-seven cents for each additional. He received no fees at all if he failed to locate the witnesses, which was often the case.

This was not all. When the accounts were rendered, the marshal deducted 35 per cent of the gross amount as his fee. Then the bill was sent to Washington—and sometimes allowed! In the meantime, the deputy had to advance all moneys spent, borrowing from friends if he had no money in the bank, very happy indeed if he finally got in hard cash just half of what was legitimately due him.

Everything considered, the average deputy seldom made $500 a year unless he was lucky enough to pick up a reward. The government usually offered rewards in cases of mail robbery and the murder of federal employees, but the deputies were not entitled to these on the grounds that they were already paid fees by the government to capture these criminals.

This was a cause of much dissatisfaction among the officers, for the rewards often amounted to more than a whole year's income, as compared with the $30 to $40 they were able to collect under the fee-mileage setup. The marshals always kept an eye on the rewards offered by local and state authorities, private individuals, and the railroad and express companies. They could, and did, collect many of these.

Parker fought the inequity of the system. "The services of reliable, efficient, trustworthy men are indispensable," he told grand juries and Washington. "To secure such services the pay must be adequate. . . ."

Congress considered the pay sufficient for well-populated sections; where transportation facilities were good, the marshals could sleep in hotels and eat in restaurants, the people willing to render all assistance necessary.

"But conditions in the Indian country," argued Parker, "are exactly in the reverse. The facilities for transportation are meager and primitive. The country is sparsely settled. The deputy cannot rely on assistance from anyone, and the Indian people, by nature uncommunicative and averse to report and prosecute crimes, are rendered all the more so by fear of bodily injury and death at the hands of criminals."

Despite his appeals, there was little change as the years passed. In 1884 a bill was presented in Congress to pay deputy marshals salaries instead of fees "to attract good men who will know just what they can make and prevent trumped up cases and the wholesale subpoena of witnesses for fees whether they know anything about the cases or not"; but it was opposed on the grounds of "inequality of service to be performed by the different men." [8]

Scores of deputies quit to accept positions as detectives for express and railroad companies or to enter civilian pursuits. Why so many stayed so long is amazing.

Perhaps it was that Judge Parker, with a desire for law and order, inspired them with his zeal. The officers had to feed their families, of course, but in no other pursuit was there such great adventure and opportunity to serve the cause of justice.

"Without these men," Parker said time and again, "I could not hold court a single day." And in his later years, when he talked much of his record on the bench, he gave a great deal of credit to the deputy marshals, particularly the sixty-five of them who gave their lives in the field in the cause of peace and decency.

Too many of the outlaws were like John Billee. Billee was so ferocious that he had to be kept chained in the corner of his cell even after he was lodged in the Fort Smith jail. He knew no fear. When a neighbor ordered him off his farm, Billee told him he would return and kill him. The neighbor armed himself with a rifle and hid in some bushes. As Billee rode back, he fired. The shot missed the outlaw. There was no time for a second. Billee wheeled his horse and plunged head on into the brush, shooting his neighbor dead.

Deputies Will Ayers, James Wilkerson, and Perry DuVal started to Fort Smith with Billee and four other prisoners in custody. At a deserted, two-roomed shack near Muskogee they stopped to spend the night. Ayers bedded down in the front room with three of the prisoners chained to him and together. DuVal slept in the same room with Ayers, with Billee in custody. Wilkerson and the other prisoner shared the back room of the cabin.

In the middle of the night Billee slipped one of his handcuffs. He seized DuVal's revolver and shot the officer in the head. He then fired at Ayers, who was resting on his back, wounding him in the right nipple. Awakened by the shots, Wilkerson rolled to a sitting position. Billee shot him through the back and kidneys. Ayers grappled the outlaw, and while Billee struggled to free his arm for another shot, Wilkerson raised himself on an elbow, leveled his own weapon, and put a bullet in his body. Fortunately, Billee survived his wound. The marshals were able to collect their fees, and Billee was hanged on the Fort Smith gallows.

A writ was issued for Sheppard Busby by the United States Commissioner at Fort Smith, charging him with living in adultery with two young Indian women in the Cherokee Nation, and placed in the hands of Deputy Marshal Barney Connelley, who resided in that district at Vinita. Connelley was a highly respected citizen and a good officer. He had arrested scores of violators and was a man of extreme caution. But as he approached Busby's home the morning of August 19, 1891, to serve the warrant, the latter opened fire on him, killing him instantly. Busby was hanged for his crime April 27, 1892.

It was cold-blooded murder again in the case of William Irwin. Irwin was a widower with two children to support. He had been a mail-carrier before he tried his hand at law enforcement. He quickly became a fearless, top-flight officer. For years he arrested murderers and whisky peddlers. Then on April 12, 1886, he was shot to death from ambush by two members of the Felix Griffin gang as he was bringing Griffin himself in from the Choctaw Nation. Investigation fastened the crime on Jack Spaniard and Frank Palmer, and the government offered a reward of $500 for each of the slayers. Frank Palmer fled the territory and was never seen again, but Spaniard was taken prisoner in 1888 and executed at Judge Parker's order. Griffin was recaptured, and while out on bail was killed stealing horses.

Popular, friendly Addison Beck was another deputy with a steady stream of arrests to his credit, but in 1883 he and his guard, Lewis Merritt, went out after two ruffians named John Bart and Johnson Jacks, and neither officer came back alive. Bart got away, but Jacks was wounded in the fight and died after his capture. So Beck's murder went only partially avenged.

It was even worse in 1885, when Deputy Marshal Jim Guy and his posse went up against the Tom Pink–Jim Lee gang. Guy and three of his men were killed and the rest of the posse routed. Deputy Marshal Heck Thomas later tracked down and killed Tom Pink and Jim Lee, but the battle went on record as one of the heaviest losses sustained by the government in any one fight with outlaws during the Judge Parker era.

Many times the marshals came out of a fight with only flesh wounds, or gunpowder-burned faces, or unscathed. But these were "just breaks of luck." A deputy called on Bill Pigeon, a Cherokee outlaw wanted for the slaying of Deputy Jim Richardson, and found him at home. He was met at the door with a fusillade from a six-shooter, and when this was backed up by a Winchester, the marshal declared himself ready to retire. A bullet passed through his hat and grazed his scalp, with no more serious results. The marshal was then informed by Pigeon that he could always be found at home, and that he could come back whenever he liked. But when the deputy returned a few hours later with a posse, Pigeon had retreated into the fastness of the Flint Hills, and he was never found.

Buck Anderson had just got out of the Texas penitentiary when he stole a herd of horses in Crawford County, Arkansas, and drove them to his hide-out on Lee's Creek in the Cherokee Nation. A posse went to his house one evening. Anderson saw them and stepped out the door, gun in hand, saying: "Stop, I've killed one man and can kill another. All I want is one shot." He fired, missed his man—and before he could fire again the posse riddled him.

Deputy Marshal Scott Bruner had a warrant for the arrest of an outlaw who had robbed a woman of $6.00, and when her two-year-old child came crying to its mother, had knocked it in the head with his six-shooter. Bruner came up on the fugitive sitting on his horse with his Winchester in his hands resting on the toe of his boot. Bruner ordered him to throw up his hands, and the outlaw jerked up his rifle and fired. His bullet struck Bruner in the side just under the heart, knocking him down. The outlaw whirled to ride away, but the deputy drew his six-shooter. His first shot tore through the man's hat brim. His second bullet struck him between the shoulder blades, killing him instantly. It passed through his body and struck the horse in the head, killing the horse. Bruner always hated it "because the horse got killed."

Doctor J. C. Bland, a white man, married a Creek citizen, which gave him the right to fence land in the Creek Nation. His ranch lay on the Cimarron in the heart of the Indian county, and he was having a hard time holding his own against horse thieves. One night he lost a big bunch of mares, and Deputy Marshals Frank Jones, John McCann, Bill Tilghman, and Heck Bruner trailed them to the Shelly brothers' ranch on Carr Creek east of Choteau. At daylight they went up to the ranch house and told the Shellys to come out and surrender. The answer came immediately: "We'll shoot it out, but we're staying inside."

The officers took up positions, then told them to send out their women and children. As this was being done Deputy Mc-Cann accidentally showed himself, and the Shellys opened fire, wounding him in the shoulder. The officers returned the fire, pouring a steady stream of lead into the house for several minutes, but the Shellys didn't come out. Realizing that the outlaws were well barricaded and that the battle might last for days, Jones got hold of a wagon, took the front gear off, and loaded it with hay. Moving it around to the side of the house that had no windows, he ran it up against the wall and set the hay on fire, then hurried back to wait with his companions. In a few minutes the weather-beaten shack was in flames, and out came the Shellys and surrendered.

The papers of the time were replete with items of this kind:

Deputy Marshal Mershon and posse attempted to arrest Jim Webb near Bywater's store, in the Arbuckle Mountains, on the 15th inst., which resulted in a running fight, in which Webb was wounded and died that night. Webb was boss of Washington's ranch. He was charged with killing a negro for burning the range last winter.[9]

Important Arrest. Dan Thompson, a full blood Creek, was lodged in jail Wednesday by Chub McIntosh, who arrested him the day previous at his home ten miles from Eufaula. Thompson is one of the men charged with the murder of Deputy Marshal John Phillips and posse, for whom the government offers a reward of $500 each.[10]

Wesley Barnett, the murderer of Deputy Marshal John Phillips is reported by the *Indian Journal* as having stormed the Creek capital with a crowd and shot twenty-six bullet holes through the cupola of the building. Armed men guarded the town afterwards to prevent similar raids. Wesley is worth $500 to anyone who will lodge him in the U. S. jail here.[11]

News reached the Marshal's office Tuesday that Wesley Barnett, for whom there was a reward of $500 was killed. The following letter to Marshal Carroll explains how it was done:

"EUFAULA, C. N., JAN. 15, 1889

"HON. JOHN CARROLL, U. S. MAR.

"We killed Wesley Barnett Saturday night last about 10 o'clock, near Okmulgee. The circumstances of the killing are about as follows: I sent Salmon north of the Arkansas river with three men, then I went up North Fork with three more, sending my posse, William Sevier, up Deep Fork, accompanied by John Barnell and Wallace McNack. They stopped at John Porters to stay over night. About the hour mentioned above Wesley Barnett and Wiley Bear came in on them and commenced shooting. In the fight Wesley was killed. We turned his body over to friends. Will be in as soon as we can. The waters are very high.

"Yours, etc.

"D. V. RUSK,
"*U. S. Dep. Mar.*"

We would infer from the above that Wiley Bear escaped . . . but it is only a question of time when all of them will either be arrested or killed off.[12]

There was a bloody fight between Deputy Marshal E. L. Drake and two outlaws named William Miller and William Hostetter. Both of the outlaws were killed and the marshal mortally wounded. The fight occurred on Deep Fork beyond Sapulpa.[13]

Deputy Marshal Heck Bruner, with D. Douthit and Wood Bruner, posse, got in from the Territory Sunday night with Sam Rogers, who they captured near White Oak Station, not far from Vinita, Saturday night. Rogers was suffering from a wound in the hips, inflicted by the officers in trying to arrest him. His partner, Ralph Hedrick, was killed in the fight. Hedrick and Rogers are supposed to be two of the men who recently robbed the bank at Mound City, Kansas.[14]

And in the *Indian Journal* of December 14, 1894:

A posse composed of U. S. Marshal Neal and five other marshals, attempted to surround the house of Kizzie Lola, about 12 miles south of Eufaula, in order to capture a band of outlaws; the outlaws escaped, shooting Deputy Marshal LeForce, who later died.

It would appear that the marshals had all their difficulties with robbers, horse thieves and murderers. On the contrary, more than half their battles were with liquor-law violators:

Deputy Marshal Chilton arrested two men near here last week charged with dealing in the ardent; and pressed "Wild Bill" a noted whiskey peddler, so close that he deserted his outfit and took to the brush.[15]

On Tuesday, Deputy Marshals Tyner Hughes and West Harris, with a posse of three men, went to arrest James Hart and Henry Ewing in San Bois county, Choctaw Nation, on a charge of introducing and selling whiskey in the Nation. They came upon them about four miles above Blaine, when a fight ensued in which many shots were fired and Hart was severely, if not fatally, wounded. Hart and Ewing were brought in late Wednesday night, and as we go to press the wounded man is in a critical condition, and may be dead before this paper reaches the public.[16]

From the Arkansas side of the federal court district:

Deputy Dave Rusk came in from Montgomery county Monday with Carter Markham, Mathew Pervine and Joseph Pepper, attached witnesses in the Cogburn moonshine whiskey case, and J. D. Hollifield, a Montgomery county farmer, charged with selling moonshine whiskey. Mr. Rusk says the five men who participated in the murder of Deputy U. S. Marshal Trammell have all been arrested and released by a magistrate, as no witnesses appeared against them, and no one was present to prosecute. Their examination was a mere farce, and during its progress they were surrounded by their friends all well armed, who would have released them had they been bound over. Rusk had writs for all of them on charges of illicit distilling but did not go to the trial, as the sheriff had warned him that it would be extremely dangerous, as he would likely be killed. He then requested the sheriff to turn over to him Fayette and Franklin Cogburn, two of the alleged murderers, whom he had in custody, and assist him in getting them out of the country. The sheriff sent him word that he could not get a force large enough to take them out, as it would be impossible, and they were released.[17]

And there was a wide range of items such as these:

Thomas Jefferson, a white man, was lodged in jail on Friday by Deputy George Williams, charged with threatening to kill G. W. Dotson. It appears that Jefferson seduced Mrs. Dotson, and the husband claims he accomplished his object by giving her doctored candy, after which he run Dotson from the house by threatening to kill him, and took full possession.[18]

J. M. McDougal was lodged in jail Wednesday by Tyner Hughes, charged with attempt to murder. In this case it is set forth that McDougal and wife separated at McAlester. McDougal went to a friend and gave him some powders requesting that he not tell who sent them, but to say they were love powders and to take them, at the same time assuring his friend that such they were, and he wanted his wife to take them so she would love him. The friend delivered the powders, but told who sent them, whereupon the woman sent them to a physician who pronounced them strychnine.[19]

The most dangerous outlaw the marshals had to go after was Ned Christie. A full-blooded Cherokee, Christie had served as one of the tribe's executive councilors, but soon found the life of bandit, horse thief, whisky peddler, and killer more exciting. He fought a greater number of battles with government officers than any other outlaw in the history of Judge Parker's court.

For months Deputy Marshals Heck Bruner and Barney Connelley trailed him without success. Deputies Heck Thomas and L. P. Isabel cornered him in 1889 and shot him in the face, but Christie escaped after shooting Isabel in the shoulder, crippling him for life. In another battle with Deputies William Bouden, Milo Creekmore, David Rusk, and Charlie Copeland in the Cherokee Nation, Christie wounded three of the officers and escaped unscathed. Finally he ambushed one of Parker's deputies, likable Dan Maples, as the officer was crossing a stream on a foot log, and fled to the hills.

The marshals learned that he was holed up in a log fort at

the mouth of a narrow canyon called Rabbit Trap, fourteen miles from Tahlequah. About daylight on the morning of November 2, 1892, the place was surrounded by sixteen of the bravest men under Marshal Jacob Yoes' command, led by Heck Bruner and Captain G. S. White.

The presence of the officers was unknown to the outlaw until about sunrise, when Arch Wolf, a comrade of Christie's, started for the spring. They ordered him to surrender; he opened fire and ran into the house, and the battle began.

The fort stood high against a steep wall, commanding every approach up the canyon. One man with a rifle could have held off a posse indefinitely. The battle raged into the afternoon without results. Several deputies had holes burned in their clothing by Christie's bullets. Christie was a dead shot, and none were so foolish as to rush the outlaw's hot Winchester.

Bruner reported the situation to Marshal Yoes at Fort Smith. Yoes, determined to take the killer at any cost, assumed personal command of the venture. He dispatched Bruner and Paden Tolbert to Coffeyville, where they obtained a three-pound cannon. Hauling the cannon in a wagon, the party returned to the scene.

They set up the cannon and opened fire. They hurled thirty balls into the fort, but they were too far away, and Christie's rifle kept them from moving the cannon in where the balls could take effect. The marshals had to try something else.

They had also brought along some dynamite. A half-dozen six-inch sticks were bound together. While the rest of the posse covered him with a heavy barrage from both sides of the canyon, Deputy Copeland placed the bomb and returned to safety.

The charge exploded, blowing down part of the house and setting fire to the ruins. While the blaze was at its fiercest, Christie emerged from under the floor and started to run. A dozen shots brought him down, and the officers turned their attention to the burning building. Wolf did not show, and it was assumed that he had been wounded and burned to death. Later they learned he had escaped in the confusion of the battle, and he was caught and sent to the penitentiary for assault with intent to kill. Christie's body was placed on a slab and hauled to Fort Smith for official identification, then given to relatives for burial.

Intrepid fighting men, these marshals, picked for their ability to handle tough assignments. They always got their man, but they made no corps' boast of it as did the Northwest Mounted Police and the Texas Rangers.

The test was not always being able to bring in the criminal dead or alive. The prosecution needed evidence to convict, and often a man-sized share of courage was needed to collect it. Such a case involved Deputy Marshal John Spencer.

Martin Joseph, a Texas horse thief, murdered Bud Stephens, raped and murdered his sixteen-year-old bride, and threw their bodies into a deep crevice at the back of a cave on top of the Arbuckle Mountains. Months later, Deputy Marshal J. H. Mershon apprehended Joseph, obtained a confession, and took him to Fort Smith, where the details of his crime were placed before District Attorney Clayton. Clayton wanted evidence to corroborate Joseph's confession. He told Marshal Yoes: "We ought to have the bones of the victims."

"We'll get them," Yoes promised.

A party was dispatched to the deep hole in the mountain. Spencer volunteered to go down and bring up the bones. The others tied a rope about his waist and lowered him into the dusky pit.

What Spencer didn't know was that a den of rattlesnakes had set up housekeeping in the bones of the two victims. As his feet touched the bottom there was a sudden rattling and hissing. In the dim light Spencer saw the skeletons crawling with the mass of scaly repiles.

"For God's sake, pull me up quick!" he screamed.

A moment later he stood back on the floor of the cave, white-faced and trembling. His nerves soon steadied, however. Then, with a lantern in one hand and his revolver in the other, he asked to be lowered into the pit a second time. Taking advantage of the blinding effects of the light upon the reptiles, he aimed at the shining eyes of the largest and nearest snake as it reared to strike, and fired.

The explosion extinguished the lantern. The snake, threshing about in wild death agony, coiled itself about his arms and neck.

Spencer kept his nerve. He called for his companions to throw down a sack. The noise of the explosion had frightened the rest of the snakes from the skeletons, and Spencer was not again molested.

Quickly he gathered the bones, including the clothing of the victims, then signaled to be pulled to the top. When he appeared on the rim with one end of the huge rattler wrapped about his arms and the other around his neck, his companions almost let him fall back into the pit. The bones and clothing were produced during the trial before Judge Parker, and Martin Joseph died on the gallows.

As time went on and the officers solved crimes and brought in more and more prisoners, their daring and morale was appreciated by the law-abiding citizens of the district, and they were often commended for their tireless efforts. Once, when appropriations were short and fees delayed but their work continued, the observing editor of the *Elevator* commented, "The failure of Congress to appropriate funds for the payments of the marshals seems to have little effect in this district." [20] Again, on July 30, 1880, he wrote: "The office of the marshal in other places is kind of a matter of form, but the marshal's office in the western district of Arkansas is very different on account of its vast territory and the immense amount of business transacted." Even as early as 1875, less than six months after Judge Parker had taken his place on the bench, the *Oklahoma Star* was moved to say:

The relation this country bears to the United States government makes the marshals office for the Western District of Arkansas of the most vital importance to us. In fact we are dependent solely upon it for the preservation of our lives and our property. But for this protection no honest man could live in the Territory. The present incumbent, James F. Fagan, was raised on our border, and is well known to most of our people, and we will venture to say that nine-tenths of them would rather see him in the position than any man that could be appointed. Before he came into office we had been imposed upon to such an extent that our best citizens had come to look upon U. S. deputy marshals as a greater curse than the thieves and murderers that infested the country, and of the two evils they preferred taking their chances among the latter.[21]

Most of the seven marshals [22] appointed by Presidents during Parker's term merited and preserved general respect. The Department of Justice gave Parker free rein. Judge Story had given the department a bad name and caused all sorts of difficulty. It was such a relief to have things going smoothly again that they said nothing when Parker influenced appointments. As a judge, Parker was reluctant to interfere in such matters, but when Fagan left office in 1876, Parker wrote a letter to the White House recommending D. P. Upham for the job. "As fine a man as ever I saw," Parker said. "He is honored by all except Ku Klux, thieves, gamblers, drunkards and liars." In 1880, when President Rutherford B. Hayes gave the office to Valentine Dell, Parker described the latter as "ill natured, irascible and impractical . . . a friend of bad and reckless men who only want an opportunity to filch money from the government." A few months later he wrote Hayes: "If we had the strong arm of an able and honest and effective Marshal to protect us, we could enforce the law and make its power felt. . . . In the interest of justice and right, peace and security, send me a man who can and will do his duty."

When Hayes failed to respond, Parker went after Dell's scalp. He was aided by District Attorney Clayton and the prosecutor's brother, Powell Clayton, United States Senator and Republican boss of Arkansas. Dell was dismissed February 20, 1882.

Dell was succeeded by Judge Thomas Boles. Boles was a native of Arkansas. He had been judge of the Fifth Judicial District from 1865 to 1868, served three terms in Congress, and was receiver of the land office at Dardenelle at the time of his appointment as marshal. An able lawyer, kind and sociable in private and public life, and reliable, he became an exceedingly popular officer. He was succeeded by John Carroll,[23] appointed under Cleveland's first administration, in 1886; in 1889 he became a candidate for reappointment, and a petition circulated in his behalf bore 16,000 signatures. But for the sake of party harmony, Boles withdrew and Jacob Yoes was given the place early in 1890.

Parker had trouble with some of the deputies, too. None were angels. Many were bullies. Nearly all were coarse-talking, unsentimental individuals. The personal characters of some of his most famous officers would scarcely bear careful scrutiny. But the judge winked at that sort of thing as long as they served the cause of justice in this haven of the worst hellions on earth. As Parker aptly put it, he was "obliged to take such material for deputies as proved efficient in serving the process of this court. . . ." A coward could be highly moral, but "he could not serve as a marshal in the Indian country."

But when the time came that he could no longer wink at a deputy, Parker never hesitated to let his influence be felt. In 1896 he sentenced Deputy Bee Mellon to three years in the penitentiary because he "did more shooting than was justified in an attempt to make an arrest." Before this, in 1892, when Deputy Marshal Tucker went on a drunken spree at "Chippy Hill," a section of South McAlester devoted to prostitution, and shot and killed an inmate of one of the houses, Lulu May, who refused him admittance, Parker sentenced him to hang.[24] But President Cleveland exercised his clemency and the sentence was commuted to life.

There were deliberate efforts to discredit these officers in the eyes of Parker and the public in general. In 1877 Anna Jones, a female inmate of the federal jail, publicly announced that Jailer Pierce had many times attacked her person. Brought before District Attorney Clayton for questioning, she claimed that she had complained about the "slop" fed the prisoners and Jailer Pierce had taken her to his private office and assured her that better food could be had if she would "cooperate." "I wanted to eat," said Anna, but she had received no better food, and she had been forced to "cooperate repeatedly thereafter." Pierce wasn't the only one, she said. After her release from jail, she claimed she had been "approached" by the other guards, the deputies, and even the United States Marshal.

"She came to this jail a common prostitute," commented Marshal Upham, "and she is now following here in Fort Smith the usual vocation of her class."

"A common strumpet," said District Attorney Clayton. "The lowest of her kind."

The case was aired before Judge Parker. Anna Jones was proved "an adroit liar," and Jailer Pierce exonerated.

A petition came to Judge Parker bearing the signatures of fifty persons asking for the removal of a deputy marshal because he was partial to a certain class. The deputy was in the Indian country on assignment at the time, but when he returned, Parker called him in and showed him the petition.

"What do you know about this?" the judge asked.

The marshal read the paper. When he had finished, he looked up with a smile. "Judge," he replied, "I brought in sixteen prisoners this trip. Four of them are signers of this petition, all arrested on writs from this court."

The four men in question were arraigned, all pleaded guilty

to their different crimes, and all were sentenced to long terms in prison.

Parker appreciated the noteworthy work of these deputies and their loyal assistance to the bench. They took desperate risks, and Parker saw that they were rewarded by seeing that the men whom they arrested were tried promptly, "with a large percentage of convictions." [25]

On April 21, 1876, less than a year after he opened his first term of court, five murderers were marched onto the gallows and plunged through the trap together. [26]

"The crowd was as great, if not greater, than at any previous execution. . . . Those present must have numbered between six and seven thousand. . . ." [27]

On September 8, 1876, four men stood on the scaffold and were hanged as a quartet. [28] In 1877 ten more convictions were had for crimes of murder and rape, and ten offenders sentenced to the rope. Two of these hanged together on December 20, 1878. [29] In the spring term of 1879, four were sentenced to hang. One died in jail while awaiting his turn to model the fatal necktie, and another had his sentence commuted by the President. The remaining duet went to their deaths on August 29. [30] Nine murderers were tried in the August term, 1881, and on September 9, five of them marched onto the gallows and died simultaneously. [31] In 1882 three were sentenced to die for murder. One received a commutation to life imprisonment, and two were executed in single hangings occurring June 30, 1882, and April 13, 1883. [32] Another trio was hanged on June 29, 1883. [33] Three more died on the gallows together July 11, 1884, [34] and another single hanging occurred April 17, 1885. [35] Eight were convicted of murder in 1885, all sentenced to die on April 23. However, the scaffold was cheated of its largest scheduled set of victims. One died in jail, five were commuted to life, and the two remaining completed the first raw, red decade of Judge Parker's tenure by falling through the trap together on June 26. [36]

A draft of official records for this ten-year period shows that, in addition, 466 were convicted for assault with intent to kill; 1190 for selling liquor in the Indian country; 97 for illicit distilling; 124 for violating the internal revenue laws; 65 for violating the postal laws; 50 for counterfeiting; 24 for arson; 48 for perjury; 32 for bigamy; 27 for conspiracy to commit crimes; 59 for stealing government property; 24 for resisting arrest, and 149 for miscellaneous offenses.[37] Witnesses, always numbering into the hundreds, reached three thousand at one term of court, and witness fees, never less than $41,000 annually during this period, reached at one time the staggering figure of $137,240.[38]

The coolness that attended Judge Parker's arrival at Fort Smith gave way to enthusiastic support. The *Elevator* said: "The Judge is giving entire satisfaction to both the bar and the public. He brought with him . . . a higher appreciation of his duties than his predecessor."

"Confidence in the court has been restored," wrote the editor of the *Herald*. "Moneys appropriated are being properly applied. . . . The court and the several departments are being run in perfect order and harmony."

A later issue described Parker as "a man of coolness, calmness and great deliberation."

The *Independent,* his greatest political critic in the beginning, was most responsive to "this almost revolutionary improvement."

Even a "stroke of conscience" seemed to have effected Congress. By an act approved January 31, 1877, Section 533 of the Revised Statutes was amended to read:

"The Western District of Arkansas shall consist of the counties of Benton, Washington, Crawford, Sebastian, Scott, Polk, Sevier, Little River, Howard, Montgomery, Yell, Logan, Franklin, Johnson, Madison, Newton, Carroll, Boone and Marion, and the country lying west of Missouri and Arkansas known as the Indian

Territory. The Eastern District of Arkansas shall include the
residue of the state." [39]

Thus the portion of Arkansas attached to the Western District consisted of nineteen counties in compact form, reaching
across the state from the north to a line even with the southern
boundary of the Indian country. Although Congress had reduced the jurisdiction of the Fort Smith court, they "gave evidence of common sense . . . as commended them to all fair
minded people . . . and the work of the gerrymanders was
destroyed." [40]

The position of the marshals strengthened. "A certain esprit
de corps grew up, and it is clear that this was due to the fact
that these officers realized that their efforts were not in vain." [41]
They no longer thought of themselves as mere deputies, but
as "The Men Who Rode for Parker."

Day after day, year after year, they ranged over this vast
region of wooded hills, long-grass pastures, and creek bottoms,
past lonely houses and ranches and wigwams and through the
raw prairie towns. And with them rolled the wagon of the law
to transport their captives. A sort of prison caravan, for usually
it was composed of a chuck wagon and extra mules and horses.

Camping at night on high ground under the stars. Eating
with Winchesters across their knees. A summons here, an arrest
there, gathering a load of prisoners, and starting the long,
dangerous haul back to Fort Smith. Watching the captives
every moment, appraising them, trying to read their thoughts
as they gazed into the campfire or carelessly ate their beans or
stared somberly across the prairie where some of them would
never ride again. Guarding them while they snored in their
blankets, chained to a tree or the wheels of the wagon.

The arrival at Fort Smith was a social event. They ferried
their wagon and prisoners across the river on a boat, and the
people came down to the docks and gathered on the sidewalks
to see who they had brought in this time. Sometimes they would

string out behind the caravan, and follow it through the streets on foot and on horseback like a circus. At the jail the prisoners would push their faces against the bars and hoot and yell while the wagon discharged its cargo. Then the guards took over. The new prisoners were marched through the main gate, and the gate closed behind them. The journey was over. The horses were returned to the men who rented them, the wagon went to a local shop for repairs, and the deputies filed claims for their pay. Some went to the saloons to relax from the strain of the trip. Most of them went home to their families.

How many outlaws did they bring to justice? The records show thousands. They brought them in six and sixteen and twenty-six at a time. On one occasion Deputy Marshal Heck Thomas and his posse surprised Parker with thirty-two prisoners in a single group, nine of whom were found guilty of crimes punishable by death.

The basement jail to which they first brought their prisoners became overcrowded and vile-smelling of food, sweat, tobacco juice, and urine. It was cold in the winter, damp in the summer, and in all seasons poorly ventilated. Segregation was impossible, and young and old, innocent and guilty crowded together with desperadoes and sadistic murderers upon the unpitying flagstone floors. The sick slept with the well, and despite the efforts of physicians, who were in charge constantly, several men died and others left jail physical wrecks. The guards fought the odor and disease with whitewash and lime, but theirs too was a losing battle. Vermin infested its precincts until its very existence was a veritable curse upon the government that harbored it and a disgrace even to the rough border town in which it existed. Members of grand juries hardly dared to enter, yet for too many years human beings—though many of them the most debased characters on earth—were allowed to be thrown into this hellhole of filth.[42]

Judge Parker fought hard to remedy these conditions. So did the marshal and the district attorney. As early as 1883 the Attorney General called the matter to the attention of Congress.[43] But nothing was done. The Indian country, which furnished most of the jail's prisoners, had no representative in Congress. Most of the congressmen from Arkansas were Democrats, and they did little to help Parker, a Republican, get aid from Washington.

Finally, in 1885, the *Elevator* took up Judge Parker's cause and strongly attacked the congressman from the Fort Smith district:

> Our representative should be the exponent and advocate of those places which originate and ask something for themselves. . . . Fort Smith, for ten years, has anxiously sought a penitentiary and a U. S. jail . . . and asks for them. . . . Such a building is a public necessity, and the present one a disgrace to a civilized people. . . . Our representative need not be afraid to get up a bill and fight it through. We say we have not the least doubt that having at his back a DEMOCRATIC House, should he place this matter before them in his bold, impressive manner and with the gift of the English language that does him credit, and said to them that this court is for the whole Indian Territory, and every member of the House was as much interested in the Indian Territory as he was, and called on all to support it, not as an Arkansas but as a National matter, it must pass.[44]

And the Attorney General again told Congress:

> This place, dignified by the title United States jail . . . in which white, black and Indian prisoners are indiscriminately huddled . . . is a standing reproach. It is under the supervision of the United States Marshal. This officer has done the best he could with the materials at hand, and it is not his fault that he is a nominal warden of the most miserable prison probably in the whole country.[45]

After repeated complaints from the officials, the newspapers, and humane agencies, money was appropriated and construction begun on a new, three-story brick jail in 1886.[46] Upon completion in 1889, the men prisoners were taken out of the basement and the women brought from their little brick shack on the courthouse yard, and all confined in the new quarters. The lower floor was designated "Murderers' Row," and used for prisoners charged with severe crimes. The second floor was used for prisoners charged with burglary, robbery, larceny, assault, and similar offenses; and on the top floor were confined persons charged with selling or introducing whisky into the Indian country and all federal prisoners convicted by the United States court and sentenced to imprisonment not to exceed one year. Each floor consisted of twenty-four cells, five by eight feet in size and equipped with two iron cots, one above the other, so as to accommodate two prisoners each; but before many years passed of Judge Parker's second decade on the bench, this new jail too became overflowing.

V

FIVE HUNDRED MILES TO
FORT SMITH

"Oyez! Oyez! The Honorable District Court of the United States for the Western District of Arkansas, having criminal jurisdiction of the Indian Territory, is now in session," rolled the voice of Court Crier J. G. Hammersly.

"The court is ready for the first case," announced Judge Parker.

"The United States versus Peter House," called the clerk. "Charge, bigamy."

A bigamy case was nothing to excite even passing interest in the days when murder was commonplace. At the moment there were 204 prisoners in the federal jail, 69 of them charged with capital offenses. Attorneys took advantage of the opportunity to make last-minute preparations for these more important cases scheduled for the November term beginning Judge Parker's second ten years on the bench. The judge adjusted his spectacles and scanned the list of more than a score of terrorists as he waited for the defendant to be brought in.

Finally a thin-faced, balding man with beady eyes, heavily manacled, was led to the bar. Parker looked over his glasses at a most unprepossessing specimen of manhood.

"Who is this?" he asked. "He's not the man. This is a bigamy case. *This* man never caught a gal in his life."

The judge was right. Peter House, who was up for the crime, was a handsome man of fine physical build; the bailiff, through error, had brought in Lee Galcatcher, who faced a charge of perjury.

Later House was brought in, found guilty of the offense, and sentenced to five years in prison.

This was one of the lighter moments in this most unique court in the world. Despite his stern bearing on the bench, Judge Parker was a congenial man and enjoyed a harmless joke better than anybody.

One day an aged Irishman, charged with selling whisky in the Indian country, was arraigned before Parker.

"Plaze, yer honor, an' may I plade me own case?" he inquired.

"Certainly," replied the judge.

"Then," said Pat, "I plade guilty."

The plea brought a twinkle to Judge Parker's eye, and drew for Pat the lowest sentence the court could fix.

On another occasion a son of Erin who answered to the name of Mike was up for a minor offense. He provoked the court no end by consistently interrupting the testimony of the witnesses for the prosecution in an attempt to correct statements in his favor. Parker ordered him down several times without success. In an exasperated moment, the judge brought his gavel down hard.

"Sit down, Mike!" he commanded. "You will get justice."

"Be jazzes, an' that's what I'm scared of," Mike replied.

The proceedings were suspended until the court and attorneys recovered from a spell of laughter.

In another case a witness for the prosecution was testifying to the law-abiding and peaceful character of the complainant. The defense attorney, a shrewd lawyer, sought to lay the predicate for impeaching the witness's testimony.

"As a matter of fact," said the attorney on cross-examination, "you know that the complainant is quarrelsome and that he has a lot of trouble with his neighbors."

"Yes," admitted the witness.

"Don't you know that he gets drunk and whips his wife and that last spring he almost beat his young son to death and that nearly every time he comes to town he gets in jail?"

"That is true," the witness replied.

"What!" boomed the attorney. "You know all this about the complainant and you swear on your oath that his reputation is good in your community?"

"Yes," stated the witness earnestly. *"It takes more than that to give a man a bad reputation up where I come from."*

A smile broke the judicial seriousness of Judge Parker's face, but in a moment those grave lines had returned, and he remarked firmly:

"That indicates the class of persons this court has to contend with."

A brief but exciting scene was witnessed by more than a hundred persons attending the trial of Mat Music, a Negro charged with raping a seven-year-old child at Caddo, Chickasaw Nation, and transmitting to her a venereal disease. The case came up in the July term of court, and the summer heat was terrific. The sun beat down on the roof of the old barracks courtroom. Every window in the place was open to admit any breath of air.

The trial proceeded slowly. Attorneys and jurors wiped perspiration. Mat Music, strong, powerfully built, and quick as a cat, conceived a plan to escape. In the rear and to the right of the defendant were three large windows, but half a dozen marshals occupied positions near these. In front of him Judge Parker sat at his cherry-paneled desk, which was nearly five feet high. Behind Parker a large window opened into the jail yard. In front of the desk stood a wide, flat-topped table stacked with court exhibits, law books, and papers. By springing onto this he could fling himself over the judge's bench and leap through the window before the marshals could swing into action. They would not dare fire at him for fear of hitting the judge. So reasoned Mat Music.

While the defense idly argued a point of law, the Negro lurched suddenly onto the table. But Judge Parker was watching. As Music topped the desk and executed the leap to clear Parker's head, the judge shot out his arm and hooked it around the Negro's thick neck. The force of the Negro's jump carried both men to the floor. Music fought to free himself, but Parker held him until the marshals had him shackled hand and foot.

Afterward, the trial proceeded with great alacrity.

Although Parker "frequently gave vent to humor on the bench" [1]—or occasionally aided in preventing the escape of a prisoner—"he never hesitated to impose sentences designed to make the Indian Territory safe for law-abiding citizens of all races." [2] The juries of his court came from the Arkansas side of the district, and the people of the Indian country often complained that they were "being tried by foreigners." [3] Another matter of concern was the pay of jurors—$2.00 per day. They felt that only shiftless and incompetent men did jury service. Judge Parker influenced the grand jury to recommend that the pay be raised to $3.00 per day "to attract jurors industrious enough to have other occupations." [4] These juries were praised for the way they upheld the law. They were usually composed of high-caliber men, and the judge was "very solicitous of their welfare." But it was more, perhaps, because Parker never hesitated to let them know when he wanted a conviction. In his charge to his first jury he plainly expressed his conception of the court's judicial duties.

"The fault does not lie with juries," he said. "Juries are willing to do their duty, if they know that the judge wants the law enforced. . . ."

At the close of one murder trial there was some belief among court attachés that there might be an acquittal. The accused was a young man of considerable influence. He had been ably defended, and throughout the proceedings his mother and sister had sat clasped in each other's arms, moaning. Parker was thoroughly convinced of the defendant's guilt, but he obviously shared the doubt of the other court officers. After he had given the jury its instructions, he said: "Retire, gentlemen, and *do your duty*."

When the jury returned to the box and the foreman announced that they had found the defendant "guilty as charged of murder in the first degree," Parker turned to the manager of the hotel where the jury ate its meals. "Have you a good dinner prepared for these men?" The hotel man nodded. "Then," Judge Parker continued, "take them over and give it to them. They deserve it!"

Parker went further than this and often advised and influenced government witnesses. "Such a reign of terror exists among them," he said, "that they are afraid to talk in open court. . . ."

Once while examining a witness on the stand, the judge asked: "Don't you know you are swearing a lie?"

"Yes," the man replied.

Parker leaned down from the bench. "Don't you know what it means to swear an oath?" he snapped. "Do you know the penalties for contempt and perjury in this court?"

"Yes," grunted the witness. "But if I swear against the defendant, his pals will give me plenty when I get home."

Parker could not guarantee them much protection, but he let these witnesses know he was on their side. If they were wronged as the result of testimony they had given, and that was the evidence in the case, they would get justice.

"But," argued the witness, "what good will that do me if I'm dead?"

On the other hand, when witnesses for the defense were caught in a lie or contradiction, Parker upbraided them severely. Under the judge's vigorous attack and threats to cite them for contempt, many became confused and bewildered or forgot completely the testimony they had been "coached" to give. Too often in the Fort Smith court the defense was sustained by perjury.[5] The average killer, when arrested, would boast of his deeds; but when he came to trial, he was always "the most respectable, peaceful man in his community" while his victim was a quarrelsome individual, or lying witnesses were ready to prove an alibi.

In these interrogations District Attorney Clayton worked closely with Parker. Trying to prosecute lawbreakers under the same difficult circumstances, he, like Parker, often scouted legal procedure and precedents. Not that he was not skilled in marshaling evidence and using it to the best advantage; most of the cases coming before the court were based on circumstantial evidence, and time and again Clayton surprised the courtroom throngs with the strength of the case he was able to present. But he angered defense witnesses so that they could not testify effectively, and tried to drag out any bad record that had a bearing upon their association with the defendant. And Judge Parker reciprocated by ruling that such questions were "competent to test reputation." If the defense resorted to the same methods, Clayton would object, and Parker usually advised the defense to "stick to the case being tried."

Defeated attorneys damned Clayton as "unfair." "The judge had no right to help the prosecution," they cried. But those close to the Fort Smith court replied: "The judge and his prosecutor behaved no more badly than the defendant's lawyers."

Parker said: "It is our desire, and our duty, to uncover perjury and falsehood and bring to justice false accusers or false witnesses, wherever we can find them, whether they are upon the side of the government or against it."

Parker and Clayton were not so severe in dealing with defendants in doubtful cases. Many times they were willing to reduce a charge of murder to manslaughter. In crimes not involving homicide, Parker often handed down less than the maximum penalty and occasionally suspended sentences. His keen sense of justice made him a stickler for the right when evidence showed the defendant was innocent.

A posse of marshals had gone to a Creek Indian lease near Checotah in search of a man wanted for train robbery in Texas. Fearing their quarry might escape before they could obtain a search warrant, they invaded the defendant's home just before daylight, and the latter, not knowing they were officers of the law, shot and killed a Cherokee Indian policeman, Jim Naked-head.[6] Judge Parker instructed the jury to acquit the defendant of the murder charge; that he had a right to resist such an attack by officers who had no warrant for his arrest or to enter his home. When the verdict of "not guilty" was given, a roar of applause filled the courtroom. Men yelled and threw their hats in the air. To the judge this was sacrilege. He rapped the bench with his gravel. When order had been restored, his dark eyes flashed and his deep basso, with powerful dignity, rolled to every corner of the room.

"Justice is justice—not chivalry!"

He then ordered the arrest of every man who had participated in the outburst and fined each $50.

Although his court properly held only criminal jurisdiction over the Indian country, several civil cases came to Parker in this period. In 1875 he decided two important cases involving Indian citizenship. Did a white man who married a Cherokee Indian woman in the Cherokee Nation, and was recognized as a Cherokee citizen, become thereby an Indian in law and subject to the jurisdiction of the Cherokee courts where he and a Cherokee Indian were parties to an offense? No, Parker said, a white man who married a Cherokee woman and thereby became a citizen of the Cherokee Nation was still under the jurisdiction of the United States court. How about the Plains tribes having reservations in the Indian Territory? Were they subject to the jurisdiction of the United States court for offenses committed against the person or property of another Indian? Yes, ruled Parker; though living in the Indian Territory in their tribal capacity, they were nevertheless citizens of the United States, and "if an Ottawa should steal the horse of another Ottawa in the Ottawa Nation, in the Indian Territory, the United States court has sole and exclusive jurisdiction."

In the early 1880's he made three famous decisions of far-reaching consequence affecting the title of Indian lands, which brought him both praise and censure from the Indians. In 1882 he held that the people of the territory were without recourse against timber thieves who came from across the border. There was no law on the subject, the lands of the territory were not public lands within the meaning of the law, and he, therefore, had no jurisdiction. The Cherokees loudly protested.[7]

Later, when Congress passed the right of way for the Southern and Kansas railroad company through the Cherokee Nation pursuant to the Act of July 25, 1866,[8] the Cherokees instituted a suit in the United States court in the nature of an injunction. Congress had no power to grant such right of way, they claimed. The right of eminent domain was not in the United States when the enjoyment of whatever right or privilege flowed from it was to be had in the Cherokee Nation. Such right was in the nation alone. Railroad company attorneys filed a demurrer on grounds that the bill was without equity because the right of eminent domain was in the United States and not the Cherokee Nation. No more important question had been placed before the courts of the country for years. Said Judge Parker:

> The Cherokee Nation is not . . . sovereign, for its dependence on the United States forbids the idea of the existence of sovereignty in the Cherokee Nation as against the United States. If not sovereign it cannot as against the United States have the right of eminent domain as an inherent right. It cannot have it as it has

not been granted it by the government, as the government cannot grant away the sovereign powers of the people. . . .

He sustained the demurrer, refused the injunction, and dismissed the bill.[9] The Cherokees again protested. His decision opened the way for the construction of railroads through tribal domains.

It was different in the case of trespass upon their lands by the crusading frontiersman David L. Payne and his land-hungry followers, the "Boomers." The unsettled lands in the center of the Indian country had been earmarked for the Indians since 1866, but never assigned by the government. Payne and his Boomers, claiming they could homestead or pre-empt the land, moved in from Kansas across the Cherokee Outlet. Many times they were thrown out by the military. Finally Payne was arrested and brought to Fort Smith for trial as an intruder under the Intercourse Law.

It was by far the most important case ever to come before Judge Parker. Delegates from the Five Tribes assembled at Eufaula for a two-day meeting, in which they discussed the forthcoming trial at length and pledged $4820 to employ the best legal minds of their nations to assist District Attorney Clayton in his prosecution.[10] They were joined by the cattle kings who were using the country as grazing lands.

On the other side, with the Boomers, stood a "powerful combination of greedy St. Louis and Kansas businessmen," Kansas newspapers and railroad companies which, although already granted a right of way through the Indian country by the government, were more anxious than Payne to see the Indian titles to the lands extinguished. There was even strong support for the movement in Fort Smith. The *Elevator,* Parker's strongest advocate, gave its sympathy to Payne and screamed "Bayonet rule!" when the Boomer chief was brought in under guard.

Parker believed in territorial organization for the Indian

country. He had fought for it in Congress when he was representative from Missouri. But, like his old boss, President Grant, he believed it should come only after a period of years when the Indians had "become sufficiently advanced . . . to guard their own rights." To uphold the Boomers meant "legalizing the overwhelming of the whole territory" by the white man. Too, the question was not whether the Unassigned Lands were public domain. Payne faced a charge of trespass on the lands of the Cherokee Outlet. There was no way for the Boomers to enter these lands without crossing the Indian country and becoming intruders.

Payne's attorneys contended that he had been improperly brought to Parker's court and that jurisdiction in the case lay with the court at Wichita, Kansas. Parker ruled that only land not belonging to the Cherokees was assigned to the Kansas court. He said that the Cherokee Nation, while under the political control of the United States and dependent upon it for its political rights necessary for the protection of its people, "owns the soil of its country," and fined Payne $1000.[11]

Accordingly the Cherokee Outlet was properly within the jurisdiction of the court of the Western District of Arkansas, and the Boomers must keep out.[12] By asserting the jurisdiction of his court, Parker had also established the Cherokee's title to 8,000,000 acres of land. The Five Tribes celebrated their victory and forever afterward regarded Parker as their "powerful friend and ally."[13]

All this was Judge Parker on the bench—impartial, inflexible. "But it was in his private life where the triumphs of his character shone most resplendent."[14] Then he was plain Isaac Parker, a gentle, kind, companionable man. His "problem area" was in the Indian country to the west, so nothing prevented him settling down to a quiet existence among the people he was to live with for twenty-one years.

He lived half a mile from the courtroom and walked to work every day. He stopped to chat with the merchants up and down the street, showed an interest in their business, and passed the gossip of the day. He found them to be "first-rate people, who wanted schools, hospitals and peaceful progress," and he joined them in advancing Fort Smith to "Queen City of the Southwest, entitled to wear a gemmed crown of the superlative degree." [15]

Within ten years he saw the dirty frontier hamlet he had looked upon the morning of his arrival by boat up the Arkansas become a town with sidewalks, gas works, electric lights, street cars, and excellent railroad connections, and declared a city of the first class.[16] In his first decade on the bench its population jumped to over 11,000. By 1887 it boasted one of the largest cotton-seed-oil mills and compresses in the world, three large cotton gins, two grist mills, three large saw and planing mills, two furniture factories, two foundries, several wagon factories, an ice factory, and one of the best waterworks systems in the South. A fifty-thousand-dollar opera house and a twenty-five-thousand-dollar canning factory were under construction, and a company had been formed and a charter applied for to build a four-hundred-thousand-dollar bridge across the Arkansas. "A great agricultural, timber, coal, mineral, manufacturing and wholesale and jobbing center, with the best cotton market in the South handling 45,000 to 50,000 bales per season, and the great United States court here, in session the year around, disbursing over two hundred thousand dollars per annum." [17]

Parker worked for the general growth of the city, but he was most noted for his work with the schools. He was given special credit for preparing the bill by which Congress donated the old military reservation, adjoining the principal part of town, to the schools of Fort Smith. "A generous fund amounting to more than half a million dollars in real estate, dedicated to education. . . . If used with wisdom and advantage, Fort Smith stands pre-eminent among her sister cities." [18] From this fund, and school taxes, were constructed three large schools for whites and one for colored children. Here Parker saw his two sons receive their public education, grow to manhood, and enter the law profession. Charles, the older, began his practice in St. Louis, and James entered a law firm in Fort Smith.

While he observed the proprieties of his judicial position with regard to politics, during his last four years on the bench the voters of this overwhelmingly Democratic community twice elected him to the Fort Smith Board of Education. "There was no politics in this . . . the tribute was to the man and not to the position he held; it was a recognition not only of his sterling qualities, but also of his affectionate interest in the children of the town. . . . To the children of the day he was the very embodiment of that patron saint of childhood made famous by the 'Night Before Christmas.' " [19] In his later years, as his hair and beard turned white and his cheeks grew pink and rotund, "he had a twinkle in his eye and a little contagious chuckle which always made them think of Santa Claus." [20]

During the four years he served as director of the board, he never missed a meeting.

> In these meetings he had the courage of conviction, and in many embarrassing and perplexing questions presented he stood, always, for the integrity, purity and efficiency of the schools and the sacred preservation of the property of the district. He looked forward to the time when night schools could be organized for indigent young men and women, whose conditions imposed upon them labor during the day, and he cherished and often spoke of adding several industrial features to the system so that young men and women might not only be trained morally and mentally but also given some means of earning a livelihood when they had completed their school course.[21]

Parker's home was open for counsel to the poor and unfortunate, and he contributed liberally to charitable causes. Although he never identified himself with any religious denomination until he joined his wife's church just before his death, he went to church every Sunday, and nearly every Sunday also attended church with Mrs. Parker. He possessed a strong religious disposition, as evidenced by the admonitions given to the men he sentenced to death. On execution days he returned home and prayed. When he finished sentencing the first six men to the gallows, he bowed his head and wept.[22]

"I do not desire to hang you men," he said. "It is the law."

It seemed strange that a man with such compassion could become so relentless in his fight against outlawry. The entire district over which he presided felt the effect and wondered at his strong character. Whereas his predecessor was noted for seldom holding court, Judge Parker gained notoriety for seldom adjourning. At the beginning of his tenure there were but two terms, May and November. Parker merged one term into the other with no apparent break, and never recessed until the last case scheduled had been tried. He opened court at 8:30 in the morning and closed at dark. Often he held night sessions at the requests of attorneys. He observed no holidays except Christmas and Sundays. In no other manner could Judge Parker have disposed of the tremendous volume of work that constantly pressed him.[23]

Within the walls of the old federal courtroom, month after month and year after year, the daily grind continued, and "Tried, found guilty as charged, sentenced" was the tale repeated until the mere fact of arrest meant almost certain conviction. The sentence "To die on the gallows" was passed upon more men here than anywhere in history. So numerous were the executions he ordered and so commonplace the thunderous crash of the gallows trap that street urchins playing outside the old walls would gleefully shout: "There goes another man to hell with his boots on!"

Its crash was also a familiar sound to the prisoners in the federal jail, and "its grisly echoes should have been an unquestionable deterrent to men of violence throughout the Territory. But how vain its iron warning. . . . Always there was someone to step into the vacancy made by the gibbet. . . ."[24]

Two men were hanged together April 23, 1886.[25] Two died together July 23,[26] and one hanged August 6.[27] On January 11, 1887, the morbidly curious who gathered in the jail yard saw four murderers drop through the trap at the same time.[28] Another murderer who was to have hanged with this quartet, but was granted a reprieve until the President and Attorney General examined his case, died alone April 8.[29] Two were hanged the same year on October 7.[30] On April 27, 1888, a trio fell through the trap.[31] There were single hangings on July 6, 1888,[32] and January 25, 1889.[33] Two died April 19, 1889,[34] and on August 30 two more murderers formed a duet on the scaffold.[35] On January 16, 1890, a second sextet of felons marched up the gallows stairs.[36] A few minutes later six bodies dangled between heaven and earth.

Judge Parker became "rank poison" to the vicious and the criminal of the Indian country. His reputation as "The Hanging Judge" spread until curious witnesses throughout the land and from points as far away as London and Paris ventured to this wild region in droves, to observe the proceedings in his court and hear his pronouncements of doom.

Famous, too, became wispy, long-whiskered George Maledon, the executioner. He seldom smiled and took a natural pride in his work. His ropes were made of chosen hemp fiber, woven by hand in St. Louis, and treated with a pitchy oil substance to prevent their slipping. When he retired from his uncanny business in 1894, he took with him one rope on which he had hanged twenty-seven men, another he had used to string up eleven, and another nine. With these mementos, other gruesome instruments of his office, and numerous photographs of the most notorious desperadoes with whom he had dealt, he toured the country towns and small cities within five hundred miles of Fort Smith, pitching his tent and lecturing on the lives of the various criminals and "how they came to their deaths in the name of the law."

He was proud of his ability to always break the neck of his

victim rather than strangle him to death, and accepted with aplomb the monickers tacked on him by journalists—"Prince of Hangmen"—and on the scaffold on which he performed his duties—"The Gates of Hell." [37]

"Get out your oilcan, Maledon," was the grim jest of officers and court attachés after each capital conviction. It was Maledon's cue to oil up the squeaking hinges of the gallows traps. But they had little time to get rusty.[38] During his twenty years of service, he hanged sixty [39] of the seventy-nine men executed under Judge Parker.

Maledon was also an expert pistol shot. Although small of stature, he carried two guns, was left-handed, and could shoot equally well with either hand. He shot four prisoners who attempted to escape while awaiting trial. Another, a Negro named Frank Butler, cheated the gallows by trying to escape Maledon the night before his execution. The hangman fired one shot, and the prisoner fell dead at the feet of his parents, who were waiting for him outside the wall. Afterward it was learned that his death had been planned that way. They knew of the unerring aim of Maledon. They had agreed with their son that it was better to die in this manner than by hanging.[40]

Many stories were told of how the gallows behind the jail was haunted. Inmates claimed that they frequently saw ghosts standing on the scaffold. Others saw strange beings coming over the walls with ropes about their necks. On one night, it was reported, a multitude of spirits gathered on the platform of the death-dealing structure and seemed to be holding a meeting preparatory to making an attack upon the prison. But these stories were largely believed by Negroes and superstitious whites. Before Maledon left Fort Smith, he was asked by a lady whom he was escorting on a tour of the jail if he had any qualms of conscience or feared the spirits of the departed.

"No," he replied. "I simply did my duty. I never hanged a man who came back to have the job done over."

On execution days it was Maledon's duty to make the necessary arrangements. He picked special guards and instructed them so the condemned could not escape. He saw that they dressed neatly and inspected their weapons. After 1881 they were furnished uniforms.

He provided new suits and coffins for the prisons and arranged for transportation of unclaimed corpses to the cemetery. In 1882, because these hangings had "taken on the aspects of a carnival," Washington ordered them closed to the public. A stockade was built around the gallows and the number of official witnesses cut down to forty. Maledon received the additional duty of supervising the issuance of passes.

While these arrangements were being made, the condemned prepared themselves to die. They were urged to pray and talk to the ministers who came to their cells, to "save their souls for eternity." "No matter how many stains of blood there may be on the hands," Parker had said, "lift those hands in supplication to the Judge of the quick and the dead . . . and let the heart speak out contrition and sorrow." At first they laughed and jeered at his words, but many, on the eve of their execution, asked permission to be taken from the jail and baptized. Nearly all, in some manner, thought of their sins and salvation before the trap fell from under their boots.

A draft of official records for the first fourteen years' work of the court shows the appalling figure of ninety-three men convicted of murder and rape committed in the Indian country and ninety-two of these sentenced to hang. Of the ninety-three total, one died in jail awaiting sentence, forty-six died on the scaffold, two died in jail awaiting execution, forty were commuted by the President to terms of from four years to life imprisonment in federal penitentiaries at Albany, New York; Columbus, Ohio; Detroit, Michigan; Joliet and Menard, Illinois; Little Rock, Arkansas; and Moundsville, West Virginia; two were granted new trials, and two were pardoned by the President.[41]

Little wonder that the criminal feared Parker and his Fort

Smith justice. To the law-abiding citizens he was the frontier's "rock of security," but to the brigands he was "hell on the border."

Throughout the Indian country they denounced him as "Hanging Parker" and "Bloody Parker" and "Butcher Parker."

Out in No Man's Land on the banks of the Canadian River a sign had been nailed to a sycamore post at the crossing of two main trails. At its top an arrow pointed eastward and beneath it was the legend:

500 MILES TO FORT SMITH

A band of horse thieves fleeing the territory a few jumps ahead of the marshals paused long enough to empty their rifles and six-shooters into the board to show their contempt for Fort Smith and the federal court, then fled to safety.

One of them, returning past the sign a few days later, noticed that they had nearly riddled it with bullets. Struck by the humor of the situation, he removed his dirk, and standing high in his saddle, added two words to the legend. The sign then read:

500 MILES TO FORT SMITH—AND HELL

For most of them, Judge Parker made the distance much shorter.

VI

LADY DESPERADO

ONE OF THE ONLY TWO MURDERERS THESE FIRST FOUR-
teen years Parker served as judge of the Western District of
Arkansas to finally receive a pardon from the President was
a white man who flourished under the alias "Blue Duck." On a
drunken spree with William Christie in the Flint District of the
Cherokee Nation, he rode into a field where a young farmer
named Wyrick was at work, emptied a revolver into the farmer's body, then reloaded, whirled his horse and rode off yelling,
firing a wild shot at an Indian boy in Wyrick's employ. He
went to the house of Hawkey Wolf, a neighbor, and shot at
him three times without injuring him, then rode about the country bragging to several persons that he had killed Wyrick.
Deputy Marshal Frank Cochran arrested the pair and took
them to Fort Smith, where Christie was acquitted and Blue
Duck was convicted of murder and sentenced on April 30 to
die on the gallows July 23, 1886.[1] But through the able assistance of his sweetheart—the dashing lady desperado, Belle
Starr, who hired the best lawyers in the country—he was twice
reprieved, and in September President Cleveland commuted

his death sentence to life imprisonment.[2] For by 1886 Belle Starr figured prominently in the criminal activities of the Indian country.[3]

She was the most notorious outlaw to be sentenced by Judge Parker.

She was born Myra Belle Shirley, February 5, 1848, in Jasper Country, Missouri, on a farm to which her parents, John and Eliza Shirley, had migrated from Virginia in 1846. When she was eight the Shirleys left the farm and moved to Carthage, where John Shirley opened a combination livery stable, blacksmith shop, and crossroads cavaransary on the direct trail south from Independence to Fort Smith and west through the central part of the Indian country to Santa Fé along the route surveyed by Captain Randolph B. Marcy in 1852. Here John Shirley became prominent in politics, was highly respected, and prospered. At the Carthage Female Academy, Myra Belle learned her three "R's" and how to play the piano, and was otherwise given every chance to grow up to be a nice little girl. But her overpowering interests were horses and guns, and by the time John Brown had stirred bad blood between abolitionist Kansas and proslavery Missouri, she was an expert horsewoman and a deadly shot with pistol or rifle.[4]

Pillaging and murder swept the border states. At the outbreak of the Civil War, citizens of both commonwealths found themselves at the mercy of guerrilla bands who joined first one side and then the other for the sole reason of looting and the lust to kill.[5] Myra Belle was fifteen when the ruthless rebel leader Quantrill sacked and burned Lawrence, Kansas. She saw him build a small band into an army of hard-riding, well-disciplined raiders whose exploits attracted the cream of frontier bad men, among them Cole Younger and the two Kentucky-born sons of a Baptist minister, Frank and Jesse James; and she idolized them as dashing heroes of a lost cause.[6]

Her brother Ed led his own band of Jasper County bushwhackers operating out of Carthage. When he was killed and the town razed by Federal troops in the summer of 1863, Myra Belle flew into a rage, strapped two pistols about her waist, and rode off to join the guerrillas. She became informant for the Rebels. Many Federal troops died in broad daylight and small detachments were wiped out as the result of information furnished by this revenge-crazed girl.[7] A few months later Carthage was again raided and the Shirley home burned.

Sick at heart, John Shirley moved his family to Texas, "where the social atmosphere was more to his liking," settling between Mesquite and Scyene, east of Dallas. He reverted to his old profession of farming and raising fine horses. He placed Myra Belle back in school and tried to cure her of her flamboyant ways; but in 1866, dark, handsome, twenty-four-year-old Cole Younger rode into the Shirley ranch with his three brothers and Frank and Jesse James, fresh from their first bank job at Liberty, Missouri, and Myra Belle fell in love with Cole. When the outlaw rode back with his gang to Missouri in 1867, he left her pregnant with a child.[8]

Myra Belle never saw Cole Younger again. The gang startled the nation with its daring bank and train robberies. Sheriffs and Pinkerton detectives were hot on their trail. At Northfield, Minnesota, the gang was nearly annihilated; only Frank and Jesse escaped; Cole and Bob were wounded and captured and sentenced to life terms in the state prison at Stillwater.[9]

Meanwhile, Myra Belle's scandal swept the Texas countryside. Scyene society ostracized her. When the child was born, a daughter whom she named Pearl Younger, she left it in her parents' care and "entered the saloon life of Dallas." For a while she sang in the dance halls, dealt monte, faro, and poker. She dressed "spectacularly," but "within the conventions," and did "very well financially."[10] But she got a craving for a successor to Cole Younger, settling finally on Jim Reed, an "obscure but proficient" young horse thief operating around Dallas.

Reed was twenty-eight years old, five feet eight, and slender, with a Roman nose and sandy hair. He had migrated to Texas from Vernon County, Missouri, in 1872, settling on Coon Creek in Bosque County.[11] A few months later he sold his farm and moved to Scyene. He made love to Myra Belle, and over the "violent opposition" of John Shirley, married her and took her, with her illegitimate child, back to Missouri and his family at Rich Hill.[12]

This was the beginning of her career in banditry. Reed was a member of a large band of horse thieves led by the Texas outlaw John Fischer. The band preyed on Texas herds and ran them north. Myra Belle found in these activities the freedom her soul craved, and aided his aspirations until the Shannon boys, members of a competitive outfit, ambushed Jim's brother, Scott Reed, mistaking the latter for John Fischer. Jim went after the Shannons and killed them, and had to flee the country to avoid arrest on two warrants charging murder. He sent for Myra Belle and little Pearl, and for a while they found refuge in California. Here her second child, Ed Reed, was born in Los Angeles. Then a local constable learned there was a reward offered for Reed. A matter of a stage robbery near San Diego also helped hasten their departure from the state.

Myra Belle returned to Texas. The birth of this second child had somewhat reconciled John Shirley.[13] He took in his daughter and the children, but Reed, "being an asset of too much value for him to remain long in one place," sought refuge in the Indian country and made periodic visits to his family by stealth.[14]

He hid out on the ranch of Tom Starr, a Cherokee, who had the reputation of being the worst Indian with whom the tribal government ever dealt.[15] A strong advocate of the Southern cause, he had stirred up such an outburst of robbery and murder against the Ross faction of the nation that the Cherokee Council made a treaty with him, granting him amnesty for his past crimes and a good slice of tribal wealth to be a good boy. Tom and his sons, Sam, Cooper, Molsie, Tuxie, William, Ellis,

Jack, and Washington, including two daughters, Nettie and Sophie—together with their numerous cousins and in-laws— all had taken land between Briartown and Eufaula on the bend of the Canadian. It was a remote region rarely traveled by people not friendly with the Starr clan, and therefore a safe retreat for outlaws of the Reconstruction disorder. Jim Reed had made old Tom's acquaintance about the same time the Jameses and Youngers used his place as a hide-out after the breakup of Quantrill's guerrillas. Here Belle came to meet her husband, and thus became acquainted with handsome young Sam Starr, Jack Spaniard, Jim French, Felix Griffin, Blue Duck, and a host of others whose names were to grace the most spectacular period of her life.

During one of her visits, in November, 1873, Belle, dressed as a man, accompanied Jim Reed and Daniel Evans [16] in the robbery of Watt Grayson, a wealthy Creek Indian living west of Eufaula not far from Tom Starr's home. Grayson and his wife were tortured by the robbers until he revealed the hiding place of over $30,000 in gold coins.

The following April, in 1874, when Jim was paying one of his visits to Belle, he teamed up with two of his old Missouri pals and held up the Austin–San Antonio stage north of Blanco,[17] obtaining $2500 in cash and four gold watches.[18] Abandoning their jaded ponies, the trio took the "spirited animals belonging to S. T. Scott & Co.'s stages," and headed "in a northwestern direction, keeping between the settlements and the Indian country." [19] On April 28, 1874, the Dallas *Daily Herald* announced the arrest of "two of the participants in the robbery" in Dallas, and on August 6, 1874, Jim Reed was slain by Deputy Sheriff John T. Morris of Collin County in a cabin near Paris.[20]

Belle now embarked upon that part of her lurid career for which she became notorious in Judge Parker's court. She took her son Ed to Rich Hill, Missouri, and placed him in the care of Grandmother Reed; shipped little Pearl to other relatives in Arkansas; and returned to the Indian country to "practice the profession she knew best." She joined the Reed gang of "rustlers, highwaymen, Indian half-breeds and cowboys" and dominated them with her "scathing tongue, superior intelligence and sex appeal." They stole cattle and horses, highjacked the tribal treasuries, ran whisky to the Indians, and burglarized stores. Belle never participated in the raids herself, but served as the "brains" of her ruffianly crew, and became so successful in securing "the quickest possible release" of any member of the gang who got arrested by the marshals that they regarded her as a sort of magician.[21]

She disposed of the loot they brought her through "fences" and helped them whoop off the profits at the seasonal stomp dances, horse races, and near-by Indian Territory "boom" towns in general "fornication and merriment."

Tulsey Town (Tulsa) had one two-story hotel from which drunken cowboys shot out the window lights regularly, and its share of "masculine social centers." Saloons being prohibited in the Indian Territory, the pool hall, with its merry click of balls and loud merriment, the back room with its card games and liquor and swirls of tobacco smoke, became the centers of cheerful talk, amiable profanity, and the dampening of one's jollity. Claremore was a "bad" town, but Catoosa, on the branch of the Frisco railroad running out of Missouri through it from Vinita to Tulsa and the crossroads of two important cattle trails, was the "hell-hole" of the whole territory.[22]

Hotels, stores, the livery stable, not to mention the wily bootlegger, all did a rushing business. Occasionally inebriated riders raced their ponies up or down Main street, whooping mightily and emptying their revolvers at the sky, though sometimes the aim was careless and store windows or false fronts suffered as a result. The noisy celebrants often kept up the rattle of pistol shots far into the night. Not infrequently arguments or smouldering grudges flared up, ending in fist fights or gun smoke. Except for a United States marshal or a deputy who occasionally rode through, there was no constituted authority of law and order. . . .[23]

Here Myra Belle caroused and made love to the characters she liked best, finally marrying young Sam Starr, and thus she became Belle Starr, the name by which she is best known to posterity.

Sam's ranch was in the bend of the Canadian River under Hi-Early Mountain. The only approach was over a narrow canyon trail set with boulder-guarded caves. By this marriage, Belle had "acquired dower rights to Sam Starr's share in the communal lands" of the nation; she moved right in and named the place "Younger's Bend," obviously in token of her "sentimental rememberances of her first lover." [24] It became a new refuge for fugitives, and so inaccessible was her stronghold and so smooth her operations, she was not arrested until she and Sam were caught stealing horses from a neighbor's corral on April 20, 1882. They were taken to Fort Smith to face Parker.

The trial began February 15, 1883. It lasted four days and became a national sensation. Reporters seized upon Belle as "copy," and Eastern journals and newspapers headlined her "Queen of the Bandits," "The Lady Desperado," "Wild Woman of the Wild West," "The Petticoat Terror of the Plains." She had achieved the notoriety of her childhood playmates—the Jameses and Youngers. She was convicted on two counts, Sam on one. Judge Parker sentenced her to two six-month terms and Sam to a full year in the House of Correction at Detroit. [25]

In nine months both were back at Younger's Bend. They took into the gang a new member named John Middleton, a cousin to Jim Reed. Middleton was wanted in Arkansas for larceny and arson and in Texas for murder. A few nights before his arrival at Younger's Bend he had gone to the home of Sheriff J. H. Black of Lamar County, called him to the front door, and shot him down in cold blood.

Meanwhile, Sam Starr and Felix Griffin held up the Creek Nation treasury. The marshals captured Griffin [26] and obtained a warrant for the arrest of Starr. Starr fled from Younger's Bend, but with the marshals and Indian police so thick in the neighborhood, Middleton began worrying about his safety and decided to head for a mountain hide-out in Arkansas near his mother's home at Dardanelle.

Belle's love had grown cold for Sam since their stay at Detroit. With Sam on the dodge and her left alone with Middleton, it soon became "enkindled." She decided to accompany Middleton and "give Sam the slip." They rode together as far as Keota. Here they separated, continuing on different routes to allay suspicion and meet later near Dardanelle. Middleton never reached his destination. A few days later his horse, still saddled and bridled, was found tangled in the brush on the bank of the Poteau in the Choctaw Nation. Near by, washed up on the bank and half-buried in mud, lay the outlaw's body. His face had been blown away with a shotgun, Sam Starr "having trailed him silently." [27]

Belle returned to Younger's Bend. Whether she gave Sam an excuse for her actions, or whether even she considered it necessary, is a matter of conjecture. Sam knew the "kind of slut she was" and that he was "sharing her" with the other outlaws, but he had to stay on the dodge. Belle's attentions had centered on Blue Duck when he went on a rampage and murdered the farmer Wyrick. Even after she succeeded in getting his sentence commuted, she was unable to spring him from prison, and found herself again "lonesome" for male companionship.

Sam ventured back to Younger's Bend in March, 1886, and was surprised to find Bill Vann, chief of the Cherokee Lighthorse, and a posse waiting for him. In their raid on Belle and Sam, they captured a white man named Jackson, but nine others escaped, Sam Starr by jumping his horse off a bluff over twenty feet high and swimming the river. "These officers are determined, however, to break up this band of cut-throats, robbers and horse-thieves, and say they will never let them rest in peace. This is certainly a bad gang, and we would rejoice to know that they were out of the country. . . ." [28]

On May 28, 1886, Deputy Marshal Tyner Hughes arrested Belle on a charge that, dressed in male attire, she had led a party of three men who robbed an old man named N. H. Farrell and his three sons forty miles from Fort Smith in the Choctaw Nation. At the hearing, however, neither Farrell nor his sons were able to identify anyone, and Belle was released. A few weeks later she was arrested for stealing horses from one Albert McCarty. Belle again successfully fought her case, and was discharged when the jury found her "not guilty as charged in the within indictment."

Sam Starr was still at large. Late in September, Chief Vann, his brother R. P. Vann, Frank West, and Deputy William Robberson, sighted him riding through a cornfield. Vann called on him to surrender. Starr set spurs to his mount and started shooting. The posse returned his fire, knocking him from the saddle and killing his horse.

With the outlaw in custody they proceeded to a farmhouse near by. While they were dressing his wounds, preparatory for the long ride to the tribal council, the Starr gang raided the farm, overpowered the officers, and then escaped with the prisoner.

Belle learned that Vann was organizing a huge posse to wipe out Younger's Bend and recapture Sam. She prevailed upon Starr to surrender to the United States marshals, explaining that he would have a much better chance defending himself on robbery charges in federal court than before a tribal council. Furthermore, if he gave himself up to the marshals, the Indian officers could not arrest him.

It was good advice, considering how the chiefs hated old Tom Starr and all his family. Too, Sam did not fancy the punishment dealt out to offenders of tribal laws. So Deputy Marshal Tyner Hughes was surprised on October 11, when the long-hunted Starr rode unarmed through the streets of Fort Smith and surrendered to him at the federal jail. As usual, Belle immediately employed the best lawyers. In a short time Sam had been arraigned, released on bail, and sent on the way back to Younger's Bend to await the date of his trial.

On Friday night, a week before Christmas, Mrs. Lucy Surratt, who lived near Whitefield on the Canadian, gave a dance at her home and invited the neighborhood. Belle and Sam decided to attend. They arrived at the place after dark. Sam was drinking and in a bad mood. The moment his eyes fell upon Frank West, who was also attending the dance, he said:

"You are the son of a bitch who shot me and killed my horse that day in the cornfield!"

West denied both charges. Starr drew his gun. He shot West in the neck. As the policeman fell he pulled his own revolver from the pocket of his overcoat and sent a bullet through Starr's heart. Both men were dead within two minutes after sighting each other.

With Starr's death, things quieted down at Younger's Bend. Pearl Younger and Ed Reed, Belle's daughter and son, now grown, came to live with their mother in her log cabin under Hi-Early Mountain, and readily took up with the wild and criminal associates they found there. In April, 1887, Pearl gave birth to an illegitimate daughter in Siloam Springs, where Belle had sent her, telling her she never wanted to see the child. Pearl left the child in Arkansas and returned to Younger's Bend, refusing to disclose the name of its father. Meanwhile Ed evinced a fondness for liquor and began selling it to the Indians. On July 22, 1888, he was convicted of horse stealing and sentenced to seven years in the federal penitentiary at Columbus. But through the efforts of his mother and the attorneys she hired, he received a pardon within a few months. When he returned to Younger's Bend, Belle had married again, this time to a tall young Creek named Jim July, who was only twenty-four years old but was well educated and could speak the languages of all the tribes fluently.

July was under indictment in Judge Parker's court for horse stealing when Belle moved him in at Younger's Bend. On

February 2, 1889, he left for Fort Smith to answer the larceny charge. Belle, riding her favorite white horse Venus, accompanied him as far as San Bois, a distance of fifteen miles.

On her return she stopped at the home of a man named Rowe to visit his wife, and while there met E. A. Watson. The rumor was that Watson was wanted in Florida for murder. He had been in the neighborhood about a year. He had been dickering to lease a part of Belle's acreage for farm land, which Belle had declined to do. On the occasion of her visit at the Rowes', they renewed the argument, during which Watson remarked about the frequency with which federal officers came to look her over.

Belle replied: "Maybe the officers in Florida would like to know where they could find you?"

It was believed that Watson decided Belle was going to turn him in; that he went home, armed himself with a shotgun, and waited in a fence corner for her to ride past as she left the Rowe place.

That afternoon two men at the ferry on the south side of the Canadian heard shots, and a moment later Belle's horse with an empty saddle ran down the trail and swam the river. One of the men, Milo Hoyt, hurried up the trail and found Belle lying face down in the mud. A charge of buckshot in the back had unhorsed her. A charge of turkey-shot had been fired into her face and neck. When the animal reached home, Pearl, fearing something had happened, mounted and rode back, soon reaching the scene of the murder.[29]

July was in Fort Smith when he received the wire about his wife's death. He bought a quart of whisky, saddled his horse, and headed for home with bad blood in his eyes and the ominous promise: "Somebody is going to suffer." [30]

The distance was about seventy-five miles. He arrived at Younger's Bend in nine hours. The story of Belle's quarrel with Watson at the Rowes' had been circulated. A set of tracks similar to those of Watson had been discovered leading from his house to the point where the assassin stood, then by a circuitous route back again, and his shotgun had been found in his home with both barrels freshly discharged.[31] July threw his Winchester on Watson and accused him of murdering his wife.

"If you kill me," Watson told him, "you will kill an innocent man."

He denied any knowledge of the crime.[32]

July informed him that he was under arrest, and Watson agreed to accompany him to Fort Smith without the formality of a warrant. The small party of witnesses, including July and his prisoner, accompanied by Pearl Younger, arrived in Fort Smith the following day, and July swore out a charge against Watson.[33]

The testimony was taken before United States Commissioner Brizzolara. The evidence was all circumstantial. No one seemed anxious to secure an indictment against Watson except July. Watson's neighbors refused to testify against him. They swore he was a quiet, hard-working man, well liked by everyone, and had caused no trouble since coming to the community. The rumor that he was wanted in Florida proved to be false. Commissioner Brizzolara ordered the defendant discharged.[34]

July jumped the bond on the horse-theft charge pending against him. Judge Parker issued a warrant for his arrest, and on January 23, 1890, Deputy Marshal Heck Thomas brought him back to Fort Smith, badly wounded. He had been shot by Deputy Marshals Bud Trainor and J. R. Hutchins near Ardmore in the Chickasaw Nation. And this is how that happened.

After Watson was released, he called Deputy Hutchins to his home and told him he had been framed by Jim July; that July had come to his house at three o'clock the afternoon he supposedly had been en route to Fort Smith and asked to borrow his shotgun "to kill a wolf that has been catchin' my chickens." When July returned the gun an hour later, both barrels had been fired. Shortly afterward Watson had learned that Belle Starr had been murdered and that he was suspected.

Watson gave Hutchins the empty shells, and the marshal took them, with his new information, to Judge Parker. It was Watson's word against July's, but Parker saw no reason for the farmer to lie now that he had been freed on the charge. He authorized Hutchins to go to Younger's Bend and find out what he could.

From Milo Hoyt the deputy learned that a short time prior to the shooting, July had offered him $200 to kill Belle. Hoyt had declined, and July, spurring his horse savagely, had ridden away, shouting: "Hell—I'll kill the old hag myself and spend the money for whisky!"

"Why would July want to kill his own wife?" Hutchins asked Hoyt.

"I reckon because Belle caught him playing around with a little Cherokee gal over at Briartown. She told him she would do nothing to help him fight that case he had coming up at Fort Smith."

This, one may conclude, was the reason Belle rode with July only as far as San Bois.

Obviously July sensed that Hutchins was finding out too much. Rumors came to the marshal that the outlaw intended to kill him. While Hutchins was on another assignment down in the Chickasaw Nation, an Indian woman sent her young son to warn him that the outlaw had stopped at her home near Rock Creek making inquiries for him, and had left heading for Ardmore.

Hutchins and Trainor proceeded to the woman's home at once and picked up July's trail. At daybreak they overtook him and demanded his surrender. July reached for his guns and set spurs to his long-legged sorrel. Hutchins opened fire, wounding him seriously with the first shot, and July surrendered.

Four days after the outlaw arrived at Fort Smith he was removed from jail on the verge of death. He asked for Hutchins, stating that he had an important confession he would give only to the man who had shot him. Hutchins was notified to come to Fort Smith at once, but before he arrived, July was dead.

The deputy was confident that July would have told him: "I killed Belle Starr." [35]

Whoever was guilty, July or Watson, Belle Starr was dead. And she died as she had lived, ingloriously and ignominiously.

Pearl Younger had her mother taken to the Bend and buried behind one of the cabins, and erected over her grave a monument of native stone. At its top, chiseled in relief, is the image of her favorite horse Venus with a B–S brand on its shoulder. Above and to the right is a star, and below, to the left, is a bell. At the bottom is a clasped hand filled with flowers, and the following inscription:

BELLE STARR
Born in Carthage, Mo.
Feb. 5, 1848
Died
Feb. 3, 1889
"Shed not for her the bitter tear,
Nor give the heart to vain regret;
'Tis but the casket that lies here,
The gem that filled it sparkles yet."

VII

"AFTER I AM KILLED!"

ON THE EVENING OF JUNE 1, 1892, THE SOUTHBOUND
Santa Fe pulled out of Arkansas City across the Cherokee Outlet
en route to the Unassigned Lands, which had been opened to
white settlement on April 22, 1889, and named "Oklahoma."
The train was loaded with passengers. Conductor Harry Wilcox
was in charge. In the express car behind the engine rode E. S.
Whittlesey, the express messenger, and John A. Riehl, a Wells
Fargo Express guard.

It was 1 o'clock when the train reached Red Rock, in the
northwest corner of the Otoe and Missourias reservation in the
Cherokee Indian strip. Just as it was pulling out a few minutes
later, two men with black masks covering their faces jumped
suddenly into the engine's cab from the tender, and covering the
engineer and fireman with revolvers, commanded them to run
the train down to the stockyards and stop there at a given signal.
Mack, the engineer, and Frank Rogers, the fireman, obeyed the
command. To have resisted would have meant their death. When
the train stopped, the two robbers were joined by five masked
companions.[1]

99

The train was in the hands of the Dalton gang—the most desperate band of robbers to infest the Indian Territory.

Whittlesey and Riehl, anticipating what was going on when the train came to a standstill, had blown out the lights in their car and refused to allow anyone to enter. The gang opened fire on the car from all sides, sending lead whipping through the wooden sides and windows, even getting under the car and shooting through the floor. But the two men bravely stood their ground, returning the fire courageously, and drove back the robbers.

Finally the leader seized a coal pick from the engine. He handed it to the fireman and ordered him to go forward and open the door. This placed Rogers literally between two fires, and engineer Mack, seeing that it meant death to his companion, explained the situation to the men inside and told them to cease firing.

Whittlesey and Riehl allowed Rogers to approach the car. He chopped a hole in the door large enough to admit a man's body, and was told to crawl through it into the car. The moment he was inside, Riehl ordered him to go to the opposite end of the car and lie down. Then the guard shouted to the bandits that the first one to enter the opening would be shot dead.

Another fusillade poured through the car while Riehl and Whittlesey hugged the floor, with their guns trained on the doorway. During the siege, the fireman kept begging the men to give up, and after each volley the leader outside would shout: "If you lay down your guns and come out with your hands up, you won't be hurt."

Realizing that they all might finally be killed, the two men surrendered. When the robbers entered the car, they covered them with their guns, and with a sledge hammer and chisel broke open both the "way" and "through" safes and robbed them of everything of value. After taking a gold watch from Riehl and both men's weapons, they mounted their horses and escaped in the night.[2]

The year before, on May 9, 1891, the Dalton gang had held up the Santa Fe express at Wharton, in the Outlet.[3]

When the robbers boarded the train . . . the messenger was looking out the door of his car, and seeing what was going on, immediately closed and locked it. . . . While the bandits were detaching the engine and express car from the rest of the train and were running it to the place where the robbery occurred, two miles distant, the messenger disposed of most of the valuables in places of safety. . . . When the robbers appeared at the door, he made a show of resistance, but finally admitted them. They immediately made for the safe and demanded that it be opened. With feigned reluctance the messenger opened it, and at the command of the leader handed over the contents, among which was a package . . . containing $500. . . .[4]

On Tuesday night, September 15, 1891:

The southbound passenger train on the M. K. & T. was flagged at Lillietta, a cattle station a few miles north of Wagoner, and the express was robbed of about . . . $3000. The robbers did not molest the passengers and only detained the train a few minutes. So quietly did they do the job that the passengers did not know the train had been robbed until after they had pulled out and were nearly to Wagoner. Reports are conflicting as to the number of robbers, one being that there were only three and another that there were seven. . . . It is the general opinion that the job was done by the Dalton boys, and it is more than probable that they were 'in it'. . . .[5]

Following the Red Rock robbery, they held up the northbound Missouri-Kansas-Texas passenger train near Adair in the Cherokee Nation. This holdup, which occurred the evening of July 15, 1892, was as daring a feat as any accomplished in the band's career. The train carried an armed force of Indian police and railroad detectives, who poured a withering fire into the bandits as they broke into the express car. Several police and passengers were wounded, and Dr. W. L. Goff, who was sitting in a drugstore near the depot, was slain by a stray bullet.[6]

The wildest rumors concerning the lightning rapidity and secrecy with which Bob Dalton conducted the band's operations spread over the territory and into the bordering Kansas towns, and every act of particularly bold outlawry was placed to their credit.

> The James boys, with all their deeds of outlawry, surpassed in no way the crimes that the devilish Daltons have been known to commit. Schooled in vice and sin through older associates, serving apprenticeships under some of the greatest criminals the world has ever known, they now have blossomed out the peer of any gang that makes a living purely and alone from appropriating other men's honest gains at the point of knife and gun.[7]

Hardly had news of the Adair robbery hit the papers when the robbers appeared in El Reno, on the Choctaw Coal and Railway Company's lines, one morning when the streets were crowded with people, and entered the leading bank of the city. The only person in the bank at the time was the wife of the president, who fainted at the sight of their guns. The bandits leisurely helped themselves to all the money in sight, remounted their horses, and rode away. The raid netted them $10,000, which was such a severe loss to the bank it was forced into liquidation.[8]

The Dalton brothers who formed the gang—Grat, Emmett, and Bob—were the three youngest of a family of fifteen children born to Lewis and Adeline Dalton. Lewis Dalton was a Kentucky man who had fought in the Mexican War. Later he moved to Jackson County, Missouri, near the home of the notorious Jameses and Youngers, and married Adeline Younger, an aunt of the Younger boys. They moved some years later to Kansas, settling finally near Coffeyville. Here the children, except two, a boy and girl who died in infancy, grew up. Of the remaining thirteen children, eight boys and five girls, the three older brothers, Charles, Henry and Littleton, drifted to Texas and Montana. Another son, Bill, went to California, married, and settled down in respectability. In 1882 Lewis Dalton moved the rest of his family to the Indian Territory, leasing land in the Cherokee Nation near Vinita until 1889. Unsuccessful in obtaining a farm in the Oklahoma land rush, his temper soured, and he returned to Coffeyville, doing odd jobs about the country until his death in 1890. Charles, Henry, and Littleton returned to Oklahoma and settled down with their mother on some good claims they obtained near Kingfisher. Their sisters married well and located on farms near by. Another brother, Frank Dalton, had seen service as a deputy United States marshal under Judge Parker as early as 1884, and was known as a brave and effective officer. On November 27, 1887, he was shot and killed attempting to arrest three whiskey peddlers in the river bottoms west of Fort Smith.[9]

Marshal John Carroll appointed Grat Dalton to fill Frank's boots. Bob joined Grat as a posseman and soon thereafter was himself appointed deputy marshal under Jacob Yoes. Emmett, still a boy, was employed on the Bar X Bar ranch near the Pawnee Indian agency. He never held a federal commission but served as posseman under Grat and Bob.[10]

The three brothers were deadly fast with their guns, knew no fear, and rode like imps from damnation. They became known the length and breadth of the territory as dangerous men to affront. But the time came when it was another case where Parker could no longer wink at the Daltons as deputies.

Grat and his brothers became involved in several shady transactions, and finally "overstepped the bounds of official decency" by stealing and running away a herd of horses, which they sold in Baxter Springs, Kansas. They fled to California to avoid arrest on federal warrants, and here, on the night of February 6, 1891, they joined brother Bill in a daring but unsuccessful attempt to rob an express train at Alila in Tulare County. The fireman was killed, and the Daltons were charged with robbery and murder. Bob and Emmett fled back to the Indian country. Grat and Bill were captured and charged as accessories. Bill won an acquittal. Grat was convicted and

sentenced to twenty years in the state penitentiary, but escaped
from the train while being transferred to prison. Aggregate
rewards to the amount of $6000 were offered by both the rail-
road and express companies for the arrest of the Daltons and
their delivery.[11]

In the Indian Territory, Grat rejoined Emmett and Bob.
Bob, wilful and impetuous, became their leader. They added
two members to their band, Dick Broadwell and Bill Powers,
alias Tom Evans—two typical Territory outlaws. Within a
year they had successfully looted trains at Wharton, Lillietta,
Red Rock, and Adair, and been charged with numerous other
crimes.

The Daltons were familiar with the operations of the United
States marshals. They avoided capture by hiding in caves on
the Canadian River and in the Creek Nation.[12] Then, on the
crisp fall morning of October 5, 1892, they attempted the bold
task of robbing two banks at once in broad daylight at Coffeyville, where they had been raised from childhood and were well
known to most of the citizens. This was the last raid of the
Daltons, and according to the proud boast of Bob, their leader,
it would have eclipsed anything ever pulled by the James boys
and the Youngers.[13]

The gang was recognized the moment they rode into town
at nine o'clock. Word spread among the three thousand residents swiftly and silently. When the gang split and entered the
two banks, armed men took strategic positions.

As the outlaws emerged, they were met by a deadly barrage
of gunfire. Bill Powers was shot dead in the street. City Marshal
Charles Connelley wounded Grat Dalton. As the outlaw lay
on the ground dying, he lifted his six-shooter and killed the
marshal as the latter approached. Two citizens, Lucius Baldwin and George Cubine, rushed to the aid of Connelley, and
Dick Broadwell fired on them, killing both men instantly. As
Broadwell fled to his horse, a charge of buckshot caught him
in the right side and arm. Blood gushed from his wounds, but

he mounted and started out of town. He was hit again by a rifle bullet fired from the livery barn. Still clinging to his horse, he rode a mile from Coffeyville before he fell from the saddle into the road, dead. When Bob and Emmett rushed from the First National Bank, they met a citizen named Charles Brown. Bob put a bullet between Brown's eyes. He and Emmett then ran to their horses in the alley and mounted. A hail of lead tore Bob from the saddle; and Emmett fell from his horse badly wounded, and was captured. The battle had lasted ten minutes. Two hundred shots had been fired and eight men—four citizens and four bandits—lay dead in the street. Had the raid been successful, it would undoubtedly have been the largest of its kind in Western history, for when quiet had been restored, it was learned that the gang had taken $11,000 from the First National Bank and $20,000 from the Condon.[14]

Emmett Dalton was removed to a hospital, where he recovered from his wounds. He was tried for murder and sentenced to life in the Kansas state penitentiary. After serving fourteen years he was pardoned and restored his citizenship. He died in California in 1937.

This ended the career of the Dalton gang, but appalling tales of their escapades still filled the border press when Bob Rogers set out "to swell the list of bandits" in 1892. With the story of how the Daltons got their start ringing in his brain, he stole a dozen horses in the Cherokee Nation and sold them in Arkansas. Deputy Marshal Heck Bruner arrested him and took him to Fort Smith.

Judge Parker sentenced Rogers to the federal reformatory, but released him on probation because he was only nineteen. Looking down at the boy from his bench, the judge said:

"This is your first offense, lad. If you continue in this path of life, death may be the penalty."

It was good advice, but young Rogers didn't take it. For a while he continued to engage in petty thefts. On November 3, Jess W. Elliott, a Cherokee, went to Catoosa to serve some legal papers in the capacity of deputy constable for the Cherokee courts. He met Rogers in a pool hall. Both men were drinking, and they engaged in a fight. Elliott was beaten and knocked down before bystanders interfered. They got Rogers out of the place and kept Elliott inside until he was able to ride. When Elliott got on his horse and started up the street, Rogers followed. He "knocked the constable off his horse, cut his throat with a knife, making three horrible gashes, and left him in the roadway." A passerby observed Elliott "leaning against a post with the blood rushing out of him as if he were vomiting" and summoned a doctor and the neighbors. Elliott died within twenty minutes. The doctor and the neighbors built a fire and "stayed to watch the body where it laid" while a messenger went after Deputy Marshal John Taylor, but Rogers returned, "rode through the fire, ran them off, kicked and stamped the lifeless body of his victim, put on and wore his hat for a while, looked through the papers in his pocket and left" just before Taylor arrived. The marshal trailed him to Sapulpa, where Rogers had his horse shod the next day and left word that he was going west.[15]

A few months later he returned to the Indian Territory riding at the head of a gang of four desperadoes, among them a killer from Colorado with a reward of $1400 on his head named Dynamite Jack.[16] Duplicating the deeds of the Daltons, they robbed the Missouri-Kansas-Texas Railroad at Kelso; held up the Mound Valley Bank in Labette County, Kansas; and on Christmas Eve robbed the Kansas and Arkansas Valley train at Seminole switch.[17]

On January 8, 1894, Deputy Marshal W. C. Smith surprised Rogers at the home of his brother-in-law, Henry Daniels, where he and a member of the gang named Bob Stiteler had stopped to spend the night. Stiteler had gone upstairs and Rogers was sitting before the fire with his boots off when the officer came in and disarmed him. At Smith's orders, Daniels went upstairs and brought the other outlaw down. As the men dressed preparatory to going with the marshal, Rogers struck Smith in the head, knocking him down, and both outlaws escaped in the darkness. Stiteler was recaptured the same night and taken to Fort Smith.[18]

Between 3:00 and 4:00 A.M. on January 24, 1894, Heck Bruner's posse surprised the rest of the gang asleep in a hideout on Big Creek. They captured Dynamite Jack and killed his brother Kiowa, and Willis Brown was so severely wounded that he died en route to Fort Smith at Vinita.[19]

Rogers remained at large. On the night of March 13, 1895, a posse under Deputy Marshal Jim Mayes learned that the youth was hiding in his father's house at Horseshoe Mound, twenty miles south of Coffeyville. They rode to the place in the early morning hours and concealed their horses in a clump of trees bordering a dry creek. Inside the house, besides Rogers and his father, were Charlie Collier and his wife, who were in the elder Rogers' employ.

Mayes deployed his men so that the building was surrounded and a shotgun or rifle trained on every door and window. With eight men, the deputy then approached the front door and knocked. Collier opened the door, saw the group outside, and summoned the elder Rogers.

"What do you men want?" the father asked.

"We want your son," Mayes said. "The house is surrounded; he won't escape this time. Light a lamp."

Rogers complied. He admitted that his son was upstairs.

Mayes called to the youth: "Come down, Bob, and surrender."

"Come up and get me!" came the defiant answer.

Deputies W. C. McDaniel, Phil Williams, and C. E. Smith volunteered. The frightened Collier and his wife, clad only in night clothes, fled from the house into the darkness and ran to the home of a neighbor.

McDaniel took the lead with Williams behind him, and Smith brought up the rear. The father went ahead, carrying the lamp. At the top of the stairs Bob Rogers met them with a revolver in each hand.

"Drop those guns!" ordered McDaniel.

Bob fired. The bullet struck McDaniel in the heart, killing him instantly. Rogers' second bullet tore Williams' right arm from wrist to elbow. He staggered against Smith, and both men lost their balance and fell back down the stairway, followed by the frightened father.

Bob Rogers seized the dead marshal's ammunition belt and his Winchester. He began pumping lead through the floor at Mayes and the possemen in the room below, and they were forced to withdraw outside. From all points, then, the posse opened a hot, continuous fire into the upper part of the building. After a few minutes the elder Rogers was sent in to talk to his son and ask him again to surrender.

"I'll give up," the young outlaw replied, *"after I am killed!"*

The posse opened another barrage. Over three hundred bullets were fired into the upper story of the house. The inch boards offered little resistance, and after the battle it was discovered that some of the rafters supporting the roof had been cut in two and hardly a square foot of the upper half of the structure remained unripped by bullets.[20] By some miracle, the desperado survived.

Finally he called to Mayes: "If you let me bring my gun, I'll come out."

"Keep the muzzle down," the marshal advised.

Dawn was just breaking, but it was still too dark to define objects easily. Mayes and his men had taken cover behind a pile of poles about twenty yards from the front of the house.

The outlaw opened the door and peered out; he saw no one. He carried McDaniel's Winchester, muzzle downward. When he had advanced a few steps into the open, Mayes rose from behind the woodpile. Rogers stopped abruptly.

"Do you have a warrant for me?" he called.

"We don't need one," Mayes replied.

The rifle in the youth's hands jerked up. Instantly a dozen guns blazed, and Rogers, with a groan, fell forward riddled with lead.

VIII

THE INFAMOUS COOKS

During his last five years on the bench Judge Parker waged an incessant war against these outlaw gangs in the Indian country. On January 17, 1895, a young desperado was arraigned before him on twelve counts of armed robbery.

His full name was William Tuttle Cook, but from June, 1894, until his arrest and capture on January 11, 1895, he was known the length and breadth of the United States as Bill Cook, leader of the vicious Cook gang. With him rode such unenviable lights as Cherokee Bill, Lon Gordon, Henry Munson, Sam McWilliams alias Verdigris Kid, George Sanders, Jess Snyder, William Farris, Thurman "Skeeter" Baldwin, Elmer "Chicken" Lucas, Curtis Dayson, and Jim French, former member of the Jim Reed–Belle Starr gangs and onetime sweetheart of the outlaw queen.[1]

Bill Cook was a docile-appearing man. He was five feet and nine inches tall and of stout but not athletic build. He had a full, boyish face, ruddy complexion, light brown hair, a small mustache, and blue eyes. The fifteen hundred people who came to get a glimpse of him in his cell at the Fort Smith jail were amazed to find a mild-mannered outlaw. While he was being interviewed and photographed by newspapermen, one young lady sketched him, and many exclaimed: "Surely this isn't the famous Bill Cook? Why, he doesn't look like a bad man!" [2]

They overlooked the fact that he had headed an outfit so tough that it became unsafe for the railroad operating between Fort Smith and Coffeyville to carry any valuable express matter or passengers over the route at night; that for the six-month period his gang functioned the company changed its schedule, going through only in the daytime and then under heavy guard; that he had raided all that country lying between Fort Gibson and Wagoner and Muskogee, and all the towns along the Atlantic and Pacific Railroad as far north as the Kansas line; that he had become so ravenous and elusive that Washington was on the verge of sending out Regular Army detachments to assist the marshals and Indian police in rounding up his gang; and that at the time of his arrest the government, railroads, and express companies had placed on his head rewards totaling over $7000.[3] All this he had accomplished before he was twenty-one.

James Cook, his father, was a Southern man. He had fought in the Civil War on the Northern side. His mother was a quarter-breed Cherokee. They had married in the territory shortly after the war, settling on Grand River, four miles north of Fort Gibson, where Bill Cook was born December 18, 1873. When he was nearly three, the family moved five miles up the river. Here his brother Jim was born. In 1878 his father died; his mother rented the place and moved to Arkansas near Fort Smith, but she soon married again and returned to the old home on Grand River, later moving to Fourteen Mile Creek, where she died when Bill Cook was fourteen.[4]

For a while Bill stayed with his stepfather, then went on his own. He worked on cattle ranches in the Osage and Cherokee Nations, and learned "to ride, shoot, drink and play cards." He spent his earnings for whisky and sold it to the Indians. In 1892 he fled to New Mexico to avoid arrest on a warrant charging sale of liquor, but he was picked up when he returned to the territory in 1893 and sentenced by Judge Parker to forty days in the Fort Smith jail.

In 1894 he was charged with horse stealing, and again became a fugitive. That same year his brother Jim got into trouble in the Cherokee Nation. He fled to the Creek Nation to avoid arrest by the Cherokee Indian police, but a warrant was issued for him at Fort Smith charging assault with intent to kill, and the marshals began to hunt for him too. He joined Bill, and together they organized a band of thieves that within two months stole more than fifty head of horses from the country between Wagoner and Muskogee.[5]

On June 16, Bill and Jim Cook, in company with Cherokee Bill, started for Tahlequah to collect their share of the Cherokee Outlet money. On June 1, 1894, more than a year after the sale of the Outlet to the government and nearly nine months after its opening to white settlement, treasurer E. E. Starr of Fort Gibson, with Captain Cochran and fifty picked gunmen to guard him, had proceeded to Tahlequah from Fort Smith with $1,000,000. On June 4 the payment had commenced, averaging $265.70 to each member of the tribe.

Cherokee Bill was also a fugitive from the Cherokee Nation. The trio proceeded to the home of Effie Crittenden, a friend of the Cook family who lived on Fourteen Mile Creek within fifteen miles of Tahlequah. They wrote her an order for their money, and she went to Tahlequah and returned with it.[6] The Indian police, realizing the three fugitives must be hiding near her place, followed the woman home. They had divided the money and were getting ready to leave when the officers opened fire on them. In the gun battle that followed, Sequoyah Houston, a Cherokee marshal, was slain, Effie Crittenden's husband Dick and his brother Zeke were wounded, and Jim Cook, too badly shot to escape, was captured.[7] Bill Cook and Cherokee Bill rode to freedom. During the next few months so many robberies were committed in the Cherokee and Creek Nations that the columns of the border press and great Eastern dailies teemed with hair-raising tales, fiction as well as fact, about "Bill Cook, the Famous Outlaw."

On July 14, 1894, the Muskogee-Fort Gibson stage was held up by six masked robbers in the Arkansas River bottoms, and the passengers relieved of their money and watches. An hour later, William Drew, a prominent Cherokee, was held up on the other side of the river and robbed of $80 and a fine belt and pistol. Two days later, on July 16, Bill Cook, Cherokee Bill, Lon Gordon, Sam McWilliams, Henry Munson and Curtis Dayson held up the Frisco train at Red Fork.

Soon after 10 o'clock on the morning of July 31, five armed men rode into Chandler, Oklahoma Territory, across the Creek Nation line, and dismounted back of the Lincoln County bank. Three rushed inside while the other two stood guard at the doors with Winchesters. Two men covered President O. B. Kees and his brother Harvey Kees, the cashier, and demanded that they "cash up purty damn quick." The third man ran into the private office where teller Fred Hoyt was lying sick. The bandit ordered him to go to the safe and unlock it. Hoyt, already weak from his illness, fell on the floor in a faint, and the bandit fired at him, the bullet fortunately missing him and tearing into the floor.

The guards outside called that it was time to go, and the three men grabbed between $200 and $300 that lay on the counter and ran to their horses. J. M. Mitchell, a barber across the street, sounded the alarm and was killed by one of the guards. The bandits left the city with a posse of citizens and two deputy sheriffs in pursuit. Numerous shots were fired. One of the gang, Elmer Lucas, was shot in the hip and captured. The others scattered and disappeared in the hills.

At ten o'clock in the evening of September 21 the gang raided the J. A. Parkinson & Company store at Okmulgee, taking over $600. On October 5 they crossed the Arkansas at the ferry between Muskogee and Fort Gibson, and held up a traveler

Isaac Charles Parker, just past 35 years of age when he arrived at Fort Smith in 1875 and took over as the youngest judge on the federal bench, where he presided for 21 years. His motto was "Do equal and exact justice."

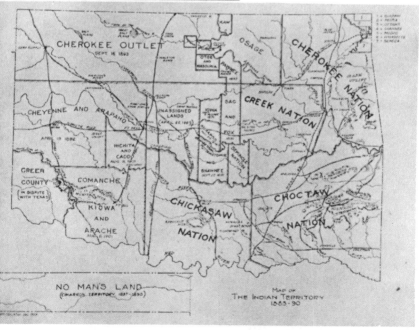

The Indian Territory, after the Civil War and the ceding of the Western lands of the Five Civilized Tribes to the Plains Indians, was called "Robbers' Roost" and "The Land of the Six-Shooter," and attracted the lawless and "the refuse of humanity."

Originally a military post on the Arkansas, built to preserve order among the Indian tribes, 1817–42, Fort Smith in 1871 became the seat of justice when an act of Congress moved the court there.

The U.S. marshals were intrepid fighting men, picked for their ability to handle tough assignments. A group of these brave men are shown with one of their wagons used to transport prisoners to the old federal jail (in background).

Each Indian tribe had its own tribal laws and sovereign government, and dispensed punishment with the whip and the rifle; but their laws did not apply to the white man. Above is a Choctaw Nation execution.

At left is a photograph of the last execution in the Seminole Nation under tribal laws. After January 1, 1898, the U.S. courts in the Indian Territory had exclusive jurisdiction over all civil and criminal cases and persons, irrespective of race.

Belle Starr, "The Petticoat Terror of the Plains," with Blue Duck, one of her sweethearts.

Belle Starr's home at Younger's Bend, Indian Territory, 1888.

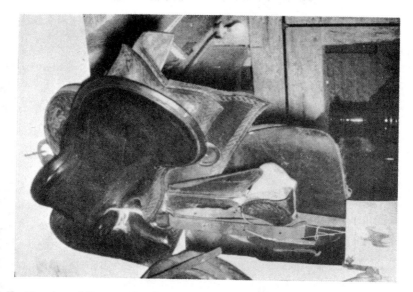

Belle Starr's saddle, now in the Fort Smith museum, is alleged to be the one she was riding the day she was shot from ambush.

Belle Starr's grave at Younger's Bend. On the tombstone is engraved an image of her favorite horse, a bell and a star, and the injunction to "Shed not for her the bitter tear . . ."

Some were taken alive: here is the Rufus Buck gang in chains, hanged as a quintet on the Fort Smith gallows, July 1, 1896.

And some were taken dead: here lie four of the Daltons—killed in the Coffey ville raid, October 5, 1892.

Taking his cue from the Dalton gang, Bob Rogers organized and led one of the fastest-riding, most dangerous bandit gangs in the Territory, until a posse riddled him with lead.

William Tuttle (Bill) Cook was known the length and breadth of the United States as the leader of the vicious Cook gang, until Judge Parker sentenced the captured outlaw to 45 years' imprisonment.

The officers' quarters at the Old Fort became the courtroom, and the basement was converted into a jail.

Judge Parker took up private quarters in the Old Fort stone commissary building, a half-mile walk from his court.

At the time of the Judge's arrival, Fort Smith was listed as the chief center of commerce and trade; but it offered little in the way of comfort or progress.

Within 10 years he saw the dirty frontier hamlet become a town with sidewalks, electric lights, and gas works, with a population increase of over 11,000.

Henry Starr, who at 18 had been a crack cowboy and looked like a man who could be trusted, became leader of the Starr gang and a notorious bank robber.

Paul Curry, the 14-year-old youth who wounded and captured Starr after a double bank robbery, posed for this picture, holding Starr's rifle.

"Kid" Wilson, companion of Starr in robberies, looked like a mere boy, was a ruthless outlaw.

Ned Christie (dead), a full-blooded Cherokee, was the most dangerous bandit the marshals had to go after.

Here are 10 members of the 17-man posse that brought in Christie. They had to use a three-pound cannon and a half-dozen sticks of dynamite to blast him from his hideout.

The hanging of Cherokee Bill on the Fort Smith gallows brought masses of people only too relieved to see the doomed man swing. Here is one artist's impression of that fateful afternoon execution.

The title page of S. W. Harman's incomparable book, *Hell on the Border*. It was published in 1898 and is today a collector's item and exceedingly rare.

This strange farewell poem, written on the back of a picture of his mother, was found in Rufus Buck's jail cell after his execution.

Heck Thomas, deputy U.S. marshal, once surprised Judge Parker by bringing in 32 prisoners in a single group. Nine were found guilty of crimes punishable by death.

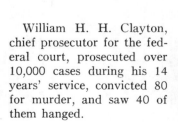

William H. H. Clayton, chief prosecutor for the federal court, prosecuted over 10,000 cases during his 14 years' service, convicted 80 for murder, and saw 40 of them hanged.

Executioner George Maledon, who achieved fame as the "Prince of Hangmen," seldom smiled, took a natural pride in his ability to always break the neck of his victim, and after retirement toured the West with rope and other gruesome instruments of his office.

The last person to die on the Fort Smith gallows was 26-year-old James C. Casharego, alias George Wilson, on July 30, 1896. In pronouncing the death sentence, the eloquent Judge Parker said: "Even nature revolted against your crime . . ."

Symbols of Crime and Punishment: The Winchester automatic, *at left,* once belonging to Henry Starr, was a spokesman for lawlessness. The chair, *below,* was Judge Parker's, from which he dispensed justice and brought the law west of Fort Smith.

near Fort Gibson and relieved him of $19. The following day they robbed Ed Ayers, a Cherokee, of $120 on the road.

On October 10, "the record of bold and desperate deeds" was broken when the gang held up and robbed the depot of the Missouri Pacific Railroad at Claremore and, less than two hours later, relieved the agent of the Missouri, Kansas-Texas of his "surplus" at Choteau, twenty miles away.

On Saturday night, October 20, they exceeded even this feat with the wrecking and robbery of the Kansas City and Missouri Pacific express at Coretta, a blind siding five miles south of Wagoner:

> The train was going at a speed of about twenty-five miles per hour and when within 100 feet of the switch a man sprang from behind an embankment and threw the switch for the side track, running the train into a string of empty box cars. Engineer James Harris applied the air and reversed his engine, but did not have time to jump before the engine struck the cars on the siding. The robbers commenced firing at the train and engine as soon as it struck the siding. Two of the robbers ran to the engine and commanded Engineer Harris and Fireman Cottrell to come down, and as soon as they had dismounted, marched them to the baggage and express cars, where, by firing through the doors, they forced Messenger Ford to admit them. Meanwhile, two more of the robbers had taken up positions at the rear of the train to prevent anyone escaping through the rear doors of the sleeper, two more mounted the platform between the smoker and the baggage car and two more the platform between the first and second coaches, all keeping up a continual firing. During this time the two in the express car were ransacking it. They got all the money in the local safe and Messenger Ford's gun, and then commanded him to open the through safe. He told them it was impossible, and after hearing his explanation as to how it was locked, they left the express car.
>
> The two robbers on the front platform started through the second coach demanding money and valuables. As soon as they reached the rear of the coach the two men on that platform started

through the second coach. When they were about half way through this car, a freight train following close behind whistled and Bill Cook, the leader, who had all the time remained outside issuing commands, swearing at the passengers and shooting, called for all hands to come out. The men on the cars jumped out, and when all were outside, fired a last volley at the train and disappeared in the darkness.

Jack Mahara, an advance agent for Mahara's minstrel Company, was struck in the forehead by a bullet and seriously injured. Walter Barnes of Van Buren, Arkansas, was slightly injured by a piece of bullet striking him in the cheek . . . Special officers Helmick and Dickson of the Missouri Pacific were on the train, also Deputy Marshals Heck Bruner and Jose Casaver, but the attack was so sudden that they were all covered by Winchesters in the hands of the bandits before they had time to make a move. Casaver lost a watch and his six-shooter in the fracas . . . The train was backed to Wagoner for assistance and to give medical attention to the injured. The entire train was completely riddled with bullets, every window being broken and the engine cab shot to pieces, even the steam gauge and gauge pump being shot away.[8]

On October 25, the Vinita *Indian Chieftain* reported:

The Cook gang . . . has opened a thriving highway robbery business along the road between this city and Fort Gibson, and within the past week three "knights of the grip" have contributed towards its support. James Wood of the Shibley-Wood Grocery Company, Van Buren, was met by two men near Menard and relieved of all his money and a valuable watch. Later, L. A. Wakefield of the Jacob Dold Packing Company, Kansas City, and F. B. Mittong of the Daughtery-Crouch Drug Company of St. Louis, were confronted near the same place by two highwaymen and made to fork over what money they carried. The two latter gentlemen had taken the precaution to leave their watches and all their money except $15 at Fort Gibson, for which they were roundly reprimanded by the outlaws.

On the same date a dispatch was received by the marshal's office at Fort Smith that the gang were again in the vicinity of Claremore and intended to sack the town. Citizens cooperating with Indian police and aided by the deputy marshals and special officers of the railway and express companies, found themselves "unable to encompass the gang or drive its members from the country." [9] "There is apparently no effort being made to capture the gang or suppress their depredations," charged the *Eagle-Gazette* on November 1, 1894, after repeated appeals to the United States Army to intervene. "The capture of the desperadoes responsible for the depredations in the Territory cannot much longer be delayed." And Dew M. Wisdom, Union Agent at Muskogee, sent another telegram to the Office of Indian Affairs, in which he stated:

> My police force is not equal to the emergency and Marshal Crump at Fort Smith writes that he has not money to keep marshals in the field for a campaign. Affairs here are in a desperate condition; business is suspended and the people generally intimidated and private individuals robbed every day and night. I renew my recommendations and earnestly insist that the government, through the proper channel, take the matter in hand and protect its court and citizens of the United States, who are lawful residents of the territory. Licensed traders are especially suffering and they are here under suspense. The state of siege must be broken and something done to save life and property. [10]

The telegram was referred to Secretary of the Interior Hoke Smith, who called the attention of the Secretary of War to the numerous previous requests. Marshal Crump was summoned to Washington to give a full account of the holdups of the Cook gang, and Attorney General Richard Olney thought that the government "should do everything legitimately within its power to prevent the interruption of interstate commerce and the detention of the United States mails."

"Abrogate the treaties; abolish the tribal relations; establish a territorial government," replied Secretary Smith. "If a territorial government were established, judges would be sent there to administer the laws and the governor who was appointed could see that they were enforced."

"The Cook gang must be killed out at once with Winchesters, at the cost of the government," said Marshal Crump.

The Attorney General authorized Crump to post a reward of $250 for each known member of the gang and advised Judge Parker "if these efforts fail, it is assumed that the military will be called into requisition." C. J. Harris, Principal Chief of the Cherokees, offered $500 for Bill Cook's head. "All the Lighthorse guards and all Indian police have been summoned for duty, and all United States marshals of the Territory have been put on the trail," reported the *Eagle-Gazette* of November 8. "In addition, there are special officers of the railway and express companies making a total of between five hundred and six hundred men ready to commence concerted action immediately."

The following day, November 9, the Cook gang held up the Schufeldt and Son store and post office at Lenapah, and Cherokee Bill deliberately shot and killed a prominent citizen, Ernest Melton. Standing in the store, looking through the glass door, he saw Melton watching from a window of a restaurant across the street. "Without warning he fired. The ball struck Melton just below the eye and came out the back of his head." [11]

Judge Parker issued his ultimatum: "Bring them in alive—or dead!"

The marshals and Indian police surrounded three of the gang in the house of Bill Province, fourteen miles west of Sapulpa. Lon Gordon and Henry Munsen were shot and killed as they fled, and Curtis Dayson was captured. He was taken to Fort Smith and tried with Elmer Lucas, who had been captured in the Chandler bank robbery. Judge Parker sentenced Dayson to ten years and Lucas to fifteen years in the penitentiary at Detroit. [12] Bill Province was brought to Fort Smith and questioned as to the possible hide-outs of the rest of the gang, and six other citizens of the Creek Nation were arrested for harboring the bandits on various occasions.

The marshals began making the territory hot for Bill Cook. He decided to cool off in Texas. En route the gang held up a German emigrant named Beckley, who was driving his family from Wewoka in the Seminole Nation to Tecumseh, Oklahoma. They robbed him of his valuables and brutally assaulted his eldest daughter, and one of the band unhitched a horse from his wagon and rode off with it.[13] The marshals picked up their trail and wired ahead to Texas authorities. Texas Rangers intercepted the gang in Clay County near Wichita Falls; Baldwin, Snyder, and Farris were captured and returned to Fort Smith, and Parker sentenced Baldwin to thirty years and Snyder and Farris to twenty years each in the Detroit prison.[14]

The remaining members of the Cook gang never united. Hunted like a wolf with a fabulous price on his head, Cook headed for Mexico. The Rangers were still on his trail, so he rode west. Captain Bill McDonald gave his description to New Mexico officers, telling them he was headed in their direction; and on January 11, 1895, in a sod house on an isolated cattle ranch a few miles southeast of Old Fort Sumner, where Pat Garrett had killed Billy the Kid, Sheriff C. C. Perry of Chaves County and two deputies surprised Bill Cook and took him without a fight.[15]

Cook arrived at the Frisco depot at Fort Smith at one o'clock in the morning of January 22 in custody of the New Mexico officers. Notwithstanding the lateness of the hour, a large crowd had gathered to see him escorted to jail. In less than ten minutes after he stepped off the train he was securely behind bars, and the next day a full force of guards were kept busy managing the throng bent on seeing the noted outlaw.

When arraigned before Parker, Cook entered a plea of not guilty to all charges against him. At his trial, however, he offered no defense, except on two counts, and the evidence against him was so clear even in these cases that his attorneys were unable to do anything for him. On February 12 the jury brought in a verdict of guilty, and Parker sentenced him to forty-five years' imprisonment at Albany, New York.

While Cook was still in jail awaiting transfer to prison, three other members of his gang—Jim French, George Sanders, and Sam McWilliams, alias Verdigris Kid—were brought in to Fort Smith, shot to death.

French was a half-breed Cherokee, his mother being a white woman. He had graduated with honors from the seminary at Tahlequah and learned the saddler's trade. In an altercation at Fort Gibson in 1891 he killed a Negro, and from that time on stole horses and sold whisky until after the big payment, when he joined the Cook gang and took part in their numerous hold-ups and train robberies. After the Texas fight he returned to Catoosa, his old stamping grounds, where he had first made love to the outlaw queen. He joined forces with a small-time burglar named Jess Cochran, alias Kid Swanson, and on the night of February 7, the pair broke into the W. C. Patton & Company general store. Too late they discovered the manager, Sam Irvin, and a night watchman named Wilkens on hand and armed. The watchman blew off Cochran's face with a shotgun, and French opened fire on Irvin with a Winchester. Irvin sank to the floor, and though fatally wounded, raised himself on one arm and fired two bullets into French's neck below the ears. The outlaw dropped his gun and fled from the store with blood spurting from his wounds. He mounted his horse and rode to a house three-quarters of a mile away, ran inside, and fell on the floor before the fire. The frightened occupants of the house hurried to Catoosa and reported what had happened, and a posse proceeded to the place at once. They found French dead on the floor. He had fallen with his body half in the fireplace. His boots were burned off and his feet and legs half-burned away.[16]

Irvin died at ten o'clock the next morning. He was given a

Masonic funeral and buried at Vinita. The remains of the two outlaws were shipped by train to Fort Smith for identification. Cochran's body was identified en route at Claremore and left there. The body of Jim French arrived at Fort Smith on Saturday morning, February 9, and for several hours lay in an open coffin at the United States jail. After it had been satisfactorily identified, it was turned over to a brother, who took it to Fort Gibson for burial.

At eight o'clock in the morning of March 28, Sanders, McWilliams, and a youth named Sam Butler rode into Braggs, a small town on the railroad nine miles east of Fort Gibson, and held up T. J. Madden's store. They were "taking things easy and had picked out a suit apiece" when warned of the approach of John Manning and Hira Stevens, Indian deputy sheriffs. They ran to the door. Butler fired first, killing Manning's horse. The deputies returned the fire almost simultaneously, and McWilliams fell dead, shot through the center of the breast. Sanders and Butler retreated toward their horses, keeping up a steady fire. Joe Morris, a clerk of Madden's, tried to intercept them and was slain for his efforts. At this moment Deputy Marshal Ed Barbee arrived on the scene. He ran between the deputies and the outlaws, grabbed up McWilliams' Winchester, and joined the fight. Sanders died with a bullet hole in his temple and several wounds in his body. Butler reached his horse and escaped. The dead outlaws were taken to Fort Smith and turned over to Marshal Crump. The guards brought Bill Cook up to see the bodies. Laying his hand affectionately upon the coffin of his former comrade, Sam McWilliams, he said: "This is the Kid." [17]

A warrant was issued at Fort Smith charging Sam Butler with the murder of Joe Morris. On the night of August 1, 1895, Deputy Marshal John Davis trailed Butler to the Henry Chambers place near Island Ford on the Verdigris River, the home of Butler's wife and mother. When Davis approached, Butler was lying under an apple tree. The moment he recognized the deputy, he sprang to his feet and fired, the ball striking Davis under the second rib on the right side. Davis fell from his horse, but regained his feet and returned the shot, striking Butler in the breast and killing him instantly. Davis died an hour later.[18]

Cherokee Bill became the most wanted outlaw on the marshals' list.

His real name was Crawford Goldsby. He was born at Fort Concho, Texas, February 8, 1876. His father, George Goldsby, was a soldier in the Tenth Cavalry, U. S. Army, of Mexican extraction, mixed with white and Sioux; his mother, Ellen Beck, was half Negro, one-fourth Cherokee and one-fourth white. His parents separated when he was seven, and he was raised by an old colored woman named Amanda Foster at Fort Gibson. At the age of twelve he killed his brother-in-law in a quarrel over some hogs. At eighteen he was a lusty, burly, brawling fellow who could not be curbed. Though charged with the slaying of agent Richards in the robbery of the depot at Nowata, he was never indicted. He was also alleged to have killed a young man named Henderson and wounded a brakeman on a freight train at Fort Gibson in the summer of 1894. He was on the scout for firing three bullets into the body of Jake Lewis, a young Negro with whom he had quarreled at a dance, when he joined the Cook gang. After that his crimes became so numerous that "working up cases against him became unnecessary, and no effort was made to get evidence." The problem was to effect his arrest.[19]

That he killed principally for the love of shedding blood was apparent from the manner in which he shot down Ernest Melton, and though rewards offered for him aggregated $1300, he was more dangerous and fierce than his white companion, Bill Cook, and few of the officers who pursued him cared to engage him in combat.

Only once did they make contact with him after the breakup

of the gang in Texas. Marshals Heck Thomas, Heck Bruner, and Burl Cox had been on his trail for days when late one evening they sighted him riding to the home of his sister, who lived near Nowata. As the outlaw came within range of the point where the officers were concealed, Bruner fired at him, but missed. The outlaw's horse was shot from under him in a running fight that followed, but he escaped, leaving them without a doubt that he would fight to the last, no matter how great the odds, and his hat as a trophy.

It remained for Deputy Marshal W. C. Smith to work a scheme for his capture in which a dusky maiden with whom Cherokee Bill was infatuated was to play an unwilling part. The girl was Maggie Glass, a cousin of Isaac Rogers, a Cherokee who had done considerable service as a deputy under Marshal Crump. Smith got Rogers to invite the girl to his house for a visit and also to extend an invitation to Cherokee Bill. The arrangements were made, and on the evening of January 29, 1895, Bill came to see the girl and was cordially received.

Maggie, however, suspected treachery and warned Bill of his danger, but the outlaw refused to leave.

"If Rogers makes a play," he said, "I'll show him how long it takes to commit murder."

He kept close watch on Rogers, but the latter was wily enough not to tip his hand. While his wife and Maggie prepared supper he joked with the outlaw, offered him a drink doctored with morphine, which the latter refused, and otherwise acted the part of the perfect host. Meanwhile Clint Scales, a neighbor and ally of Rogers, "dropped in for a visit."

After supper, cards were proposed, and Bill played casino and talked with the men until past midnight, declining to retire. Toward morning, however, he was induced to lie down with Rogers.

His host feigned sleep and waited in vain for Bill to close his eyes in slumber, but every time Rogers moved, Bill was

wide awake, his Winchester ready. After breakfast all were sitting in front of the open fireplace. Bill again held his Winchester
across his lap, and began to talk of leaving.

What happened next is best told in Rogers' own statement to
the editor of the Fort Smith *Elevator:* [20]

It began to look as if the game would surely escape. I didn't
want to kill him; but I made up my mind to kill him if I couldn't
get him in another way. . . . I knowed that we had to make a
break on him pretty soon and I was afraid the girl would take a
hand in it when the trouble began, so I gave her a dollar to buy
some chickens at a neighbors, so as to get her out of the way. I
also sent my boys away, as I had not told them of my plans.

Bill finally took a notion that he wanted to smoke and he took
some paper and tobacco from his pocket and rolled a cigarette. He
did not have a match, so he stooped over toward the fireplace
to light it, turning his head from me for an instant. That was my
chance and I took it. There was a fire stick lying on the floor
near me and I grabbed it up and struck him across the back of
the head. I must have hit him hard enough to kill an ordinary
man, but it only knocked him down. Scales and I then jumped
on him but he let one yell and got to his feet.

My wife grabbed Bill's Winchester and we three tusseled on
the floor a full twenty minutes. I thought once I would have to
kill him, but finally got the handcuffs on him. He then pleaded
and begged me to kill him or release him. He promised me money
and horses, all I wanted. Then he cursed. We put him in a wagon
and Scales rode with him and I rode horseback and started to
where Deputies Smith and George Lawson were waiting at
Nowata. On the way Cherokee broke his handcuffs and grabbed
at Scales' gun and Scales had to fall out of the wagon to keep
from losing his Winchester, while I kept Cherokee covered with
my shotgun. . . .

At Nowata, Smith and Lawson took charge of the prisoner,
and that same night landed him behind the bars of the federal
jail in Fort Smith. "The news of his capture spread like wild-
fire, and a sigh of relief went up . . . his captors being regarded

as having done a noble work for the good of the country. . . ." 21

At his trial for the murder of Melton, Cherokee Bill endeavored to prove an alibi but "failed utterly," every witness he had held up in the Schufeldt store "fully identifying him as the man who fired the shot that pierced Melton's brain." Arguments in the case began at noon February 26 and ended at ten o'clock that night. The next morning Judge Parker instructed the jury, taking only fifteen minutes in his charge, and within twenty minutes after retiring, the jury brought in a verdict of guilty.22

The boy killer simply smiled. But his mother and sister, who were with him in the courtroom throughout the trial, wept loudly. "What's the matter with you two?" he snapped. "I ain't dead yet." And that afternoon, over at the federal jail, Cherokee Bill "was engaged in a game of poker with Bill Cook and several kindred spirits as if nothing had happened." 23

On April 13 he was brought before Judge Parker for sentencing. Asked if he had anything to say why judgment should not be passed at that time, he replied, boldly and defiantly, "No, sir." Judge Parker then continued:

From the evidence in the case there can be no doubt of your guilt. That evidence shows a killing of the most brutal and wicked character. . . . Melton was the innocent, unoffending victim of the savage brutality which prompted the robbery and murder. From the information that has come to me this murder is one of three committed by you, and the others were equally as wicked and unprovoked as this one. The young man you killed was . . . innocent of any wrong against you. While offending no one, you shot him down in cold blood. . . . The murderous act was of the most wanton and reckless character, showing total disregard of human life.

These murders are not the only crimes committed by you. You have aided in the commission of many robberies. Your career recently has been remarkable for the number of crimes you have committed, and yet how brief has been that career. It has been scarcely a year since you became a hardened criminal, and your life of crime, covering as it does, many of the worst crimes known to law, has all been crowded in that space. Justice has at last overtaken you, and you have been tried and convicted of several robberies, and now stand before the bar of this court, to be sentenced for a crime for which you must forfeit your life. What a lesson is here to those who have a criminal tendency, or who entertain a desire to become criminals. The law very soon overtakes. They are brought to justice, and their lives become a blank or have to be forfeited to the law. From your criminal career you are a fit representative of that spirit of lawlessness and murder which characterizes the age to such an extent that social order and personal safety are threatened by lawlessness and crime. . . . Happily for the peace of the country, the whole of the band in which you belonged has been broken up. Its members have been brought to justice or have been killed by officers while they were in the act of committing crimes, or resisting arrest, and this has all happened to them in less than a year.

Now it behooves you to prepare to meet your fate. You must reflect on your past life, and fully comprehend its wickedness, and the injuries that your acts have done others. I have no idea that you appreciate the enormity of the wrongs that you have committed, or that you comprehend your condition. Your career of crime has been a wicked, bold and bad one. You must recognize this. You must seek forgiveness for it from the author of all mercy, the good God, whose government is so much higher than human government that he can and will forgive the worst of crimes. Then I ask you to consider that no one can doubt the justice of your conviction, or the certainty of your guilt, so you can enter upon a new existence with your sins, wickedness and crime behind you.

Do everything you can to accomplish this end, and lose not a moment's time. . . .[24]

Then followed the dread pronouncement, setting June 25 as the date of execution. But Cherokee Bill's attorneys took an appeal to the Supreme Court, and Judge Parker issued a stay of execution a few weeks later.[25]

Cherokee Bill "took the sentence very calmly and disclosed no emotion whatever. The only show which he made that he regarded the matter more seriously than when he was convicted, was the absence of his smile." [26]

Back in jail, he became morose and unruly. The lower floor where the condemned were kept was called "Murderers' Row." The prisoners were allowed the freedom of the floor and permitted to mingle with each other during the day. At night they were locked in separate cells. Cherokee Bill's conduct affected the other prisoners. Among themselves they predicted that "something terrible" was going to happen. Even Bill Cook, while en route to Albany prison on May 2, expressed the opinion that "no bars can hold Cherokee."

Few men had escaped from the old jail or the new one since Parker's arrival at Fort Smith. Many breaks had been halted in the planning stage, due to the inspection system put in effect by the first head jailer, Charley Burns. Routine inspections had turned up everything from iron knucks, three-cornered files, knife blades, slingshots, and pistols to tunnels and sawed bars. Most of the weapons were smuggled in by friends, wives, and sweethearts in cakes, pies, loaves of bread, and jugs of buttermilk, or hidden under petticoats. Sometimes these persons used money and bribed a guard or trusty. Though poorly paid, the guards rarely took a bribe. The few who did lost their jobs, and at least one was arrested and sentenced to three years in the penitentiary. [27]

On December 1, 1889, five men managed to escape by cutting off the heads of the bolts to the lock on one cell, sawing the heavy chain holding the door that let them into the guards' corridors; then climbing through a steel trap door into the attic of the jail over the third tier of cells, passing into the attic of the old courthouse adjoining, and crawling through a hole between the roof and ceiling of the back porch, where they let themselves down on blankets tied together. It was the first time anyone ever escaped from the new jail, and was recorded as the biggest break in the court's history. The five convicts were never recaptured.[28]

J. D. Berry, former deputy sheriff of Franklin County, Arkansas, was head jailer during the stay of Cherokee Bill, Bill Cook, and others of their ilk, and was perhaps the most alert and competent of any who served in this capacity during the tenure of Parker. When he took charge on November 1, 1894, there were 209 prisoners in jail, and the number increased during his term to 244 in February, 1896. Hardly a day passed that some scheme was not afoot for a single escape or a wholesale delivery. Matters grew worse following the confinement of Cherokee Bill.

Berry read the mood of the prisoners, sensed trouble brewing, and ordered a search of the entire prison. In Cherokee Bill's cell the guards found several .45 cartridges. They found a .45 revolver in the bathroom in Murderers' Row and arrested Sherman Vann, a Negro trusty serving ninety days for larceny, who confessed to a conspiracy on the part of several prisoners to break jail and to smuggling in the weapon and ammunition in a bucket of lime.[29]

They failed, however, to find a second gun that had been smuggled to Cherokee Bill. The killer had hidden it in the wall of his cell where he had removed a loose brick. The inside half of the stone had been broken off and the whitewashed end replaced, and the trick was not discovered.

At seven o'clock in the evening of July 26, guard Lawrence Keating and turnkey Campbell Eoff began checking in the prisoners for the night. The two rows of cells ran north and south on each side of the "bullpen." By pulling a lever connected to a long bar all the cell doors on each side could be closed and fastened at the top. It was Eoff's job, after pulling the levers, to enter the corridors flanking the cells and lock each door separately with a key. Guard Keating, wearing his six-shooter, walked along outside the corridor to ascertain that each prisoner had closed his cell door so that the locking bar would work properly. The bar could be thrown, however, by a stick or similar object in the hands of any of the prisoners in either row of cells. Cherokee Bill shoved up the bar with the barrel of his smuggled revolver and released all the doors to the cells on his side after Eoff had entered the corridor and locked the door behind him.

Eoff locked all the cells on the east side, Keating keeping pace outside the corridor. When the turnkey passed around the south end and started locking the doors of the west row of cells, Keating was even with him. Cherokee Bill waited with gun ready.

In the cell next to the outlaw was Dennis Davis, a half-witted Negro who had murdered his best friend. The keyhole of his cell lock had been stuffed with paper. When Eoff inserted the key, it lodged in the lock, and he called to Keating:

"Hold up. Something is wrong here."

As Eoff leaned forward to examine the lock, Keating stepped closer to the bars, and for a moment his attention was attracted to the turnkey. At that instant Cherokee Bill leaped from his cell and shoved the muzzle of his revolver between the bars at the guard.

"Throw up your hands and give me that pistol damned quick!" he commanded Keating.

The guard reached for his six-shooter instead, and Cherokee Bill shot him through the stomach. Keating ran toward the front of the jail and Cherokee Bill fired a second shot at him. He fell dead at the foot of the stairs leading to the jailer's office.

When Cherokee Bill leaped from his cell, Eoff tried to jerk the keys from the lock. Failing again to dislodge them, he left them hanging and ran around on the other side of the door. George Pearce, one of the ringleaders of the desperate plot, had come out of his cell when Cherokee Bill threw the brake. As the young killer followed Eoff, firing four shots at him, Pearce, thinking Eoff had the keys, joined in the chase, brandishing a broken table leg for a club. George Lawson happened to be at the door of the jail and ran in. He emptied his revolver at Cherokee Bill, chased him to his cell, drove Pearce back around the south end of the row of cells, and saved Eoff's life.

Guards Will Lawson, Bras Parker, Tom Parker, and William McConnell were soon in the jail, and jailer Berry arrived to take command. Heck Bruner and several other deputies heard the shooting and hurried to the jail to join the fight. They began a sniping match with Cherokee Bill. Every time the outlaw fired, he gobbled. It was an unearthly sound, half way between the bark of a coyote and the gobble of a turkey cock. It was the death cry among the territory Indians.[30]

> The great excitement prevailed from the time of the first shot which killed Keating until late into the night. Crowds gathered in an incredibly short space. They heard the cannonade going on within the jail and some were frantic. Not less than 100 shots were fired, Winchesters, shotguns and revolvers being brought into play. To the person entering the jail after the firing ceased, excitement and confusion was apparent at every hand. Firearms were at every step and the place was redolent with the smoke of gunpowder. The prisoners were for the most part badly frightened and huddled in the corners of their cells. On the west side in the outside corridor, were twenty or more men, all armed to the teeth. Standing in the inside corridor was the vile murderer himself, Cherokee Bill. Captain Berry, the jailer, was vainly endeavoring to induce him to tell who furnished him the weapon. A steady refusal was the only response. . . . Outside the crowd continued to increase until it assumed alarming proportions. The cry "Lynch him!" "Hang him!" was frequently heard. The guilty wretch himself heard the shouts; he saw the temperament of the men; he feared he was about to be brought out to a terrible death. . . .[31]

Marshal Crump arrived from his home in the suburbs and took personal charge of the situation. He ordered the cell blocks surrounded. Keating was a popular citizen of Fort

Smith and one of the oldest officers of the court. He had served as guard at the jail for nine years. "Vengeance boiled in many breasts" and a "short but earnest consultation was held . . . to kill the outlaw then and there." One word from Crump and "justice, swift and certain," would have been "meted out," but the outlaw pleaded with the officers:

"I didn't want to kill him; I wanted my liberty. Damn a man who won't fight for his liberty! If I hadn't shot him, he would have shot me. If I could have captured the jail . . . no one would have been killed."

He then "pleaded for the protection of the law which he had so many times and so lately outraged," and told Marshal Crump, "If you promise they won't kill me, I will give up my pistol."

"Shooting is too good for him," ordered Crump. "Save him for the gibbet."

The killer surrendered his weapon. His cell was searched thoroughly before he was handcuffed and chained and locked back inside, and the jail cleared of spectators.[32]

The rest of the night the marshals and guards worked about the jail, dispersing the crowds and discouraging talk of lynching. District Attorney James F. Read also made his way quietly among these enraged citizens, arguing against mob violence, promising that the case would be vigorously prosecuted and that the crime would not go unavenged; and the night passed without incident. But these people remained in a waiting, sullen mood. They talked of nothing else in public places the whole week that followed, and Read moved swiftly to make good his promise.

The autumn term of court opened Monday, August 5. For the first time in three years the petit and grand juries were empaneled on the opening day, and the first case taken up was the murder of Keating. The grand jury returned the quickest indictment in the history of the court, considering the evidence

only thirty minutes, and at one o'clock in the afternoon Cherokee Bill was arraigned before Judge Parker.[33]

When his shackles were removed, the killer threw back his
head with a quick jerk, taking in every detail of the courtroom
at a glance. What he saw was a dozen armed marshals and a
court bailiff with a heavy billy. Finally an expression of resignation settled over his Satanic countenance, and he entered a
plea of not guilty.

Parker set his case for the following Thursday, August 8,
and on that date Cherokee Bill was again brought into court
in chains and under heavy guard.

Never had the courtroom been jammed with so many visitors.
His defense attorney fought the case with every "hook and
crook" from the beginning. He made a motion for continuance
on grounds that public sentiment and prejudices of the people
of Fort Smith would not allow his client to get a fair and impartial trial at that time, and filed a demurrer alleging that
the court did not have jurisdiction because the killing had occurred in jail. Judge Parker ruled that "there is no question
as to the jurisdiction of the court in this case"; he became
"highly indignant" that a fair and impartial trial could not be
had in his court and stated that "the allegations in the demurrer
are wholly false and without foundation." He ordered the panel
of jurors called. Twelve men who lived no closer than forty
miles to Fort Smith were chosen. He questioned each man
closely and, satisfied that they were not prejudiced and could
render a verdict in accordance with the law and the evidence,
pronounced them "qualified jurors."

The trial lasted three days, the prosecution being handled
by District Attorney Read's able assistant, J. B. McDonough.
In the closing arguments in the case, McDonough delivered the
most lengthy, hair-raising appeal ever made to a Fort Smith
jury.

First he spoke of the evidence the prosecution had produced,
then of the renegade band of which the defendant had been a

member and the reign of terror they had spread "under the very eaves of this court!" Of Cherokee Bill, as recorded in Harman's *Hell on the Border,* he said:

"Life, honor, property, all were unsafe, so long as this red-handed fiend stalked abroad, unmindful of another's rights or another's life. His love of crime was his controlling passion, and even the mighty power of the law seemed almost unable to keep it in check. Failing to work out his plan for escape, he deliberately . . . let out the life-blood of a fellow being . . . who had been the best friend he had known in his incarceration; then, nerved by the very scent of the fresh blood he had spilled . . . he stood at bay and fired shot after shot at the brave officers who gathered to prevent him from adding other and heavier burdens upon his soul that was already foul with crime.

"Now he comes here, with his hands steeped in human gore, with a long list of misdeeds that should cause even the imps in hell to shudder, with a plea that is untenable, asks mercy at your hands; mercy! for a series of crimes that knows no equal among men of the nineteenth century; with his heart reeking with infamy, he pleads for mercy; this most ferocious of Monsters . . . whose very existence is a disgrace upon nature, a grievous burden to the atmosphere from which he draws his breath. . . ."

McDonough grew "intense in his masterful eloquence." His blue eyes "flashed and seemed to become as black as night." He threw back his head and his breast "heaved" as he "pounded blow after blow upon crime and its perpetrators" in a deep voice that "reached the far corner of the court yard where were massed many who were unable to secure entrance to the courtroom."

Finally he paused, like a man who had "reached the limit of his endurance," yet "showing no signs of fatigue." When he again faced the jury, he was "strangely calm" and his blue eyes were mild and filled with sympathy. Quietly he spoke of "poor

Larry Keating" and his "untimely death," of his kind heart and his wife and fatherless children. He then concluded:

> We all loved Larry Keating. . . . He loved his family, idolized his children; few men were ever blessed with his splendid temperament. He had always a kind word for those he met, always a smile and a hearty handshake for his friends. We cannot allow his murder to go unavenged. . . . There is nothing complex about this case, no technicalities to be cleared away; all is as plain as the noonday sun. You will do your duty, I have no fear of that . . . I feel it . . . I can read it in your faces. . . . And may God bless you for it.

A "subdued ripple of admiration passed over the crowd" as he finished, and all faces turned toward Judge Parker. They expected him to deliver a similar, lengthy charge, but in all his years on the bench, the judge had never had before him a case where there was "not a particle of doubt that the crime was committed" or "as to who committed it." His charge was brief. The jury brought in a verdict of guilty within thirteen minutes. Judge Parker sentenced Cherokee Bill to be hanged September 10.[34]

Again his case was appealed to the Supreme Court, and Parker granted another stay of execution. But, on December 2, the Supreme Court affirmed the decision of the Fort Smith court in the Ernest Melton case. For the third and last time Judge Parker sentenced Cherokee Bill to die on the gallows and fixed the date as St. Patrick's Day, March 17. There was "no avenue of escape left except executive clemency by the President, who was appealed to in vain." [35]

The *Elevator* [36] carried the following account of his execution:

> [Cherokee Bill awakened] this morning at six, singing and whistling. He partook of a light breakfast about eight o'clock, which was sent to him by his mother from the hotel. At 9:20,

Cherokee Bill's mother and the old negress who raised him were admitted to his cell, and shortly after Father Pius, his spiritual adviser, was also admitted. The usual noise and hubbub that is always heard within the big iron cage that surrounds the cells was noticeably lacking this morning. Cherokee Bill's fellow-prisoners, many of them under sentence of death, seemed to be impressed with the solemnity of the occasion, and an air of subdued quiet pervaded the jail. Many of the men who are already standing within the shadow of the gallows gathered in a group near the cell occupied by the condemned man and conversed in low tones. To his most intimate associates since his confinement Cherokee distributed his small effects. . . .

By 10:30, the corridor in front of Cherokee's cell was crowded with newspaper representatives, deputy marshals and other privileged individuals, all taking note of every passing incident. Occasionally the condemned man would throw aside the curtain which concealed the interior of his cell and make his appearance at the grated door in order to give some instructions or to make some request of the officer who stood guard.

About 11 o'clock Marshal Crump, after a short conversation with Cherokee, announced that the execution would be postponed until 2 o'clock, in order to give his sister an opportunity to see him before the death sentence was carried out. She was coming in on the east-bound Valley train, and would not arrive until one o'clock. The 2000 or 3000 sight-seers surrounding the big stone wall and within the enclosure dispersed.

It was a struggling mass of humanity that had gathered on and around the steps and walls and when the time came there was a scramble even among those who were provided with passes. There was a crush and a jam for a few minutes but order was at last restored in a measure and all awaited the moment when the door should open for the coming of the condemned man. On the inside there was a repetition of the scenes of the morning. Bill's mother had packed up several belongings of her son and was ready when called upon to take final leave. Her parting was an affectionate one but she strove as much as lay in her power to restrain her emotion.

Bill was affected by it, but following the example of his mother, gave little or no indication that he was other than perfectly composed.

"Well; I am ready to go now most any time," said he, addressing the guards.

He was taken at his word, and the jail was cleared. The crowd outside had swelled to increased numbers, all the available buildings and sheds being occupied. A pathway was cleared through the crowd, and very shortly after the clock struck two the door opened and the doomed man was brought forth, a guard on either side. The march to the gallows was taken up, and at Col. Crump's suggestion, Cherokee's mother and the old colored Aunty walked alongside Bill. Father Pius came next, the newspaper men following and the crowd bringing up the rear.

"This is about as good a day to die as any," remarked Cherokee as he glanced around. Arriving at the south end of the jail, he looked around at the crowd and said, "It looks like a regiment of soldiers."

He continued to look around at the crowd, eyeing them curiously.

At the door of the enclosure there was a jam. Everybody crowded up and there was a stop for a few moments. It took several minutes for everyone holding tickets to gain admittance, and by this time the condemned man and guards had mounted the scaffold. Bill walked with a firm step and, taking up a position near the west wall of the gallows, waited for the end.

Turning slightly and seeing his mother standing near, he said:

"Mother, you ought not to have come here." Her reply was: "I can go wherever you go."

Colonel Crump suggested to him that he take a seat until all was in readiness, but he replied: "No, I don't want to sit down."

The death warrant was then read, during which Bill gazed about as if a little impatient to have the thing over with. He was asked at its conclusion if he had anything to say, and replied: "No sir, without he (meaning Father Pius) wants to say a prayer." The Priest here offered a short prayer, the condemned man listening attentively the meanwhile, and then as if knowing what was to come next, he walked forward till he stood upon the trap. Deputy

George Lawson and others arranged the ropes, binding his arms and legs, and it was while this was being done that Bill spoke to different ones in the crowd below.

"Good-bye, all you chums down that way," said he, with a smile. Just then he caught sight of a young man in the act of taking a snap shot with a kodak and pulling it sharply back. There was a creaking sound as the trap was sprung and the body shot downward. The fall was scarcely six feet, but the rope had been adjusted carefully by Lawson and the neck was broken. The muscles twisted once or twice, but that was all. . . . Twelve minutes from the time the trap was sprung, the ropes that bound his limbs were removed, also the handcuffs and shackles, and the body was lowered into a coffin and borne away and the crowd dispersed. At Birnie's, the coffin was placed in a box and then taken to the Missouri Pacific depot and put aboard the train. His mother and sister took it back with them to Fort Gibson.

On May 18, 1896, the Supreme Court disposed of the second appeal case of Cherokee Bill as follows: "Crawford Goldsby, alias Cherokee Bill, v United States, No. 728. In error to the circuit court of the United States for the Western District of Arkansas. The Attorney General, for the United States. No opinion. Dismissed, the cause having abated, on motion by Mr. Solicitor General Conrad, for the defendant in error." [37]

IX

APPEALS AND REVERSALS

For fourteen years from the day Judge Parker stepped to the bench and took the fate of civilization's outpost in brave and willing hands, there was no appeal from his pronouncements of doom. In cases of homicide, his tribunal functioned as a circuit court, and federal statutes made no provision for having his findings reviewed by the Supreme Court of the United States. To that extent his court was greater than the Supreme Court, for it possessed both original and final jurisdiction. His decisions were absolute and irrevocable. A murderer could ask for a new trial, but Parker could deny the motion. A murderer could be pardoned or commuted by the President, but in these years Parker had considerable influence in Washington, and the White House was little inclined to issue pardons over his judgment. "It reminds one of the famous argument between the Judge and the Bishop," says Harry P. Daily.[1] "The Bishop asserted that his power was the greater because, while the Judge could merely say, 'You be hanged,' the Bishop could say, 'You be damned.' The Judge retorted, 'Yes, but when I say, "You be hanged," you *are* hanged.' "

Parker held still another advantage. The United States had

few laws and practically no precedents. State legislatures, however, had passed many statutes, and state courts of appeal had rendered numerous decisions on murder and manslaughter, but Parker was not compelled to follow decisions of these state courts. He must adhere only to the old English common law, which was obscure and doubtful and could be construed variously. He made his own rulings and established precedents that became the law. No jurist in America has ever been invested with so much power.

"Tyranny!" cried his critics. Others asked: "Is there any country on earth even one-half civilized that gives one man the power to commit judicial murder with no hope of appeal?" Multiple hangings were played up more and more, and newspapers placed much stress on the title "The Hanging Judge," until in distant states and modern cities, where citizens had never faced the atrocities committed against the people of the Indian country, Judge Parker was given the reputation of being "heartless and blood-thirsty."

More than this, Parker felt the pressure of the tide of white immigration. From the beginning he had fought against "this temporizing process—this sugar-coating the inevitable destiny that awaited the Indian country." As early as 1878, of its population of 85,000 people, 20,000 were whites and 6000 to 7000 were Negroes. Already there was $10,000,000 worth of railroad property in the territory and half as much more of other owned by whites and Negroes not members of the tribes.[2] More than thirty different tribes, with all this outside population, were without any law to regulate and control intercourse, except Indian law. Commissioners, Presidents, and committees had for years recognized this "analogous condition of affairs," and had recommended the establishment of some kind of civil government. So had Parker. But he did not believe, as many of these officials of note believed, that "the false theory that the Indian tribes are so many independent nationalities, with whom it is necessary or competent to make treaties, may as well be abandoned now, as at any future time, for abandoned it must be." Parker was emphatic in regard to the titles held by the leading tribes of the territory, and thought that Congress could furnish a form of government for them that would not disturb existing rights and institutions; that the government could make such laws as would give to every tribe "full protection in person and property, and in the enjoyment of his homestead in his full right, to use, occupy and own, and with it prosper."

But his critics took the opposite view, pointing to the activities of the Fort Smith court as "strengthening our convictions that the Indian country should be by Congress organized into a territory of the United States, and that beautiful land made the home of civilization and refinement, instead of the rendezvous and refuge of the thieves, murderers and desperadoes of all classes from the states as it now is." The so-called Indian nationalities that they clung to "with such pertinacity" were but "myths and shadows," they said, having in reality "no existence worthy of the name." They complained of the jurisdiction the United States court exercised over all white people in that country for offenses committed by them and over all Indians for offenses committed upon white people, and that the result was that they were brought by the hundreds from their homes in all parts of the territory to Fort Smith and tried by juries not of their own race or nation, but by strangers. "If they were organized into a territory and made citizens of the United States, such would not be the case; but courts could be established in their midst and their criminals tried by their own people," [3] to say nothing of the "enormous expense incurred by the government and the loss of time and money imposed upon witnesses and accused persons in reaching its portals, nor the trivial charges and offenses that come within its comprehensive grasp, nor of the interests of Fort Smith, of the bar, the jurors and tradesmen and boarding house keepers to hold fast to the benefits derived from the presence of the court. . . ." [4]

To alleviate the pressure, Congress, by an act approved January 6, 1883, took the western half of the Indian country from the jurisdiction of the Western District of Arkansas. This western section was in turn divided at the Canadian River, shifting cases from the northern half of the area to the United States Judicial District of Kansas, giving the federal courts at Wichita and Fort Scott "exclusive, original jurisdiction"; the southern area being annexed to the Northern District of Texas with the federal court at Graham.[5]

Judge Parker kept quiet. The larger number of crimes were committed in the eastern half of the Indian country, and the loads of offenders coming to Fort Smith did not slacken.

The howl for patronage from Kansas and Texas subsided, but there was no improvement of conditions in the Indian country, and Senator George Vest of Missouri took the floor of Congress in behalf of locating a United States court in the territory. Pointing again to the Fort Smith tribunal, he stated that "here it has been shown by experience that it is poor practice to take [these people] from the Territory for trial" and declared, "It is high time to stop experimenting with courts in the states."

He pointed out that with courts in Kansas and Texas, guards and the same means of transportation had to be employed as before, that it was no closer to Paris for the Choctaws and a good half of the Chickasaws than to Fort Smith, and that when going to the courts in these states the territory witnesses were still surrounded by the same debasing influences. Very few went to Fort Smith or to the Texas cities "without indulging in a big drunk, and many a gallon of vile whiskey finds its way back by these same witnesses to swell the crime of the Territory. Hotel keepers rob them of the last cent of their mileage and fees as at present and they are still tried by juries not of their own race or nation."

Senator Vest closed his argument with the following appeal:

So long as we treat the Indian as a dependent, helpless being, fit only to be used for the purpose of plunder and greed, we may expect the result which has attended our Indian policy for the last hundred years. Instead of dragging them off to other states to be tried by juries made up of strangers, instead of impressing them with the idea that they are fit only for the punishment of the law and not its administration, let us rather seek to teach them the self-respect which comes as [sic] free men as both makers and administrators of the laws.

The *Indian Journal* commented that "as the United States is teaching the Indian civilization, what would be better to give them than practical lessons in the workings of our laws and courts?" 6

Congress struck another blow at the Fort Smith court. By two acts approved July 4, 1884, it granted rights of way through the Indian territory to the Southern Kansas & Gulf and the Colorado & Santa Fe railroads, and gave the circuit and district courts of the District of Kansas and the Northern District of Texas concurrent jurisdiction with the Western District of Arkansas in all controversies arising between the railroads and the tribes through whose nations they should be constructed, regardless of the amount in controversy and "without distinction as to the citizenship of the parties." 7 But these acts went "so little noticed that some of the deputy marshals were unaware of their provisions for several years thereafter." 8 Again Parker said nothing.

He took notice, however, that Congress "seemed determined to keep haggling away at his jurisdiction" when, on March 3, 1885, it approved another act providing that "any Indian committing against the person or property of another Indian any of the crimes, as follows: Murder, manslaughter, rape, assault with intent to kill, arson, burglary and larceny, in any Territory of the United States and within or without an Indian reservation, shall be subject . . . to the laws of such Territory relative to such crimes, and . . . tried in the same courts and in the same manner and . . . subject to the same penalties as are all other persons charged with the commission of said crimes, and said courts shall govern and have jurisdiction in all such cases." [9] This began the "breaking down of the barrier protecting the Indian in the Indian territory in the right to punish the members of their own tribes for offenses committed against each other." [10]

Added to Judge Parker's burdens was "the arrested state of development of the whole federal judicial system." There were yet several courts of original jurisdiction having no superior appellate courts, and some, like Parker's, were loaded with both district and circuit court jurisdiction. The Attorney General had urged Congress to reorganize these jurisdictions "because such conditions are causing delays that amount to a denial of justice." [11] Too much territory was under one court. For instance, the eighth circuit, in which the Fort Smith court was located, comprised nine states, twelve districts, and twenty-five divisions. "It is impossible to administer justice efficiently under such conditions." [12]

A grand jury report to Judge Parker in 1887 summarized the conditions in the Western District of Arkansas as follows:

> The task of law enforcement in this district is too great for Marshal Carroll and his trusted deputies. The dangers are too great to risk. It would require the might of the United States Army backing the marshals to efficiently cope with the conditions. . . . The task is too great for yourself, your honor, and your pay is insufficient for the vast duties you perform.[13]

From 1883 to 1889 criminal cases and court costs increased so steadily that Marshal Yoes, in his annual report of 1889, stated that "further reduction of the territory" was the "most likely" means of cutting expenses and the volume of work coming before the court.

Apparently all agreed that conditions were "bad" in the Western District of Arkansas. They were unable, however, to agree upon a solution. In the "turmoil of dissatisfaction" they focused their attention upon the tribunal's "character as a court of both original and final jurisdiction," and settled down to attacking the fact that "in its constitution by Congress, certain great principles of law which lie at the very foundation of common justice" had been ignored.

> The Judge of the Fort Smith district alone has passed the sentence of death upon more convicted criminals than we care to guess at, not one of whom, red, white or black, ever had the poor privilege of having his case reviewed in any manner. . . . The law vests the judges of these border district courts with almost unlimited power; human nature prompts them to use it.[14]

And in Washington, Representative John H. Rogers and Senator James K. Jones of Arkansas took the lead in advocating appellate courts for the districts that had none, and called the Fort Smith tribunal "a burning shame on American civilization." [15]

Finally, in 1889, Congress acted upon their recommendations, abolishing the circuit-court powers of the district courts of the Western District of Arkansas, the Northern District of Mississippi, and the Western District of South Carolina, three of the four districts complained of by the Attorney General, and providing that, after May 1, "in all cases of conviction of crime, the punishment of which by law is death, tried before any court of the United States, the final judgment of such court against the respondent, may be re-examined, reversed, or affirmed by the Supreme Court of the United States upon a writ of error, under such rules and regulations as said court may proscribe." [16] Thus the Fort Smith tribunal was stripped of its right as a court of last resort.

Judge Parker was piqued. "Like a huge monolith supporting the temple of justice," he had borne alone the great burden, originally placed upon his shoulders by Congress, of passing finally upon the guilt and innocence of those arraigned before him and of sentencing men to death. Why was it necessary now to share the responsibility with the United States Supreme Court? Judge Parker spoke out.

"Back of this change," he said, "is a maudlin sentimentality that condones a crime on which the blood stains have dried. . . . Take the good ladies who carry flowers and jellies to criminals. They mean well . . . but, oh, what mistaken goodness! What motives of sincerity, pity and charity, sadly misdirected. They consider alone the prisoner chained in his cell . . . the convict on the scaffold and his fatal plunge to death. . . . They forget the crime he perpetrated and the family he made husbandless and fatherless by his assassin work.

"I have no objection to appeal. I even favor abolition of the death penalty, provided there is a certainty of punishment, whatever the punishment may be, for in the uncertainty of punishment following crime lies the weakness of our halting justice.

"The murderer must be punished as an example to others. Screening him from punishment by releasing him . . . on some technicality . . . is the greatest calamity to the members of society. . . . The murderer must look to a Higher Court, to a Higher Power, to a Higher Law, for mercy, for absolute forgiveness.

"This court," he concluded, "is but the humble instrument to aid in the execution of that divine justice which has ever decided that he who takes what he cannot return—the life of another human being—shall lose his own. . . ."

This seemed to settle it. The judge had shed few tears for those who had died on the gallows. His tears were for the innocent, the victims, the murdered men and their families, and most Fort Smith attorneys, as familiar with conditions in the Indian country, respected Judge Parker's views. It was not until ten more men had been sentenced to hang that the right of appeal was exercised in behalf of a client.

The defendant was William Alexander, a Mexican convicted for murder committed in the Creek Nation, October 21, 1889.

His attorney was J. Warren Reed, a newcomer to the Fort Smith bar.

Reed had been born December 9, 1849, in Parkersburg, West Virginia. Like Judge Parker, he spent his childhood on a farm and in early life chose law as a profession. Through the "same energy and perserverance which distinguished him in later years," he secured a fair education and was admitted to the bar in 1879, when he was thirty, practicing in Wood County, West Virginia, and southeastern Ohio, where he soon gained notoriety as "That Lawyer, Who Always Wins His Cases." In 1886 he was admitted to practice in the Supreme Court and in the United States District and Circuit Courts of West Virginia. In April of the same year he went to California, and was admitted to the bar there by the Supreme Court, in full session at San Francisco. For a while he successfully handled many important mining, land, and criminal cases, then became interested in criminal law and decided to specialize in it. He made a tour of Mexico, the United States, and Canada, and returned to his native state to settle down to permanent practice; but he was called to Fort Smith to defend a prominent case and, noting the volume of business being transacted in the famous court, decided to stay. He associated himself with the law firm of Boudinot and Barnes. When Boudinot died a few months afterward, the firm continued under the name of Barnes and Reed. Three years later, Reed began practice alone. For by this time he already was well on his way to becoming one of the most successful lawyers in the Southwest.[17]

Reed was shorter in stature than Parker, but of stout build and stronger physically. He wore a thick black mustache, in contrast to Judge Parker's whitening beard and goatee, but had the same cold, calculating, and piercing blue eyes. Wearing only the most fashionable clothes, affecting a "claw-hammer" coat, a silver-headed cane, and a high silk hat, he was "something of a dandy" to the citizens of Fort Smith, and appeared out of place on this rough frontier. But he soon became known as an indefatigable worker for his clients, and a "bold, ruthless schemer" who won cases.

He began defending scores of criminals, specializing in defending those charged with murder. Whether his clients were guilty or not, he fought hard to free them and was not too particular about his methods. His sole interest was to win their cases. And when juries found them guilty and Judge Parker sentenced them to die, Reed went directly to the President. He began getting executive clemency and pardons in nearly every case he took to the White House. His ingenuity was "uncanny, almost diabolical," and word swept the Indian country: "Hire Lawyer Reed."

Parker was wondering what to do about him when Congress allowed appeals in all cases carrying the death penalty. It was too late then for the judge to do anything.

Alexander's conviction stemmed from "wholly circumstantial" evidence that he killed his partner, David C. Steadman, and appropriated his horses and money. The chief indication of his guilt was a statement he made concerning the disappearance of his partner to J. G. Ralls, a Muskogee attorney whom he consulted in regard to the ownership of the horses a few days after the slaying. Over the objection of the defendant, Judge Parker admitted the statement "as a matter of public policy when such statements tend to prove the guilt or innocence of the person accused." Reed was certain there were errors in the ruling and took a bill of general exceptions to the Supreme Court.

His move attracted national attention. He scorned the notion that he might incur the displeasure of the court, and maintained and urged that "it is the duty of any attorney, under his oath, to avail himself of every right and advantage provided by law in the interest of a client. . . ."

The Supreme Court agreed. In delivering its opinion, Mr. Justice Brown accused Parker of scouting the established rule that "whatever facts are communicated by a client to a counsel solely on account of that relation, such counsel are not at liberty, even if they wish, to disclose," and added: "While, if he were guilty of murder, [his statement] may have had a tendency to show an effort . . . to make profit out of his death by appropriating to himself the partnership property, it did not necessarily have that tendency" and "is perfectly harmless upon its face." Ralls' testimony, therefore, was incompetent. The judgment of the Fort Smith court was reversed, and the case remanded for a new trial.[18]

Alexander went on trial again a few months later. The skillful, perservering Reed more plainly developed the circumstances of the case, and the jury stood five to seven for acquittal. At a third trial a year later, the jury again failed to agree, and on the day before Christmas, 1892, District Attorney Clayton, convinced that he could not secure a conviction, consented to nolle prosequi.

Reed's success caused him to muster courage to appeal more cases, and more reversals followed.

On the night of June 15, 1888, the southbound Missouri-Kansas-Texas passenger express had been held up at Verdigris tank and Benjamin C. Tarver, a cattleman from Rose, Texas, en route home from Chicago, had been slain. Four men were involved in the robbery. One of them, Jim Johnson, was arrested in Texas on another charge and sentenced to twenty-five years in prison. A second, Kelp Queen, a notorious bandit, was killed near Claremore by Deputy Marshal Bud Sanders of the Cooweescoowee District. And later a third member of the gang, John Barber, was slain by Deputy Marshal Connelley and Captain White. In December, 1890, a youth who had been raised in the home of Alexander Lewis, fifty miles from the scene, confessed to J. J. Kinney, a railroad detective, that Lewis was the fourth member of the band, that plans for the robbery had been made in Lewis' home, and that Lewis had ridden away with the gang and returned with them following the holdup and slaying.

Detective Kinney and the marshals worked up a mass of corroborative evidence, and Lewis was indicted, tried, and sentenced to hang. Attorney Reed appealed to the Supreme Court on error that, during the trial and after the defendant had pleaded not guilty to the indictment, Judge Parker had directed secret challenges to be made, not in the presence of the prisoner and the jurors. At least Reed discovered that the clerk had failed to indicate in the record that the jury was present in the box, face to face with the defendant, when he was called upon to make his challenges, and the Supreme Court, in reversing and remanding the case, held that "nothing can be presumed for or against a record, except what appears substantially upon its face." [19]

The second trial was "hotly contested." Reed depended "very little" upon his witness for defense. He "assaulted the government witnesses in cross examination. . . . In his plea to the jury, he was concise, logical, keeping the minds of the jury fixed upon the discrepancies in the testimony of the prosecution." He literally tore down the case the government had built up, and "the lengthened faces of the jurors betokened how true to the mark Reed's logic and argument had been fired" when he maintained that at no time during the robbery had the prosecution been able to place his client on the scene as one of the members of the gang. Reed won his point and Lewis' acquittal. [20]

Joseph Wilson was a fearless young Texan riding as deputy United States marshal in the Muskogee district. On September 21, 1891, he went to the home of Sam Hickory, alias Downing, on Fourteen Mile Creek near Tahlequah, to serve him with a warrant for a violation of the liquor laws, and after arresting him in the field, proceeded to the house with the outlaw to get his saddle. Once inside the house, Hickory decided to escape. He picked up his gun and returned to the door, and Wilson, drawing his revolver, fired into the door facing above his head. Hickory returned the fire, shooting the deputy's horse in the leg and Wilson from the saddle. Then the outlaw loaded the marshal's body into a wagon, hauled it a mile from his home, and dumped it in a ravine, where it was found, badly decomposed, by a searching party three days later. The deputy's horse lay dead a quarter-mile in the opposite direction, saddle and bridle missing, its throat cut, and the bullet wound in its knee.

Hickory pleaded self-defense, claiming that while en route to the house, the marshal began firing at him; that he ran into the house; and that the affray occurred there, in which there was shooting by both, until the marshal was slain.[21] The evidence, however, failed to bear out his story. He was convicted of murder and sentenced to the gallows.

Attorney Reed objected to the manner in which Judge Parker instructed the jury, and appealed. In reversing the case (*Hickory v United States*, 151 U. S. 303), Mr. Chief Justice Fuller of the Supreme Court wrote:

The "experienced" trial judge told the jury that the mere fact that a killing is done willfully does not necessarily make it murder; that it is also done willfully when done in self-defense; and explained the characteristics of that malice the existence of which is the criterion of murder . . . pointing out that the requisite malice exists when the act is perpetrated without any provocation or any just cause or excuse . . . that the time of prior consideration will vary as the minds and temperaments of men . . . that there is no time so short but that within it the human mind can form a deliberate purpose to do an act. . . .

And in this connection, the "learned" judge charged, among other things, as follows: "You see, a man is required to discharge certain great duties under all circumstances, and especially is this law of duty incumbent upon him when he is put in . . . the position of a judge sitting on the bench, deliberating upon what the law is, and of a jury sitting in the jury box, listening to the facts, and finding as coolly, deliberately and dispassionately as possible under the circumstances what the facts are. When a party is in such a condition, he is the judge upon the bench and the jury in the box; and not only that, but he is the executioner. He finds what the facts are as a jury, and he makes an application of the law that he finds as a judge to these facts that he finds as a jury, he enters up a judgment, and then and there, he, as a marshal, kills in the furtherance of the judgment. Suppose that the judge of this court had that power, how long would the people of this land permit him to sit on this bench? Suppose that you, as twelve dispassionate citizens, had that power, how long would these people permit that system to exist? Suppose that the chief executive officer of this government, the President of the United States . . . how long would these people permit one man to exercise a power of that kind? Exercise it, too, when he wasn't inflamed with acts that confronted him, but exercised it when he was an intelligent man, and just man . . . and a fair-minded man? We have divided this power when it comes to be executed deliberately. We have a court that performs one office, and the jury another, and the executive arm of the government another. Yet the law of self-defense puts all of these mighty elements of power into the hands of one man. . . . He is required to avoid the necessity of killing if he can with due regard to his own safety. He must do that. He must forget that he is judge, jury, and executioner when he is sitting in that tribunal out in the woods or country. . . . He is required to know what the facts are that confront him, and . . . make correct application of what this law is . . . to these facts . . . and if he does not do that when he might do it he makes a mistake in that regard, and he would be guilty of manslaughter. . . ."

To enlarge upon the magnitude of the power of slaying in defending against an attack as being a power which in itself would not be tolerated in the chief executive of the country or in the judge then passing upon the issues of life and death, and to advise the jury to inquire, not into the existence of defendant's belief, or the reasonableness of the grounds on which it rested, but into the character of the deliberation which accompanied it, tested by the standard of that of the judge, the jury, and the executioner, in the discharge of their appropriate duties, manifestly tended to mislead. Nor does this view impute a want of intelligence in the jury. They might find a verdict in disregard of the instructions of the court, but this is not to be presumed; and, if that strict attention to judicial direction were paid which the due administration of justice requires, we are constrained to the conclusion that such instructions as these under consideration could not but have a decided influence upon their action.[22]

At his second trial a year later (*Hickory v United States,* 160 U. S. 408) Hickory was again convicted and given the death penalty. And again Reed objected to Parker's charge to the jury. The language of this charge to which Reed took exception was as follows:

There is no man who has arrived at the years of discretion who has not been so created that he has that in his mind and heart which makes him conscious of an act that is innocent upon his part; and his conduct, when connected with an act of that character, will be entirely different from the conduct of a man who is conscious of wrong and guilt. In the one case he has nothing to conceal; in the one case his interest and self-protection, his self-security prompts him to seek investigation, to see to it that it is investigated as soon as possible. This is no new principle. I say it is as old as the days of the first murder. There is a little bit of history on that, and I apprehend the gentlemen won't take any exceptions to reading from this book [the Bible]. There are a great many exceptions filed here to almost everything said by the court, but I hope they won't take any exceptions to this. There is a little bit of history illustrative of the conduct of men:

"And Cain talked with Abel, his brother; and it came to pass, when they were in the field, that Cain rose up against Abel, his brother, and slew him.

"And the Lord said unto Cain, where is Abel, thy brother? And he said, I know not. Am I my brother's keeper?

"And He said, what hast thou done? The voice of thy brother's blood crieth unto Me from the ground."

"Am I my brother's keeper?" From that day to the time when Professor Webster murdered his associate and concealed his remains, this concealment of the evidence of crime has been regarded by the law as a proper fact to be taken into consideration as evidence of guilt, as going to show guilt, as going to show that he who does an act is consciously guilty, has conscious knowledge that he is doing wrong, and he therefore undertakes to cover up his crime. . . .

The questions for you to pass upon is whether or not . . . there were acts upon the part of this defendant . . . that looked toward concealing this act of the killing of Wilson; what these acts were; if they were cruel, if they were unnatural, if they were barbarious . . . that men who are conscious of innocence do not usually characterize their conduct after a killing by that sort of acts . . . the concealment of this body, the concealment of this horse, the killing of the horse, and the concealing of everything that pertained to that man . . . that they might be discovered afterwards as evidences of the killing.

And bear in mind that the other witness in this case cannot appear before you. He cannot speak to you, except as he speaks by his body as it was found, having been denied even the right of decent burial, by the dead body of his horse, by the concealed weapons and the concealed saddle, by the blood stains that were obliterated. . . . You are to see whether [these circumstances] harmonize with the statement of this transaction as given by the defendant, bearing in mind that he stands before you as an interested witness, while these circumstances are of a character that they cannot be bribed; that cannot be dragged into perjury; they cannot be seduced by bribery into perjury but they stand as bloody, naked facts before you, speaking for Joseph Wilson and justice. . . .[23]

In writing the opinion of the Supreme Court, Mr. Justice Edward D. White said:

It is undoubted that acts of concealment by an accused are competent to go to the jury as tending to establish guilt, yet they are not to be considered as alone conclusive, or as creating a legal presumption of guilt. The charge . . . magnified and distorted the proving power of the facts on the subject of concealment; it made the weight of the evidence depend not so much on the concealment itself as on the manner in which it was done . . . it practically instructed that the facts were, under both divine and human law, conclusive proof of guilt . . . the effect of . . .

the epithets and vituperation . . . was to instruct the jury to return a verdict of guilty.

The manner of contrasting the testimony of the accused with the circumstances connected with the concealment was also clearly illegal. . . . It substantially said to them, "The circumstances as to the killing and concealment cannot be bribed, but the defendant can be; therefore you must consider that these circumstances outweigh his testimony, and it is hence your duty to convict him."

Admonished by the duty resting on us, we feel obliged to say that the charge crosses the line which separates the impartial exercise of the judicial function from the region of partisanship where reason is disturbed, passions excited, and prejudices are necessarily called into play.[24]

In the third trial the crime was reduced to manslaughter, and Hickory received a five-year sentence in the penitentiary at Columbus.

These reversals and Reed's temerity encouraged other attorneys. More than that, Fort Smith in these years was crawling with lawyers; and with clients demanding such service as Reed's, it was good business to climb on the Supreme Court bandwagon. Numerous other cases were appealed, Judge Parker's decisions reversed many times, new trials granted, charges reduced, and acquittals won.[25]

During his first seven years at the Fort Smith bar, the enviable Reed alone defended or assisted in the defense of 134 persons charged with murder and other capital offenses, besides over 1000 cases of lesser importance, such as assault with intent to kill, robbery, larceny, and whisky violations. Of the 134 charged with capital offenses, he lost only 2 on the gallows; the others were discharged by commissioners' courts upon examination trials, acquitted by juries after second or third trials, the grade of their crimes reduced, or were commuted or pardoned by the President.

Besides William Alexander, Alexander Lewis, and Sam Hickory, the most important murder cases with which he was

connected were those of Charles Bullard, Ed Alberty, Buzz
Luckey, Frank Carver, Jake Harles, Isaac Yustler, John Alli-
son, A. H. Craig, Berry Foreman, Rufus Brown, Jess Miller,
Thomas J. Thornton, Frank Perry, and John Gourke. He was
defense attorney for Cherokee Bill at the time of his conviction for the slaying of Ernest Melton, and it was the consensus
that this savage would never have hanged if he had not, while
awaiting the review of his case by the Supreme Court, attempted
the wholesale jail delivery and murdered Lawrence Keating.

Obviously these appeals did not set well with the Fort Smith
press. The editor of the *Elevator* wrote in his issue of September 13, 1895:

> For the benefit of those who may not understand why Cherokee
> Bill was not hanged (why he was allowed to remain alive long
> enough to commit another brutal murder), we will say that his
> case was appealed to the Supreme Court of the United States upon
> what is known in law as technicalities—little instruments some-
> times used by lawyers to protect the rights of litigants but oftener
> used to defeat the ends of justice. It will remain there until the
> bald-headed and big-bellied respectables who compose that body
> get ready to look into its merits. . . .

Keating's slaying also affected Judge Parker deeply. At the
time, he was in St. Louis with his family on a brief vacation.
On July 30 he issued a statement to the St. Louis *Globe-
Democrat,* commenting on the affair and sharply criticizing the
Supreme Court in its handling of appeals. He said:

> At this moment the Fort Smith jail contains over fifty mur-
> derers. They have been tried by an impartial jury; they have
> been convicted and sentenced to die. But they are resting in jail,
> awaiting a hearing of the Supreme Court.
> You ask why that, while crime in a general way has decreased
> in the Indian country very much in the last twenty years, murders
> are largely on the increase? Why, I attribute the increase to these
> reversals. First, the convicted murderer has a long breathing spell

before his case comes before the Supreme Court; then, when it does come before that body, the conviction may be quashed; and wherever it is quashed it is always upon the flimsiest technicalities. The Supreme Court never touches the merits of the case. As far as I can see, the court must be opposed to capital punishment, and therefore, tries to reason away the effect of the law.

In speaking as I do, I am mindful, of course, of the wise and merciful provision of the law which declares it is better that ninety-nine guilty ones escape than that one innocent man should suffer. Nor am I devoid of human sympathy because I have endeavored to carry out the law justly and fearlessly. . . . Sympathy should not be reserved wholly for the criminal. I believe in standing on the side of the innocent. Take that man Keating. Is there no sympathy for him and for the wife and children who have been deprived of his support and protection? Wasn't his life worth more to the community and to society at large than the lives of a hundred murderers?

During the twenty years that I have engaged in administering the law here, the contest has been one between civilization and savagery, the savagery being represented by the intruding criminal class. The United States government, in its treaties from the days of Andrew Jackson, stipulated that this criminal element should be kept out of the country, but the treaties have only been made to be broken. . . . Thus this class keeps on increasing; its members marry, and the criminal population keeps ever growing larger. . . . At the present time there seems to be a criminal wave sweeping over the country, the like of which I have not seen before.

It is due to the laxity of the courts.

I have this much satisfaction, after my twenty years of labor; the court at Fort Smith, Arkansas, stands as a monument to the strong arm of the laws of the United States, and has resulted in bringing to the Indian Territory civilization and protection.

X

THE SAVAGE BUCKS

EIGHT MEN WERE HANGED IN 1896 FOLLOWING THE
execution of Cherokee Bill. Three were hanged together April
30,[1] and little more than two months later, on July 3, the entire gang of Buck outlaws were marched onto the scaffold.

The Buck gang sprang up in the Creek Nation in July, 1895,
and flourished thirteen days. But in that thirteen days they
made a criminal record that, considering the time they operated, faded the Starrs, the Daltons, the Rogers and Cook
gangs combined. Their acts were heinous and terrifying. They
never rose to the level of bandits. They were simply ravishers.
Undoubtedly they were the most depraved band of outlaws in
America.[2]

Rufus Buck, a full-blooded Euchee Indian, was their leader.
The other members were Sam Sampson and Maoma July,
Creek renegades, and Lewis and Lucky Davis, Creek freedmen
—a mixture of Creek and Negro (a cross considered the most
dangerous of all the types of "mixed-blood" desperadoes to
infest the Indian country). These four had been lawbreakers

159

for months, Buck for years. All had been before Judge Parker for minor offenses and served time in the Fort Smith jail.

On July 28 they shot and killed a Negro deputy marshal, John Garrett, near Okmulgee. Buck is credited with having done the job personally. It was the first act of a carefully laid scheme to get rid of the officer who was watching them in the district before starting their campaign of terror and destruction. In fact it was Rufus Buck's boast that his outfit would make a record that would sweep all the other gangs of the territory into insignificance.

Riding from Okmulgee, four of them met a Mrs. Wilson, who was moving from one farm to another with two wagons. Her fourteen-year-old son and a young man who was with her were ordered to drive on with the wagons, while they kept the woman. Then each member of the band brutally assaulted her, releasing her afterward and firing at her feet as she fled from their abuse half dead with fright.

On Berryhill Creek, eight miles from Okmulgee, they met a man named Staley and robbed him of his horse and saddle, fifty dollars in cash, and a gold watch. They then discussed the most feasible method of killing him, but finally released him after three of the gang voted to let him go.

They rode in the night to the home of Gus Chambers on Duck Creek near Sapulpa to steal some horses. Chambers put up a fight, and they filled his house with lead.

They robbed a stockman named Calahan, even taking his clothing and boots, and fired at him as he fled naked, at the same time badly wounding a Negro boy who was with him.

Two days later the whole gang appeared at the home of Henry Hassan between Duck and Snake Creeks, and after forcing his wife to prepare dinner for them and gorging themselves like ravenous wolves, they seized and tied her down with a rope, and each took his turn assaulting her while the others held her husband at bay with Winchesters. They then amused themselves by making Hassan and his hired man, who also was present, fight each other and dance, shooting at their heels to make the affair more lively.

On August 9 they robbed Norberg's store near McDermott and Orcutt's store in the same locality. By this time the people of the Creek Nation had become thoroughly aroused. Captain Edmund Harry of the Creek Lighthorse, with Lighthorsemen Tom Grayson, George Brown, and Skansey, accompanied by Deputy Marshals Sam Haynes and N. B. Irwin and over one hundred irate citizens, took their trail. Shortly after noon the following day, the huge posse came upon the outlaws camped in a little valley at the foot of a high knoll several miles south of the village.

The sky was clear; the sun beat down; not a breath of air stirred. In wide-brimmed black and white felt hats, jean trousers, high-topped boots with long-shanked spurs, vests flung open, fancy colored bandannas about their necks, and heavy cartridge belts around their waists, they squatted in the shade of a clump of trees around a big pile of ammunition, tobacco, clothing, and other merchandise they had carried from the two stores. A dozen yards away their horses switched flies and fed on the half-dead prairie grass. They were so occupied in dividing the loot that they were unaware of the posse until it had surrounded them from the other side of the knoll and opened fire.

Strangely, none of the gang were wounded by the first volley. The fierce, unexpected onslaught brought them into action. Unable to reach their horses, they grabbed their rifles and fled to the top of the knoll, where they sought cover in some grass roots in the center of a little plateau and opened fire on the posse below. For seven hours the battle raged, while the "brave and desperate" Indian police, deputy marshals, and Creek citizens sought to ascend the hill, and the outlaws, shooting down from their vantage ground, drove them back.

At Fort Smith, shortly after court had convened at one

o'clock, the first dispatch reached the city that the big posse had made contact with the Buck gang and "a furious battle" was in progress.

Everybody in Fort Smith had heard of the Buck gang, the report of whose dare-devilishness had spread over the entire country. Coming so soon after the Keating murder, their acts had filled the people of the city and country with horror, and women and children feared to step out of doors after dark. The news of the "round up" spread like wild fire; "The Buck Gang" was upon everybody's lips. The news reached the court house. There were in the yard and corridors over 400 persons who had been summoned before the court as witnesses. The court room was crowded, to listen idly to the numerous petty cases that were invariably called up after the disposal of a noted murder trial. Inside the court room word was passed from lip to lip, to the effect that officers had corralled the Buck gang; almost instantly all was in a bustle. A bailiff whispered the news to Judge Parker; he nodded pleasantly, called for order in the court and proceeded with the regular business. Soon another dispatch came; it read:

"Deputy marshals and Indians are engaged in a *hand to hand* conflict with the Buck gang."

Like a flash the contents of this second dispatch found its way to every nook and cranny in the city. In the court room the bustle increased; attorneys for once forgot to ask questions, and witnesses to answer them, and again and again Judge Parker called for the bailiffs to preserve order. His tone was kindly, however, and he seemed to join in with the crowd in secret exultation at the fact that the murderous and unholy gang had been tracked to their lair. All through the afternoon this eager uneasiness continued and Judge Parker's voice would sing out ever and anon . . .

"Bring in the prisoner; swear the witnesses; order in the court!"

And when court finally adjourned everyone hurried to the streets to learn of any possible later news of the fight and gathered in little knots to discuss the probable outcome.[3]

Shortly after dark a dispatch was received that the battle was over and all five outlaws had been taken alive.

They were shackled and chained together and returned to McDermott. Marshal S. Morton Rutherford of the northern district of the territory arrived to take charge. It was decided to place the outlaws under heavy guard during the night and transfer them to Fort Smith the next day.

Citizens and settlers throughout the Creek Nation swarmed into the little village to get a look at these men who had spread such terror among their people in so short a time. At first there were only whispered threats, then lynching was talked openly.

Marshal Rutherford spoke to the people. He assured them that the bandits would be delivered to Fort Smith and that they would get justice in Judge Parker's court, and the mob quieted down for a while. Then talk began about cases being long-drawn-out affairs that went to the Supreme Court. They talked also of the White House criticism of the tribes in general, and the Creeks in particular, for their laxity in upholding the law and their failure to assist in its enforcement as a cause for much of the crime in their nation. The Creeks had smarted under these accusations, and they saw an opportunity for retribution.

Rutherford realized that if he waited until morning none of the prisoners would leave there alive. The noise of the mob increased, more threats, more curses. One large group of Creeks gathered near the marshals' camp and began posting sentries to see that neither the officers nor their prisoners escaped.

Rutherford consulted with his deputies. In the darkness, he believed, they could steal through to safety but for the noise of the heavy chains that bound the bandits together. He told the outlaws that the only way they could remain alive was to cooperate, and if they would pick up their chains and carry them without sound, his officers would try to slip them away. Anxious to save their own lives, although they had little regard for the lives of others, the renegades picked up their chains and carried them silently for half a mile. From there the officers whisked them to Muskogee, placed them on the train, and took them to Fort Smith.[4]

They reached the Arkansas city on Sunday morning, August 11. Seven hundred people had gathered at the depot to gaze upon "these fiends in human form." As the prisoners were escorted off the train with the officers in front and behind them, the crowd fell back on either side, and the outlaws shot furtive glances, taking in every face, every detail, as if at any moment they might attempt a break. One contemporary in describing the situation wrote that "if by some manner or means these men" could have been "unshackled and all provided with Winchesters," what a "scattering" there would have been.[5]

Quickly the deputies marched their prisoners up Garrison Avenue, with the crowd close behind them following silently, "while the church bells tolled a requiem to the dead victims of this blood-thirsty gang." The only other sound was the clanking of their chains upon the sidewalk. Three blocks away the iron gate opened into the old government barracks enclosure, the marshals and their prisoners passed through, and the gate screeched closed behind as the territory's most savage band of criminals walked within the majesty of Judge Parker's law.

The case was assigned to Assistant District Attorney McDonough, who had prosecuted Cherokee Bill and obtained his second conviction. For a week McDonough collected evidence surrounding the gang's "most shocking, dastardly crime"—the rape of Rosetta Hassan—which was placed before the grand jury and an indictment returned as follows:

UNITED STATES OF AMERICA, WESTERN DISTRICT OF ARKANSAS.

IN THE CIRCUIT COURT, MAY TERM, A. D., 1895.

UNITED STATES
     vs
RUFUS BUCK AND LEWIS DAVIS AND LUCKY DAVIS } RAPE
AND SAM SAMPSON AND MAOMA JULY.

The grand jurors of the United States of America, duly selected, empaneled, sworn and charged to inquire into and for the body of the Western District of Arkansas aforesaid, upon their oath present:

That Rufus Buck and Lewis Davis and Lucky Davis and Sam Sampson and Maoma July, on the 5th day of August, A. D., 1895, at the Creek Nation, in the Indian country, within the Western District of Arkansas aforesaid, in and upon Rosetta Hassan, a white woman, and not an Indian, feloniously, forcibly and violently an assault did make, and her, the said Rosetta Hassan, then and there, and against her will, forcibly, violently and feloniously, did ravish and carnally know, contrary to the form of the statute in such case made and provided, and the peace and dignity of the United States of America.

E. J. BLACK, Foreman of Grand Jury.

JAMES F. READ,

U. S. District Attorney, Western District of Arkansas.

On August 20 the prisoners were arraigned before Parker and entered pleas of not guilty. The judge set September 20 as the date for trial.

The trial was amply covered by the Fort Smith press and the newspapers in the Indian territory, St. Louis, Little Rock and Kansas City, and other points near and far. Yet the best account is given by S. W. Harman in his incomparable book, *Hell on the Border:*

Court opened at 8:30 A.M. Within a short time the courtroom was packed with an eager crowd, of all kinds and classes, and the whole motley throng, unmindful of the suffocating heat, sat through the trial, eagerly drinking in the loathsome details of the horrible crime . . . that they might gain a knowledge of the minutest details . . . and so work themselves to a pitch where they could more fully enjoy the punishment, even if inadequate, so certain to be dealt [these outlaws].

Henry Hassan, the husband of the injured woman, was the first witness examined. He described how, on Monday, the fifth day of August, as he lay sleeping beneath an arbor, his wife sitting nearby preparing fruit for the family larder, the gang rode through the front gate. Awakening, he greeted them pleasantly and asked them if they were hunting. Buck replied in the affirmative and called for water. Sending his wife's little brother for a pail of fresh water, he started to meet them and then discovering that one of the number was Lewis Davis, with whom he had previously had some slight difficulty, he knew he was at the mercy of the terrible band of whose recent depredations he had heard. He hesitated a moment, then started for a corner of the house, hoping to reach cover, then enter a door, inside of which hung his Winchester. He gained the corner safely, then ran towards the door and as he started to enter was stopped by Maoma July, who had entered from an opposite door and securing the coveted rifle now brushed his face with its muzzle, while Sampson at the same time covered him with a six-shooter. Hassan backed away, and the others coming up, Buck, with an air of bravado, said: "I'm Cherokee Bill's brother; we want your money." With vile curses they commanded Hassan to sit in a place designated, then ordered his wife and her mother to prepare dinner. The women hastened to cook a meal, and meanwhile Lewis Davis stayed with Hassan to keep him under control by threats of death, boastfully declaring himself to be Tom Root [a notorious outlaw sought at that time]. While the meal was being made ready the rest of the gang searched the house and appropriated $5.95 cash, a suit of clothing, some baby's dresses, together with various articles of feminine apparel, handkerchiefs and whatever struck their fancy. After having appeased their appetites, they came out and stood guard over Hassan while the Negro went in to dinner, after which the assault on Mrs. Hassan was made.

Having satisfied their lusts, they mounted their horses and ordered Hassan to go with them; just then a young man [the hired hand] came, unsuspectingly, to the house . . . and they held him up, and marched both him and Hassan two miles away and compelled them to jump into a pool of water, then forced them to wrestle and fight, then amused themselves by making the men dance while they fired random bullets at their bare feet. Finally, when their ideas of fun were exhausted, they ordered the men to go home, warning them: "If you ever appear against us our friends will kill you." Hassan hurried to his home as soon as released, but found his wife missing. She had been so wrought up over the ordeal through which she had passed, believing it the only means of saving her husband's life, the continued absence of the latter had caused her to believe her sacrifice had been useless, and that he had already fallen a victim to their love of crime, and finally, overcome with fear, she had fled to a nearby cornfield and hid. After a continued search, her husband found her, in a paroxysm of fear, nearly dead from apprehension.

Hassan's story, as related on the witness stand, was straightforward, and was given with but little interruption on the part of the prosecuting attorney and none whatever by the attorneys for defense. Through it all the members of the gang sat unmoved, pretending an inability to understand English. If the testimony of the husband was listened to by the vast assemblage with thrilling interest, then there is no adjective capable of describing the interest shown during the time that the injured wife and mother was giving a recital of her wrongs.

The murmur of indignation that ran through the crowd when Hassan stopped speaking and retired, ceased as Mrs. Hassan was escorted into the courtroom and took her position on the stand, and but for the bustle occasioned by the shifting and craning of necks by the members of the crowd to secure a view of the witness, all was silent. Mrs. Hassan was a well proportioned woman with beautiful features, and a look that betokened a kindly disposition. She appeared to be about 30 years of age. She was very nicely dressed, and wore nothing that could be considered gaudy. Her appearance was most modest and it was evidently with a great effort that she was able to sit there, cynosure of so many curious pairs of eyes. She still showed the effects of her frightful experience. She spoke slowly and in low but tremulous tones showing the strong nervous tension under which she was still laboring; at times her breath came quick, her bosom heaved, the hot blood surged to her temples with her head bowed low she would give way to heart-rending sobs, as the questions propounded by the prosecution or the court brought back with awful vividness the horrible scene through which she passed but a few weeks before. She related, much as her husband had done, the coming of the gang to her home to ask for water, of her fears for the life of her husband, of the hastily prepared meal which she hoped might be the means of saving him. Urged to tell what occurred after they had eaten, she described between sobs how Lucky

Davis, the Negro, had told her: "You have to go with me," and how she pleaded with him not to take her away from her babies; how he had replied, "We will throw the G— d— brats in the creek"; how he had commanded her to mount his horse and ride away with him, only desisting when she declared she could not ride; how he then ordered her to go with him a little way, and she hesitated and had finally obeyed, believing if she refused they would kill her and the rest of her family, and marched on, while the colored brute held the muzzle of his Winchester close to her head. She told how they continued until they reached the back side of the barn, out of sight of the house and 200 feet away, and of Davis then laying down his rifle and drawing a pistol from his belt—then paused.

Judge Parker said kindly, "Just go on and tell everything that occurred there. The law makes it necessary to tell it. It is a very delicate matter, of course, but you will have to tell about it."

"Did he tell you what to do?" asked Mr. McDonough.

"Yes sir," in a tone barely audible.

"What did he say?"

"He told me to lie down"; and the witness broke down completely, while her frame shook with convulsions and she sobbed like a child, yet as a child could not. The effect upon the audience was magnetic. They had listened with sympathetic eagerness, forgetful of their own existence even, and the result when the climax was reached is indescribable; during the several minutes that elapsed before the witness could regain her composure there was the most profound silence, broken only by her sobs; the conditions, the awfulness of the crime committed, the story so clearly told and the woman in tears, had a reflex action upon the auditors, and a wave of sympathy swept through the room, and left scarcely a dry eye. Not one of the jurors, accustomed though they were to recitals of brutality, somewhat hardened no doubt, but who shed tears, sympathetic, manly, noble tears, of which they were not ashamed, neither had reason to be. It was a supreme moment such as I never expect to experience again. The few women in the crowd gave way to a mighty surge of grief, and even Judge Parker, notwithstanding that he had been inured by many long years of experience with brutal crimes, removed his spectacles and while a suspicious moisture twinkled upon his

lashes, drew a handkerchief from his pocket, wiped the lenses, then spoke a few words of gentle encouragement to the witness.

Let us draw a charitable veil before the remainder of her testimony, her unwilling description of what followed, and was repeated, one, two, three, four times, each one of the brutal ruffians taking their turn at the revolting crime while at all times three of the gang remained on guard over the husband, ready to send a bullet crashing through his brain if he attempted a remonstrance or made an outcry. Gently the court drew from her that it was only for the sake of her husband and children and through fear that they would kill her loved ones that she submitted to the indignities, and as she proceeded, the terrible iniquity of the deed came upon him with such power that Judge Parker became livid with rage; it were well for the prisoners that the law prevented him dealing out punishment then and there.

Without cross-examination Mrs. Hassan was allowed to step down from the witness stand and retire; the attorneys standing aside and bowing reverently as she passed out, bearing the sympathy of every one in the courtroom. At the conclusion, Assistant District Attorney McDonough rose and in a subdued tone said to the jury:

"Gentlemen: You heard the evidence. It was so plain it is unnecessary to argue the case. The court will give all necessary instruction, and we will expect a verdict of guilty at your hands."

Wm. M. Cravens, one of the five attorneys appointed for the defense, arose and said, simply, "May it please the court and you, gentlemen of the jury, you have heard the evidence. I have nothing to say," then resumed his seat. It was probably the shortest plea for defense ever recorded.

Judge Parker then delivered a short but impressive charge and the jury retired. It required no effort on the part of any member of that jury to arrive at a verdict of guilty. They did not even take time to ballot. One of their number was chosen foreman, his signature was affixed, and the jury at once returned to the courtroom, where in silence, the verdict was awaited. It read: "We, the jury, find the defendants, Rufus Buck, Lewis Davis, Lucky Davis, Sam Sampson and Maoma July guilty of rape, as charged in the within indictment. (Signed) John N. Ferguson, Foreman." [6]

Harman continues:

> Immediately after the finding of the indictment for the rape of
> Mrs. Hassan, the grand jury had returned a true bill charging
> the Buck gang with murder . . . of the Negro marshal . . . the
> first crime committed by them as they started out on their short
> and terrible career. As soon as the verdict convicting them of rape
> was read, Judge Parker excused the jury and at once another
> panel was drawn, a new jury was selected, and, without being
> allowed to leave their seats, the prisoners were placed on trial
> for murder. The case continued until the next day, resulting in a
> verdict of guilty.[7]

On Wednesday, September 25, a huge crowd again gathered
in the courtroom to hear Judge Parker pronounce their sentence.

"Rufus Buck, Lewis Davis, Lucky Davis, Sam Sampson and
Maoma July, stand up.

"You have been convicted by a verdict of the jury, justly
rendered, of the terrible crime of rape. It now becomes the duty
of this court to pass sentence upon you which the law says shall
follow a conviction of such crime. Have you anything to say
why the sentence of the law should not now be passed in your
cases?"

"Yes, suh," Lucky Davis replied. "I wants my case to go to
the Supreme Court."

"I don't blame you," commented Judge Parker, then he continued, speaking to all of them:

> I want to say in this case that the jury, under the law and the
> evidence, could come to no other conclusion than that which they
> arrived at. Their verdict is an entirely just one, and one that must
> be approved by all lovers of virtue. The offense of which you have
> been convicted is one which shocks all men who are not brutal.
> It is known to the law as a crime offensive to decency, and as a
> brutal attack upon the honor and chastity of the weaker sex. It is
> a violation of the quick sense of honor and the pride of virtue
> which nature, to render the sex amiable, has implanted in the
> female heart, and it has been by the law-makers of the United

States deemed equal in enormity and wickedness to murder, because the punishment fixed by the same is that which follows the commission of the crime of murder . . .

Your crime leaves no ground for the extension of sympathy. . . . You can expect no more sympathy than lovers of virtue and haters of vice can extend to men guilty of one of the most brutal, wicked, repulsive and dastardly crimes known in the annals of crime. Your duty now is to make an honest effort to receive from a just God that mercy and forgiveness you so much need. We are taught that His mercy will wipe out even this horrible crime; but He is just, and His justice decrees punishment unless you are able to make atonement for the revolting crime against His law and against human law that you have committed. This horrible crime now rests upon your souls. Remove it if you can so the good God of all will extend to you His forgiveness and His mercy.

Listen now to the sentence of the law which is, that you, Rufus Buck, for the crime of rape, committed by you upon Rosetta Hassan, in the Indian country, and within the jurisdiction of this court, of which crime you stand convicted by the verdict of the jury in your case, be deemed, taken and adjudged guilty of rape; and that you be therefor, for the said crime against the laws of the United States, hanged by the neck until you are dead; that the marshal of the Western District of Arkansas, by himself or deputy, or deputies, cause execution to be done in the premises upon you on Thursday, the thirty-first day of October, 1895, between the hours of 9 o'clock in the forenoon and 5 o'clock in the afternoon of the said day; and that you now be taken to the jail from whence you came, to be there closely and securely kept, until the day of execution, and from thence on the day of execution as aforesaid, you are to be taken to the place of execution, there to be hanged by the neck until you are dead.

May God, whose laws you have broken, and before whose tribunal you must then appear, have mercy on your soul.

He then pronounced the sentence upon each remaining member of the gang, while they "exhibited no sign" and "seemed to care nothing for it." [8]

For "downright dare-deviltry" and "complete abandon" these renegades stood at the head of all "dissolute characters" who had been swung into eternity on the gallows at the federal jail. There was "no extenuating circumstance" for their counsel to offer in their behalf. The "details of the rape of Mrs. Hassan were so revolting" and "proof of their guilt so plain" that it appeared the case would not be taken to the Supreme Court.[9]

But Buck claimed that, given the opportunity, he could prove an alibi, and the case was appealed. Judge Parker issued a stay of execution, but this time the Supreme Court refused to interfere. The decision was affirmed without opinion,[10] and Judge Parker resentenced the gang to hang on July 1, 1896.

The best account of their execution appeared in the *Elevator* issue of July 3:

It was seven minutes past 1 o'clock when the doors of the jail opened for the egress of the condemned men. As they passed out, many of their fellow prisoners called to them: "Good bye, boys." They responded in a rather low tone of voice. Rufus Buck was the first to come from the jail door. He was perfectly calm. The others followed, and were equally cool. All were clad in black suits, and Rufus Buck, Maoma July and Lucky Davis wore large boutonniers upon the left lapel of their coats. Father Pius, their spiritual adviser, accompanied them. Closely following upon the train toward the gallows were the sisters of Sam Sampson and Lucky Davis.

When the prisoners entered the gallows enclosure they took a glance at its hideous paraphernalia and then ascended the steps without the least sign of emotion. They remained seated upon a bench while Colonel Crump read the death warrant. Most of the officers and the spectators seemed impressed by this part of the proceedings, and stood with uncovered heads. When this part of the preliminaries had been disposed of, Col. Crump asked the condemned men if they had any remarks to make. All except Lucky said they had not. Lucky simply said he wanted the priest to pray for him.

Father Pius uttered a short prayer in silence, during which all present stood with uncovered heads.

This over, the prisoners stepped upon the fatal trap. As they did so they recognized a number of persons among the crowd around the gallows and saluted them. Lucky Davis shouted "Good bye, Martha" to his sister, who was also present. Rufus Buck's father, a big, heavy old man, got into the jail enclosure and attempted to come up the steps to the platform where his son stood; but he was stupidly drunk, and was escorted below.

The sister of Sam Sampson entered the gallows yard and stood until the black caps were placed in position. . . .

It took but a short time to complete the work after the preliminaries had been arranged. The prisoners stepped forward . . . none of the condemned men except Lucky Davis showed any signs of trepidation. Lucky was nervous, and during the time Col. Crump was reading the warrants, showed his nervousness by restless movements and twitchings of his face. Beyond this he showed no signs of fear. When he stood upon the scaffold he was perfectly cool. He kept repeating prayers even after the black cap was placed over his head.

The trap dropped with its horrible "chug" at 1:28 o'clock. Lewis Davis died in three minutes, his neck being broken. The necks of Sam Sampson and Maoma July were also broken, and they died easily. Rufus Buck and Lucky Davis were strangled to death. . . . Davis' body drew up several times before it straightened out. Rufus Buck did not suffer, unconsciousness coming over him as soon as the rope tightened around his neck and shut off his breath; but it was several minutes before the contortions of his body ceased.

In Rufus Buck's cell, after his execution, was found a photograph of his mother. On its back he had sketched a strange farewell poem, decorated with a cross and a drawing of the Savior. It read:

MY, dreAm,—1896

I, dreamP'T, i, wAs, in, HeAVen,
Among, THe, AngeLs, Fair;

i'd, neAr, seen, none, so HAndsome,
THAT, TWine, in, goLden, HAir;
THey, Looked, so, neAT, And, SAng, so, sweet,
And, PLAY,d, THe, THe, goLden, HArp,
i, wAs, ABout, To, Pick, An, AngeL, ouT,
And, TAke, Her, To, mY, HeArT;
BuT, THe, momenT, i, BegAn, To, PLeA,
i, THougHT, oF, You, mY Love,
THere, wAs, none, i'd, seen, so, BeAuTiFuLL,
On, eArTH, or, HeAven, ABove,
gooD, By, My, Dear, Wife, anD. MoTHer
all.so.My. sisTers

RUFUS, BUCK
Youse. Truley

I Day. of. JUly
Tu, THe, Yeore
off
1896

H
O
L
Y
FATHer   Son
g
H
O
S
T
virtue & resurresur.rection.
RememBer, Me, ROCK, OF, Ages:

XI

⋆THE WICKED FLEE⋆

MEANWHILE, JUDGE PARKER WAS EXPERIENCING great difficulty suppressing his indignation at having his opinion reversed by the Supreme Court in the case of the notorious desperado Henry Starr.

Henry was born December 2, 1873, in a log hut near Fort Gibson. His father was George "Hop" Starr, half-breed Cherokee son of the old Cherokee outlaw, Tom Starr, and brother of Sam Starr, husband of Belle, the outlaw queen. If there was an inherent criminal instinct in Henry's nature, it was a dark heritage from the Starr strain. His mother was half-Irish and a highly respectable woman. At sixteen he went to work on the Half Circle Box ranch south of Coffeyville. In the fall of 1890 he worked on the Open A, and when their cattle were shipped in the spring of '91, he got a job with the Roberts brothers near by.[1] By this time he was a crack cowboy—five feet nine inches tall, strong, of athletic build, with straight black hair, dark brown eyes, and handsome with just a tinge of swarthiness. He didn't use tobacco, coffee, or liquor. He looked like a man who could be trusted.[2]

Then, in June of '91, Henry was arrested for introducing whisky to the Indian Territory. Starr always claimed that the whisky the marshals found in his buggy belonged to a friend who had asked him to haul it to Nowata. Official records do not bear him out. The supposed friend was never identified. Starr pleaded guilty, and was fined and released.

In February, 1892, he was arrested for horse stealing, but the case was dismissed in commissioner's court. In August he stole two horses and was released on bond furnished by a cousin and the chief of the Cherokee Nation. He failed to appear for trial; the bond was forfeited, and his bondsmen offered a reward for his capture. While a fugitive on this charge he began the series of crimes that graduated him into the full-fledged outlaw class of the James, Youngers, and Daltons . . . "a well fit type of his distant kinsmen and as daring a devil as ever terrorized peaceable citizens." [3]

Accompanied by a Delaware half-breed, Ed Newcome, and Jesse Jackson, a white man, he held up the Missouri Pacific at Nowata. He robbed the Schufeldt and Son store at Sequoyah.[4] Meanwhile Detective H. E. Dickey of the express company, investigating the Nowata affair, had gone to Fort Smith, obtained a warrant for Starr's arrest, and accompanied by Deputy Marshal Floyd Wilson had gone out to hunt the youthful bandit. It was while being pursued by Wilson and Detective Dickey that he committed the murder for which he was tried before Judge Parker.

On December 13 they picked up his trail south of Lenapah and traced him to the ranch of Albert Dodge in the California Creek country. Dodge reported he had seen the outlaw ride past his place several times. The officers began scouring the country for him.

Wilson came upon Starr alone in an opening on Wolf Creek. They sighted each other the same instant, and Starr dropped from his saddle. Wilson dismounted also, and the pair stood facing each other only thirty paces apart, Winchesters in their hands.

Wilson ordered Starr to surrender. "The reply was a shot from Starr's rifle." [5] Wilson fired once and then "an empty shell became clogged in his Winchester, and throwing down the weapon, he tried to defend himself with a revolver." [6] Starr "discharged his Winchester several more times at the brave marshal," [7] knocking him down; and while the deputy lay on the ground, too badly wounded to defend himself, the outlaw calmly strode forward and fired another shot into his breast, holding his gun so close that the blaze spouting from its muzzle burned the officer's clothing.[8] Dickey heard the shooting and hurried to the scene. But Starr had escaped.

The slaying of Wilson "established" Starr among the remaining desperadoes of the West. He now organized a "hard-riding, fast-shooting gang" that, under his planning and leadership, committed robberies in a short time as follows: the People's Bank at Bentonville, Arkansas, in which a fierce battle was waged with citizens and the gang took $11,000; the Chelsea railroad station; the Missouri-Kansas-Texas train at Pryor Creek; stores at Nowata and Choteau; the bank at Aldrich, Missouri; and the Caney Valley Bank at Caney, Kansas. Three thousand dollars were obtained at Aldrich and $2000 at Caney.[9] "Always on the go, always pursued, but somehow always managing to avoid capture," the gang experienced only one brush with the marshals. In a fight with Deputies Isaac Rogers and Rufe Cannon near Bartlesville, one member, Jesse Jackson, was shot three times. Henry Starr and Ed Newcome escaped. Rogers, in a message to Marshal Yoes at Fort Smith, stated that "about two hundred shots were fired; we are still on the trail of Starr and his confederates and will yet run them down." [10]

With the law "literally breathing down their necks," the gang decided it wise to break up and go their separate ways. Starr, accompanied by Kid Wilson, the only other survivor of the Bentonville raid,[11] departed for Colorado Springs. On July 3, 1893, they were captured by the Colorado Springs police:

It had been rumored for several days that Starr was in the city, but his identity could not be determined. Monday morning Mr. William Feuerstine [a resident of Fort Smith who was in Colorado Springs attending to private business] happened to step into the Spaulding House . . . and saw Starr. He at once informed Capt. Dana, chief of police . . . and a search was instituted at the Spaulding House, where the following entry was made late Saturday night:

Frank Jackson, Joplin, Mo.
John Wilson, Joplin, Mo.
Mary Jackson, Joplin, Mo.

As surmised, Jackson proved to be Starr, and Mary Jackson his alleged wife. Chief Dana, knowing the character of the men he had to deal with, planned to attack them separately. Four men, heavily armed, were located in a convenient room on South Telon street. Detective Joe Atkinson was detailed to remain at the Spaulding House and keep the game in sight. . . . Shortly after noon Starr and Wilson sauntered up Telon street. They entered the store of Oppenheim Brothers, bought a lot of clothes and a good gold watch and chain and impressed the proprietors they were from the East to see the sights. The Oppenheims were asked to accompany them, which they did. Mrs. Jackson was picked up at the Spaulding House, and the party drove to Manitou Springs and spent the day, closely followed by officers in citizens' garb, who watched their every movement. They returned about dark. Starr and the woman got out at the Spaulding House, but Wilson accompanied the driver to the stable. An hour later Starr descended to the hotel office, and being informed that the supper hour had passed, he started out to get a lunch. The hour anxiously awaited for had come. The desperadoes had separated. Starr sauntered up the street, with Chief Dana and Captain Gathright behind him, and Detective Atkinson and two deputies on the opposite side of the street.

After walking about two squares, Starr entered the Cafe

Royal, and ordered a lunch, which was served. While he was engaged in disposing of the meal, Dana and Gathright sauntered in leisurely, but turned suddenly and pinioned Starr's arms and wrists. Meanwhile, Atkinson and his deputies entered and leveled their revolvers on Starr, who, after being relieved of a .45 Colt's revolver, surrendered. After being taken to the police station, he asked:

"Who do you think you've got?"

"Henry Starr," was the answer.

"You're right," was his reply.

Wilson, "the Kid," had taken the street car for Colorado City, in company with the Oppenheims. The officers were soon in pursuit. One of the Oppenheims said Wilson had entered a house of ill fame close by. The landlady opened a door of one of the rooms and the officers rushed in, calling on Wilson to throw up his hands. He did so, and his capture was effected without a struggle. Wilson's revolver was found under his pillow. The last of the trio, the woman known as Mrs. Starr, was found in bed at the Spaulding House a few minutes later. Under her pillow was $1460 in bills, and in a valise near by $500 in gold.[12]

Starr, with Wilson, was taken to Fort Smith, where four indictments for robbery and one for murder awaited him.[13] Wilson was convicted for participation in the Pryor Creek train robbery and sentenced to twenty-four years in prison at Brooklyn.

Henry Starr was tried for murder of the deputy marshal. He did not deny killing Floyd Wilson, but claimed it was in self-defense . . . that he did not know Wilson was an officer and that the latter had given him "no notice of his character or mission." That Starr knew Wilson was an officer and knew he was being pursued was evidenced by the testimony of one Mrs. Padget, who witnessed the slaying from near her home and testified that she heard Wilson say, "Hold up; I have a warrant for you," and that Starr said, "You hold up." In answer to a question put by the District Attorney, she also stated that three or four weeks before the shooting Starr had remarked to her that he guessed the marshals were hunting him "for jumping his bond." [14]

Parker charged the jury accordingly:

> If a man stands up and obstructs arrest, prevents arrest, armed with deadly weapons, and using them in a way that is threatening, then the officer has no time, nor is he called upon to make proclamation. The officer must stand on the offensive and overcome the danger and take his man or overcome him by violence, if necessary.

The judge added:

> When we enter upon the execution of as grave a design as the taking of the life of individuals, we must enter upon it with clean hands and a pure heart. If we have created a condition that leads to a deadly result, the law of self-defense does not apply . . . if we create that condition by doing a wrongful thing upon our part, which would naturally or reasonably or probably produce a deadly result . . . because we are wrong in the first place.

Referring to the defendant, he said:

> He was a fugitive from justice . . . he had forfeited his bond and was up in that country, hiding out from his usual place of abode, to avoid arrest. . . .

And continued:

> It is a fact that becomes pertinent to you to take into consideration . . . from what transpired . . . that he knew Floyd Wilson was an officer, and was seeking to arrest him. . . . It takes men who are brave to uphold the law here. There is no protection unless the law is upheld by men of this kind. . . . If you are satisfied of the fact, beyond a reasonable doubt, that Floyd Wilson was a man of this kind, that he was properly in the execution of the high duty devolving upon him, and while so properly executing it, by the light of these principles of the law I have given you, his life was taken by this defendant, your solemn duty would be to say that he is guilty of the crime of murder, because . . . the law is to be vindicated. You are to

stand by the nation. You are to say to all the people that no man can trample upon the law, wickedly, violently, and ruthlessly; that it must be upheld if it has been violated.

Parker concluded his charge "in strong terms, expressed indignation at the homicide, and urged argumentatively the necessity of vindicating and upholding the law." [15]

In pronouncing sentence upon Starr, he said: "You tried this brave officer, condemned him to death and executed him with a Winchester; and now it is only simple justice that you should die at the end of a rope." [16]

Starr's attorney quickly sued out a writ of error on grounds that Parker's remarks were "not consistent with due regard to the right and duty of the jury to exercise an independent judgment," and Chief Justice Fuller, in handing down the opinion of the Supreme Court, said:

Whatever special necessity for enforcing the law in all its rigor there may be in a particular quarter of the country, the rules by which, and the manner in which, the administration of justice should be conducted, are the same everywhere; and argumentative matter of this sort should not be thrown into the scales by the judicial officer who holds them. . . . The judgment is reversed, and the cause remanded, with a direction to grant a new trial.[17]

Parker demanded:

Does it mean that it is the part of the government to send a man out into that Golgotha to officers, and command them, in the solemn name of the President of the United States, to execute these processes, and say to them: "Men may defy you; men may arm themselves, and hold you at bay; they may obstruct your process; they may intimidate your execution of it; they may hinder you in making the arrest; they may delay you in doing it by threats of armed violence upon you; and yet I am unable, as chief executive of this government, to assure you that you have any protection whatever!" What a mockery, what a sham! What was this posse to do? What was he commanded to do? To go into the Indian country and hunt up Mr. Starr, and say to him that on a certain day the judge of the federal court at Fort Smith will want your attendance at a little trial down there, wherein you are charged with horse stealing, and you will be kind enough, sir, to put in your attendance on that day; and the judge sends his compliments, Mr. Starr? Is that his mission? Is that the message from this court that is to be handed to Mr. Starr upon a silver platter, with all the formalities of polite society? Is that what Floyd Wilson was employed or engaged to do?

No. This court did not have anything to do with that command.

In the fall of 1895 Starr was retried before Parker. After being granted a new trial by the Supreme Court, the outlaw feared nothing more than a conviction of manslaughter. Friends of the dead marshal were also uncertain of the result, and many thought it would be impossible to secure another conviction. Starr went on the stand and corroborated the most damaging testimony against himself. He admitted that he advanced on Wilson all the time, and was standing almost over his prostrate body when the fatal shot was fired.[18]

"The wicked flee when no man pursueth," charged the white-haired Parker, "but the righteous are as bold as a lion. A man is to be judged by his consciousness of the right or wrong of what he does. . . . If he flees from justice, if he goes to a distant country and is living under an assumed name because of that fact, the law says that is not in harmony with what innocent men do, and jurors have a right to consider it as an evidence of guilt . . . a presumption of fact . . . a silent admission by the defendant that he is unwilling or unable to face the case against him . . . a confession that comes in with other incidents, the corpus delicti being proved, from which guilt may be cumulatively inferred."[19] And Starr was again convicted of murder and sentenced to die.

"Reversed and remanded for a new trial," ruled the Supreme Court. Flight of the accused did not raise a "legal presumption" of guilt so that an "inference of guilt" could be drawn therefrom. At the most, wrote Justice White, it was only one of a series of circumstances to be considered by the jury with the reasons that prompted it, and even then "its force is slight." The law on the subject of the weight to be given to the evidence of flight of the accused was "identical with instructions heretofore held by this court to be fatally defective." [20] The high tribunal had corrected Parker on this matter in the cases of Alexander Allen and Sam Hickory, in which the judge's language was "substantially similar." So Parker "should know the law."

A review of the thirty-seven reversals of his court shows that most of the errors he made were the outgrowth of his philosophy that law was a subject beyond the experience of the average frontier juror and that they needed guidance. The polyglot section of American society, so entirely different in its legal setup than any other in the United States—with many nations within the western district and each possessing its own system of laws and courts—created judicial difficulties that required extensive explanations to juries. When an offense occurred in which whites, blacks, foreigners, and Indians were involved, jurisdiction could not be determined by color or race alone. The reconstruction treaties of 1866 had freed the Indian's slaves. Previous treaties had established the immunities of adopted or naturalized citizens, and the slaves when freed and adopted became Indians in the sight of the law, with the immunities of the Indian. Evidence had to substantiate the significant statement of the indictment, "a white man and not an Indian," or "a Negro and not an Indian"; for if it was proved during the trial that the parties to the crime were Indians, either by blood, treaty, or adoption, the indictment was quashed. The judge of the United States court had to know the laws of the Indian nations, and they were not the same in bestowing citizenship. Parker had to explain these treaties and laws to the juries; he quoted Scripture, gave illustrations, and used figures of speech to employ language within the grasp of these lowly trained men;

and consequently his charges amounted to from twenty to fifty pages of material. On one occasion Solicitor General Edward B. Whitney complained that "in one case on my desk his charge contains 70 large and closely typewritten pages where five pages would have been ample." [21]

The Supreme Court knew these conditions, but the majority of the justices felt that his lengthy discourses from the bench "infringed upon the rights of the accused"; that his charges went beyond mere exposition and became "inaccurate, prolix and prejudicial toward the defendant"; and that his strong feeling against corrupt and lawless characters often caused him so to explain the rule of evidence as to take the evidence away from the jury and "confuse the law as to its weight and competence." [22]

On the other hand, the Supreme Court reversed Parker many times on points not raised by defense attorneys. Instead of insisting that they specify the exceptions, the justices allowed "general exceptions," as in *Alexander v United States,* the first case appealed. In *Hicks v United States,*[23] November 27, 1893, Justice David J. Brewer, dissenting, scored the court because errors "were challenged by only a single exception running to them as an entirety; which was not noticed in the motion for a new trial, or in the assignment of errors, and is evidently an afterthought of counsel, with the record before them, studying up some ground for a reversal"; and added that "the opinion and judgment of the court proceeds in disregard of rules long ago established in regard to the conditions under which an appellate court will review the instructions given on the trial." Several other cases were sent back to Parker where "no sufficient exception was taken."

Often, too, the court "sacrificed justice to the merest kind of objection." In *Lewis v United States,*[24] December 5, 1892, Justice Brewer stated that "the discretion vested in the trial court as to the manner of challenges" was no error sufficient to justify a new trial. Justice Brown concurred. Justice R. W. Peckham, dissenting in *Crain v United States,*[25] April 20, 1896, thought the judgment of the court "seems to proceed, not alone upon the merest technicality, but also upon an unwarranted presumption of error arising from a formal statement in the record showing that the defendant was duly arraigned and pleaded not guilty," and declared the reversal of the trial court "without an allegation, or even a pretense, that the defendant has suffered any injury by reason of any alleged defect of character in question . . . a result most deplorable."

Justice Brewer wrote an even more vigorous and caustic dissent when the court saved John Brown from the gallows the third time because it said Parker had committed reversible error in stating that "reputation must grow out of the dispassionate judgment of men who are honest men and good men, and able and competent to make up a judgment of that kind. It is not the judgment of the bad people, the criminal element, the man of crime, that is to fasten upon a man and blacken his name."

Said Justice Brewer:

> This part of the charge is, as a whole, unobjectionable. . . . The admonition was just and sound. Reputation is the general judgment of the community in respect to the witness whose reputation is challenged, and is not made up by the flippant talk of a few outlaws. . . .
>
> The testimony discloses an outrageous crime, showing the defendant, in connection with another party, in the nighttime called from their slumbers two officers of the law and shot them down, without provocation. . . . Three juries (36 jurors) have agreed in finding a defendant guilty of the crime charged, and such finding has each time been approved by the trial judge, the judgment based upon the last verdict ought not be disturbed unless it is manifest that the verdict is against the truth of the case. . . . Justice and the protection of society united in saying that it is high time such a crime was punished. . . .[26]

In *Isaacs v United States*,[27] November 11, 1895, the court admitted the assignments of error were "so obviously frivolous that no discussion of them is necessary."

In *Garland v State of Washington*,[28] in 1914, Justice William

R. Day, referring to the identical question of law on which the Supreme Court reversed Parker in the Crain case, said:

> Technical objections of this character were undoubtedly given much more weight formerly than they are now. . . . Notwithstanding our reluctance to overrule former decisions of this court, we are now constrained to hold that the technical enforcement of formal rights in criminal procedure in the Crain case is no longer required in the prosecution of offenses under present systems of law, and . . . is not in accord with the views herein expressed. . . .

Strange to say, the court in later years also departed from the rule of flight and upheld criminal cases containing substantially the same language as used by Parker in Starr's case.[29]

Under the federal judicial system a federal judge could express rather freely his opinion on the weight of evidence in a criminal case. Parker was "prone to emphasize first the government's and then the defendant's theory . . . and often used strong statements favorable to the prosecution," which were reversible error except where cured by "equally vigorous statements favorable to the accused." It was "difficult for him to frame his charges in colorless language." [30] The practice is still followed in the federal courts, and Judge Parker's remarks "would probably seem mild compared with the remarks of some present day federal judges." [31]

Perhaps if Parker had not so openly criticized the Supreme Court, it would not have been so inclined to ferret out technical points to his disfavor. It was more than the judge could bear. For six years his irritation smouldered. The reversals in the Starr case [32] sparked it to flame.

He intimated that he was more familiar with criminal court procedure and criminal law than were justices of the appellate court. "I am not," he stated, in February, 1896, "opposed to the right of appeal. I merely prefer that my decisions be reviewed by courts specializing in criminal law, and that all technicalities not affecting the guilt or innocence of the accused be ignored. The convicted criminal should have the right to have his case reviewed upon a writ of error, but . . . the case should be passed upon according to its merits. The Supreme Court, being learned in the civil law and not the criminal law, looks to the *shadow* in shape of technicalities instead of the *substance* in the form of crime." [33]

And later in the year he stated, "I have given every criminal a chance to prove his innocence, but I never made hair-splitting distinctions in favor of the criminal at the expense of life." He characterized the appellate court as "knifing the trial judge in the back and allowing the criminal to go free." [34]

While denouncing the Supreme Court, Parker also vigorously assailed Attorney General Judson Harmon and Solicitor General Whitney. In an open letter published in the St. Louis *Globe-Democrat,* dated February 3, he said: "They are supposed to speak for this court when cases go up on appeal, but they have blundered badly and let the opposition run off with the show." A bitter controversy arose, through letters and the newspapers, in which the issues developed into personalities.

The Solicitor General described Parker's interpretation of the law of self-defense "obsolete and applicable to an age in which swords, spears and knives were used as deadly weapons" and labeled the idea that a defendant when attacked "must use every means in his power otherwise to save his own life, such as retreating as far as he could, or disabling his adversary without killing him" as ridiculous. "If the learned judge would confine himself to statements of the law instead of going into the merits of the case, he could avoid innumerable errors."

And Parker, in reply to the Solicitor General's open letter, labeled his charges "a string of falsehoods" made by "a legal imbecile" who spoke a "personal screed . . . croaked by every foul bird of evil, hissed from every wicked serpent of crime . . . for all these twenty years."

He contended further that Whitney "knew nothing of the

frontier," and therefore "was unable to cope with experienced frontier criminal lawyers." He hadn't even tried, Parker added. "On five occasions [35] he has given up without a struggle, confessing error and agreeing with the opposition."

"I have actually argued at the Supreme Court eight murder cases coming from Judge Parker," the Solicitor General stated to the President, "and I have been, to some extent, cognizant of the facts of seven others."

"Whitney knows this is not true," Parker replied. "He has never argued one case, and he could not do so, for he has never tried a murder case in a trial court." And he added that the only time Mr. Whitney had "exercised his gigantic intellect before the President of the United States" was in asking for some outlaw's pardon.

"Is he a pardon broker?" demanded Parker. "This brings me to the conclusion that he is on the side of the man of crime, the man of blood. . . ."

And Whitney scathingly retorted that the judge was "ignorant and careless" and only trying to cover up for his "gross errors." *He* was the best friend of the criminals, Whitney said, for he "assures them reversals and thus gives them chances of escape which the most adroit criminal lawyers could not possibly accomplish."

"A lame attempt at the suppression of facts!" Parker fired back. "The feeble and childish reply of a legal simpleton . . . who knows no more of criminal law than he does of the hieroglyphics of the Great Pyramid."

Thoroughly aroused, the judge cracked down at Attorney General Harmon:

> I have, for four lustrums, been aiding the battle between the law and human rights on one hand, and wicked and unrelenting men of crime on the other. . . . Do you not think, my dear sir, that if instead of the solicitor general in hot haste confessing error, he would have looked into the cases far enough to understand them, and that someone in your department would have

orally argued these cases before the Supreme Court, that that
court might have had a better understanding of them? Sir, do you
know that no murder cases going to the Supreme Court under the
law as it now stands has ever been orally argued before that
court? . . . Liberty and life are precarious unless those in authority have sense and spirit enough to defend them under the
law.

The controversy was one of the most bitter and vituperative
ever conducted in the border press. Parker's action in not sending a copy of his letter to the Attorney General, allowing the
latter to learn of it from the newspapers, caused considerable
speculation. The St. Louis *Republic* charged that the judge
aspired to an appointment to the Supreme Court bench, and
that his motive was politics.

Parker had plainly stated his motive in his letter to the Justice
Department:

> I think my duty to the public, my duty to the law, my duty to
> peace and order, my duty to the innocent and unoffending people,
> and my duty to the murdered dead, all demand that I should,
> in the name of right and justice, protest against this extraordinary
> and unusual method of getting rid of important criminal cases
> which have been taken on appeal.

The citizens of the Indian country were behind Parker. It
was a tough job to fight "the worst bands of desperadoes, murderers and outlaws to be found in any civilized land." The
"almost necessary result" was to "shock the man of blood" into
"dread of the law" by aiding the marshals who brought in the
bad men, helping the district attorneys prosecute the murderers,
and "leading" the juries to a verdict of death. The people
wanted results, there was no time for technicalities.

The Solicitor General, however, disagreed:

> We have little difficulty in sustaining the judgment of other
> judges in murder cases, and I believe that no other judge has
> found it necessary to write open letters abusing the Supreme

Court. The continual mistrials before Judge Parker are the more
to be deplored because in most cases the prisoners are probably
guilty and would have been convicted if the court had submitted
the case with the very barest statement of law of murder and
without any denunciation or attempt to usurp the jury func-
tions. . . .

Where the charge of the trial judge takes the form of animated
argument, the liability is great and the propositions of law may
become interrupted by digression, and so intermingled with inference springing from forensic ardor, that the jury are left without proper instructions; their appropriate province of dealing with
the facts invaded; and errors intervene which the pursuit of a
different course would have avoided.

The Judge replied:

The truth is the administration of the civil laws has so absorbed
the attention of the court that they have been looked upon as
the greatest rights of man . . . all over the country criminal law
has fallen into disgrace due to corrupt practices which have allowed the man of influence and money to break through the
meshes and go free, and the sickly sentimentality in favor of the
criminal. . . . In the past five years 43,000 persons, more than
are in the regular army, have been murdered in the United States.
Parallel with these have been 723 legal executions and 1,118
lynchings. Think of an average of 7,317 murders a year! Last year
10,500 persons were murdered in this country; that is at the rate
of 875 a month, while five years ago the number of murders
were, for the year, but 4,290. . . . This fearful condition exists
because the bench is not alive to its responsibilities. . . . The
law must be vindicated . . . if this great government is to teach
to the people the high object lesson that they can depend on its
courts and thus secure protection to life and destroy that hideous monster which now curses the country called the "mob."

And he pointed to the fact that there had been only three
cases of mob violence in his jurisdiction in twenty years.[36]

But the controversy had been carried too far. The newspapers blazoned the affair. Friends of the offended Supreme Court

shamed Parker for bad taste. Friends of the offended Attorney General and Solicitor General complained to the President. Dissatisfied lawyers who had seen their clients' necks placed in the noose, to vindicate themselves and their clients, damned the federal court and its judge for "cruelties," "inhumanities," and "wickedness." Considering only the number of men who had died on the scaffold, others characterized Parker as "harsh" and "cruel," "a monomaniac on the subject of crime." And the "sentimentalists," sensitive to the jibes of other regions about the hangings that took place in their midst, demanded more than "reduction of territory" to modify the operation of the court in behalf of justice.

In a heated speech before the House of Representatives, Congressman John S. Little of Arkansas charged that, although "the honorable judge of the court presumes that he has hanged all the mean men and left the good ones there," the Indian country was still "the very glen of criminal miasma, the fumes of the poisons from which are not only generating the best blood of that country, but its contaminating influences are extending into the adjoining states," [37] and that the situation would not improve, regardless of the number executed, until the Indian country "has been organized into a territory."

He admitted that Judge Parker "has done more to stay the progress of murder and crime in the Indian country than any other power"; that "his name was a terror to evil doers"; but "while this court has been serving its purpose, it has done much to bring the good name of the city of Fort Smith and Western Arkansas into disrepute." He let the country know that he did not want the institution referred to as "the Parker slaughter house" retained in his district any longer, despite the fact that many of the officials belonging to the "slaughter house gang" were his best friends.

And in the Senate—before men who had never seen the desperado riding red-handed over the Indian country, unmindful of the rights of property, raiding trains, desolating homes, and subjecting defenseless women to the most unspeakable indignities—George Vest of Missouri arose to declare the Fort Smith hall of justice "a shambles, a stench and a disgrace, a butcher's domain."

Step by step, Congress had "encroached" upon the Fort Smith court, "taking away its criminal jurisdiction over the Indian country by degrees, like the slow bleeding to death of an unfortunate patient under the knife of the bungling surgeon." [38] Immediately following the act of February 6, 1889, in which appeals were allowed to the Supreme Court, it approved an act on March 1, establishing the first white man's court in the Indian country at Muskogee. Principally a court of civil jurisdiction, putting into force the civil laws of the State of Arkansas, it interfered with the criminal jurisdiction of the Fort Smith court to the extent that it was given exclusive, original jurisdiction of all offenses against the laws of the United States not punishable by death or imprisonment at hard labor. By this same act, apparently repealing the act of January 6, 1883, annexing a certain portion of the Indian country to the Northern District of Texas, the Chickasaw Nation and a greater portion of the Choctaw Nation as far north as the Canadian River were annexed to the Eastern Judicial District of Texas, with the court seat at Paris, and the Paris court was given exclusive, original jurisdiction of all federal law violations within this portion of the territory of which jurisdiction was not given to the new court at Muskogee. [39]

On May 2, 1890, Congress approved an act creating the Territory of Oklahoma, comprising all that part of the Indian country not actually occupied by the Five Civilized Tribes and the Indians of the Quapaw Agency in the extreme northeast corner of the country, except the unoccupied part of the Cherokee Outlet, together with that portion of the United States known as the Public Land Strip (No Man's Land). An independent territorial judicial system, with three judicial districts, was established with full jurisdiction of all cases originating in Oklahoma

Territory and that portion of the Cherokee Outlet not included in Oklahoma Territory. The act defined the Indian Territory as "all that portion of the United States bounded on the north by Kansas, east by Arkansas and Missouri, south of Texas, and west and north by Oklahoma." Thus the new court at Muskogee was restricted to less than one-half its area, but given increased jurisdiction and power over all civil cases in the domain remaining as Indian Territory except cases under jurisdiction of the tribal courts. Fifty-six chapters of Mansfield's Digest of the Statutes of Arkansas were put in effect; the judge of the court was given the power to extradite persons who had taken refuge in the Indian Territory and to issue requisitions for fugitives upon governors of other states and territories; and the right of appeal and writs of error to the Supreme Court of the United States were allowed.[40]

By an act of May 3, 1892, still another court was given jurisdiction in the Indian Territory. This act created a third division of the District of Kansas from portions of the First District. For judicial purposes the Counties of Miami, Linn, Bourbon, Crawford, Cherokee, Labette, Neosho, Allen, Anderson, Coffey, Woodson, Elk, and Greenwood were established as the Third District of Kansas, and all offenses against the laws of the United States within these counties and the limits of the Quapaw Agency in the Indian Territory were to be tried in the court of the Third Kansas District at Fort Scott.[41]

But of all these acts "none were so vicious, nor had such depressing effect" as the one with which Congress now "swooped down upon its victim like some monster bird of prey . . . practically demolishing this greatest court on earth, signaling the ending of its career as such, and sweeping it, almost, from its very foundation." [42] By an act approved March 1, 1895, it divided the Indian Territory into three judicial districts, to be known as the "Northern," "Central," and "Southern" districts. The northern district included the Quapaw Agency and the area of the Creek and Cherokee Nations, with headquarters at Muskogee and court towns at Vinita, Miami, and Tahlequah; the central district embraced the Choctaw Nation, with headquarters at South McAlester and court at Atoka, Antlers, and Cameron; and the southern district comprised the Seminole and Chickasaw Nations, with headquarters at Ardmore and court at Purcell, Pauls Valley, Ryan, and Chickasha. A special provision constituted the three district judges into a court of appeals, presided over by the senior judge acting as chief justice, to which could be appealed decisions of any of the trial courts, and South McAlester was designated seat of the appellate court. Appeals to the circuit court of appeals were provided in lieu of direct appeals to the Supreme Court of the United States. These courts were given exclusive, original jurisdiction of all offenses committed in the Indian Territory, "except such cases as the federal courts at Paris, Texas, Fort Smith, Arkansas or Fort Scott, Kansas, may have already proceeded against"; and September 1, 1896, set as the date when the authority of these outside courts would pass to the new federal courts within the territory. The jurisdiction of the Fort Smith court was specifically limited to the handful of counties in Western Arkansas.[43]

Judge Parker's great white head dropped. How keenly he felt this stripping of authority is shown in his famous grand jury charge of August 5, 1895,[44] when he spoke of the trust reposed in the people of Arkansas for enforcing the law in the Indian country:

> When the court was removed from Van Buren to this place, the same power of protecting remained in the hands of the people of Arkansas, and I want to say that for twenty years, since the opening of the first court here, these people have performed their duty faithfully and well. . . . Why a distrust has been entertained of them or why the jurisdiction was changed, I am not prepared to say. . . . All I have to say is that much has been falsely asserted in regard to it. I can say, in vindication of these jurors and of the people, that the law has been as well enforced by them

as affecting that country and all the rights of its people, as it is enforced in any state of the union anywhere. . . . More cases of criminals committing high crimes have been tried, a higher percentage of arrests have been made, more convictions have been obtained, more men brought to justice, the law better vindicated, better upheld and better sustained and the rights of the people better protected by the people who come to this court as jurors than in any court in the country.

To another grand jury in February, 1896, he said: "It was a desire for gain at the expense of law enforcement that caused the change."

Again in May, 1896, in referring to the administration of justice in the territory by these new courts, he added:

At my first term of court it was rather hard to get good, honest men to come out of that country and give testimony against these desperate characters. A reign of terror existed over there, and the peaceful, law-abiding citizens would rather put up with the annoyances they were subjected to than to come out and testify against the criminals and thus incur the enmity of these bad men and their friends and risk life by assassination at their hands. I fear the same reign of terror will again prevail when jurisdiction of higher crimes are taken away from strong outside courts and given to Indian Territory courts.[45]

Judge Parker was now in the full vigor of manhood at the age of fifty-eight, but the twenty-one years spent in the arduous task of this unusual tribunal had left their mark upon the man, upon the judge. He looked like a man of seventy. Yet he "presided with the same ease and dignity that has characterized his deliberations all these years. His kindly face belies the many hard things that have been said of him, and he is the same counsellor and friend to the wayward that he has always been."[46]

XII

ADJOURNED, FOREVER

THE LAST PERSON TO DIE ON THE FORT SMITH GAL-
lows was George Wilson. Wilson was a white man, twenty-six
years old. A swindler, thief, and forger, he had been out of the
state penitentiary of Tennessee less than a year when he killed
Zachariah W. Thatch, a traveling companion from Washington County, Arkansas, as the latter sat at their campfire near
Keokuk Falls in the Creek Nation, on May 15, 1895. After robbing the body, he threw it into Rock Creek, then stole Thatch's
team and wagon and camp outfit, which was still in his possession when he was arrested a few days later. Wilson claimed
Thatch was his uncle, and said that Thatch had left the property in his care and gone farther west into the Kickapoo country.[1]

Meanwhile the corpse had floated downstream toward the
North Canadian River, where it was discovered lodged among
some rocks and logs with two fingers shot away and the head
split from the blow of an ax. Wilson identified the body and
admitted that he was not the dead man's relative, that his proper
name was James C. Casharego of Conway, Arkansas. But he

197

denied that he had murdered Thatch. Several persons, however, stated they had seen the pair in camp together the night of the slaying, and that shortly after dark two shots had been fired. There was blood on Wilson's trousers and other garments, and on an ax still in the wagon.

Deputy marshals located the camp site. Wilson had burned a fire over the spot where his victim had bled on the ground, and they found no surface evidence of the slaying. But dry weather at the time of the crime had caused the earth to crack, and blood from the murdered man had run deep into one of the fissures. The officers dug deep into the crack and collected several chunks of blood-saturated earth, which were produced at Wilson's trial.

In pronouncing his death sentence, Judge Parker said:

> Even nature revolted against your crime; the earth opened and drank up the blood, held it in a fast embrace until the time it should appear against you; the water, too, threw up its dead and bore upon its placid bosom the foul evidence of your crime.

Wilson appealed to the Supreme Court, but the higher court upheld Parker's decision. Wilson was resentenced, and hanged July 30, 1896.

In Judge Parker's twenty-one years on the bench, 13,490 cases had been docketed, exclusive of more than 4000 petty crimes that got no farther than the commissioner's courts. Of this total, 9454 had been convicted by a trial jury or had entered pleas of guilty, and 344 had been tried for offenses punishable by death. Of the 344, 165 had been convicted and 160 of these sentenced to the gallows. Seventy-nine had been hanged, 2 killed attempting to escape, 2 had died in jail awaiting execution, 2 had been pardoned, 46 commuted by the President to terms from ten years to life, and 2 granted new trials and finally discharged by acquittal or nolle prosequi. Twenty-seven had been given new trials on appeal to the Supreme Court, and of these 9 had been acquitted, 15 convicted on charges of smaller degree with imprisonment from one year to life, 2 nolle prosequi and 1 commuted. Of the 5 remaining of the 165, 2 had died in jail awaiting sentence, 1 had been declared insane and transferred to an asylum, 1 returned to the Indian courts for lack of jurisdiction, and 1 out on a bond of $5000 had failed to return and his bond had been forfeited.[2]

Parker had taken pardonable pride in eradicating lawlessness from his jurisdiction. He had taught the criminal class to fear the law and respect the rights and property of peaceful citizens, and had helped the Indian advance to a higher civilization.

The Indians loved and respected him. While in general they hated the white man, they looked upon Judge Parker as their friend and protector. Although he "regarded his court as having been established for the protection of the innocent, unoffending Indian . . . he held no maudlin sympathy for the criminal Indians. They received exactly the same treatment at his hands as other criminals. But he was fair, and the Indians came to know that he was fair, and acted accordingly." [3] They expressed their "liberality" towards full jurisdiction of the United States courts in the Indian Territory with the wish that "the good name of Judge I. C. Parker would not be villified. . . . Judge Parker is good enough for any law-abiding people, and too good for some visitors we have out here . . . a well known class of land grabbers, townsite boomers and vigilantes . . . clamoring, howling and sending up to Congress such great and terrible petitions for help and mercy . . . while striving daily to rob the Indians of what they have left of that which is justly theirs. . . ." [4]

They looked upon the enlargement of federal courts in the territory as an effort to suppress them just as the South had been oppressed under the carpetbagger regime. They feared that these courts, which permitted no Indian to serve on a jury, would be used by the white men within their country to imprison them unjustly and confiscate their lands, and boldly asserted that the courts were not needed for them but for the white people in the country, and that justice would be more readily attained before Judge Parker, who was appointed for life, than in courts where judges were appointed for four years.[5] "May God grant that these courts may never get full jurisdiction until we can elect our officers by ballot. . . ." [6]

These tribes had been forcibly driven from their homes in Florida, Mississippi, Arkansas, Georgia, North Carolina, and Tennessee, cruelly driven like cattle across country over the "Trail of Tears" to the land the government had set apart to be theirs "as long as grass grows and water runs," and the white man had followed. From the time of the earliest colony, disregard for the rights, property, and life of the Indian had been practiced, and the white man in the Indian country could see no more reason for respecting Indian claims here than elsewhere. "So long as there remained on the frontier one square mile of land occupied by a weak and helpless owner, there was a strong and unscrupulous frontiersman ready to seize it, and a weak and unscrupulous politician, who could be hired for a vote or for money, to back him." [7] Parker was not so foolish as to think that he could obstruct the tide of white civilization. He did not even want to. But he knew that before their removal the Indians had been compelled to yield to mass aggression, and he "was determined that in their new home they should not be cowed, intimidated, robbed and murdered by individual ruffians." [8]

He wanted a while to protect them, to teach them that there were good white men who respected their rights and would punish their oppressors. In a little while, said Parker, the Indian would become "convinced that his true interest was to keep pace with civilization," and then he could be absorbed as a willing, devoted citizen. Twenty-one years' experience with the Indians had taught him that they were a "religiously inclined, authority respecting" people, living off the "honest fruits of their labor" and "ambitious to advance as to the development of their lands and conveniences of their homes"; in their councils were men of "learning and ability," and their "rapid progress

from a state of wild barbarism to that of civilization and en-
lightment . . . in the past hundred years . . . had no parallel
in the history of the world." [9] Was it too much to ask the white
man to wait a little longer . . . ?

After years of agitation the Unassigned Lands had been
opened, and 50,000 whites poured in. Bit by bit other strips
of the Indian country or reservations—Iowa, Sac and Fox,
Shawnee and Pottawatomie, Cheyenne and Arapaho, Cherokee
Outlet, Kiowa-Comanche—had been added to this originally
settled land. The population was now 250,000, with 200,000
whites, an increase over the 60,000 population of 1875 of over
300 per cent. [10]

Said Parker:

> Beyond this tide of immigration, and hanging like the froth
> of the billows upon its very edge is a host of law-defying white
> men—many of whom are refugees from justice—who introduce
> among the Indians every form of demoralization and disease with
> which depraved humanity in its most degrading forms is ever af-
> flicted. . . . While the Indian, in many cases copies our vices,
> he has failed to imitate our virtues because, as a rule, none but
> the refuse of our population . . . have mingled among them.

Many in high authority censored the Indians for this lawless
condition and used it as leverage to deprive them of their tribal
governments. "United States marshals and Winchester rifles
will not solve the outlaw question in the Indian Territory,"
they claimed. "Civilization will. And civilization can only come
through a change in the conduct of the Indian governments
which are crude and uncivilized, and will remain so as long as
the influence of the white man is excluded." [11] "This farce of
treating them as independent nations with whom it is necessary
to have treaties . . . is a great mistake, so early made and so
long followed. The Indian needs law and government to become
civilized, and if he has no power to procure these for himself,
he must either receive them at our hands or remain a savage." [12]

Parker replied:

Perhaps things would have been different had the government given them the protection it promised in 1828. "Not only will we give you farms and homes in fee simple," it said, "but we will protect you in your rights. We will give you every protection against lawlessness; we will see that every refugee, every bandit, every murderer that comes into your country is put out." Not one of these pledges has ever been kept, except for the work that has been done by the United States courts having jurisdiction over this country.[13]

Upon Parker and his marshals had fallen this task, and it had been necessary for him to be stern on the bench and to bring all the strength of his nature to bear upon the enforcement of law.

The court was his idol; with its fall his mission was ended; and as the final day approached, it was reported that for the first time the judge, always the example of perfect strength and health, was too ill to hold court. "Dropsy. An affectation of the heart," the town gossips called it. His physician said it was the result of the enormous amount of work he had accomplished in twenty-one years.

As the days passed the court opened each morning and closed each evening as was customary. Unable to preside in person, Parker kept in touch on all important matters and issued orders from his sickbed. The grand jury met and conducted its investigations, but withheld its report pending the judge's return.

A vast number of cases accumulated. On August 24 Judge Caldwell, who by now had risen to the position of Judge of the Eighth Judicial District, issued an order for the Honorable Oliver P. Shiras of the Northern District of Iowa, at Dubuque, to proceed to Fort Smith and preside over the court two days, August 27 and 28. The grand jury returned 187 true bills and ignored 58. On the following day, 33 of the 58 indicted entered pleas of guilty, and Judge Shiras set the remaining cases for trial during the coming term.

As the day approached designated by Congress for ending the criminal jurisdiction of Parker's court over the Indian Territory, the St. Louis *Republic* sent its famous woman reporter, Ada Patterson, to Fort Smith to interview the judge. She had been told that he was stern and cruel, and she experienced an uncontrollable dread of the meeting. She secured the interview, however, and gave her opinion of him in the following words:

> He is the gentlest of men, this alleged sternest of judges. He is courtly of manner and kind of voice and face, the man who has passed the death sentence on more criminals than has any other judge in the land. The features that have in them the horror of the Medusa to desperadoes are benevolent to all other human-kind. . . .
>
> He spoke on his personal views of crime and law enforcement with such feeling that he sat up from his pillows . . . and his weak voice grew strong. . . . "I have been accused of leading juries. I tell you a jury should be led! They have the right to expect it; if they are guided they will render justice, which is the greatest pillar of society. . . . People have said that I am a cruel, heartless and bloodthirsty man, but no one has pointed a specific case of undue severity. . . . I have ever had the single aim of justice in view. No judge who is influenced by any other consideration is fit for the bench. 'Do equal and exact justice' has been my motto, and I have often said to the grand juries, 'Permit no innocent man to be punished; let no guilty man escape.' "

She described a visit to the gallows "so inseparable with Judge Parker's name," and quoted a prominent member of the Fort Smith bar:

> "Judge Parker is learned in the law; he is conscientious of the administration of it. He has a kind heart and a big soul. He is absolutely faithful to his home ties. All I could say of him for days would be summed up in this: He is a good man."

She concluded:

> He is a good man! What a tribute that is by one man of the world to another! What music to the ears of the woman who loves

him! I am glad to have the honor of knowing this alleged cruel judge. It is darkly, indeed, the press and people view him through the glass of distance. He is a twentieth century hero, worthy of the fame of the most just of Romans. More than all, as the old lawyer said to me, while a moisture he was not ashamed of made the office belongings and the face of the visitor look misty and far away, more than all, 'He is a good man.'

On September 1, 1896, Court Crier J. G. Hammersly shouted his "Oyez! Oyez! The Honorable District and Circuit Courts of the United States for the Western District of Arkansas, having criminal jurisdiction of the Indian Territory, are now adjourned, forever. God bless the United States and the honorable courts!"

It was still the fervent hope of everyone connected with the court that Judge Parker would soon recover, and during September and October the work was allowed to accumulate for his disposition. But on Monday, November 2, the day for the opening of the November term, Parker was still too ill to leave his home. Judge John E. Carland of the District of South Dakota was ordered to Fort Smith by Judge Walter Sanborn of the Eighth Judicial Circuit, and he held court during the remainder of Judge Parker's life. For Court Crier Hammersly, in sounding the death knell of the famous jurisdiction, had also sounded the death knell of its judge. On November 17 he was dead.[14]

It was hailed as a gala day by the prisoners in the old jail awaiting trial . . . whose cases had been listed on the docket before the arrival of the time for the finale of the court's jurisdiction over the Indian Territory . . . and hoped during the months Judge Parker was too ill to attend court that he might continue confined in his bed until their cases were disposed of, that with some other judge upon the bench they would stand better chances of light sentences or of possible acquittal. The announcement of Judge Parker's death was, therefore, the signal for a jubilee. Word was quickly passed from cell to cell. "The devil's shore got de ole cuss dis time!" sang out a negro criminal. "Is he dead? Whoopee!" yelled another, and, almost in a twinkling, those prisoners nearest the ones first learning of Judge Parker's demise took up the refrain, and for a brief period it looked as if pandemonium was about to break loose, but . . . Berry, the astute jailer, was on the ground and by prompt action and energetic measures he quelled the disturbance, and the offenders were brought to understand that open contempt for Judge Parker, even when dead, would not be tolerated in the Federal jail.[15]

Throughout the Indian country, and in Judge Parker's big brick home on North Thirteenth Street, where he had lived his last fifteen years, there was mourning. The funeral was at two o'clock the next day. It was the largest ever held in the little city. Notable personages came from everywhere. Public and private business was suspended. Flags stood at half mast.

The casket was placed in the huge front parlor of the big house and covered with flowers. Mrs. Parker and Charles sat at the head of the coffin. The room was filled with other members of the family and close friends, among them officers of the court and attorneys, Odd Fellows, members of the Grand Army of the Republic, and Knights of Honor. Father Smyth conducted the brief services, and the family and close friends filed out; then large groups awaiting outside passed through the room to gaze upon the figure in the casket.

The National Cemetery, where he was buried, overflowed with thousands who accompanied the body to its last resting place. The grave was filled and sprinkled with holy water, and there were expressions of condolence.

Many proclaimed him the greatest judge in all the history of the West. "American civilization has produced a multiplicity of character, but only one Parker. . . . In the administration of the law for the Indian country, he was a necessity. . . . It is impossible to even imagine what the record of the territory might have been had not the strong arm of Judge Parker extended over it. . . ." Even his archenemy, J. Warren Reed,

added a grandiose gesture: "Our beloved judge has fallen asleep.
. . . For him the sun of existence has dropped its golden light
of eternity. When we think of his bereft family—the wife, his
sons—we long to speak words of sympathy, as we stand with
them in the shadow of a great affliction." But the most touching
tribute was paid by Pleasant Porter, Principal Chief of the
Creeks, who, in behalf of all the tribes of the Nations, placed
upon his grave a simple garland of wild flowers.

APPENDICES

APPENDIX A

Chronology of Hangings

("Chronology of Hangings" lists by date the seventy-nine executions carried out under Judge Isaac C. Parker, the names of those executed, and a resume of their crimes, dates committed, victims, and other pertinent details available. The records show that from the date of the federal court's creation, March 3, 1851, until its removal to Fort Smith in 1871, nine persons were sentenced to death at Van Buren; one was commuted to life imprisonment at Little Rock and afterwards released by Confederate soldiers; one was commuted to life imprisonment and later pardoned; four were commuted to terms of imprisonment of shorter length; and one escaped and was sought nine years before he was recaptured, resentenced, and executed at Fort Smith. Also not included in this Chronology are seven murderers hanged on the Fort Smith gallows following the execution of John Childers and before the advent of Judge Parker.)

September 3, 1875—Daniel Evans
                        William Whittington
                        James Moore
                        Smoker Mankiller
                        Samuel Fooy
                        Edmund Campbell
The first famous sextet. See Chapter III.

April 21, 1876—Orpheus McGee
                        William Leach
                        Isham Seely
                        Gibson Ishtanubbee
                        Aaron Wilson

ORPHEUS McGEE murdered Robert Alexander on April 20, 1874. Alexander's body was found in the timber about sixty yards from his home, shot through the back and the neck. McGee was arrested in possession of his victim's rifle. In his confession he claimed that Alexander had murdered a friend, for which crime he had not been prosecuted; that he had lured him from his house into the timber by gobbling like a wild turkey, and as Alexander approached through the brush, he had slain him for revenge.

WILLIAM LEACH murdered John Wadkins in the Cherokee Nation, March 8, 1875. Wadkins was an itinerant minstrel who had hired Leach to show him the road to Fayetteville, Arkansas, where he was to play a performance the following evening. Wadkins never reached Fayetteville. A month later a hunter, attracted by buzzards, discovered the burned remains of a human body. The smaller bones had been destroyed and the larger bones charred. The skull had been punctured by a bullet. From the ashes deputy marshals recovered pieces of clothing of the description worn by Wadkins, a knife and screwdriver known to have been in his possession when last seen alive, and two sections of catgut from the strings of his violin. Leach was arrested when he attempted to sell Wadkins' boots.

"SQUIRREL" FUNNY, a white farmer, lived in the Chickasaw Nation near Stonewall. He was unmarried and kept a Negro woman in his employ as housekeeper and cook. ISHAM SEELY and GIBSON ISH-

TANUBBEE stopped at his home about midnight on May 10, 1873, and were given accommodations before continuing their journey the following day. Shortly before daylight the pair arose. Ishtanubbee secured an ax from the yard. He chopped Funny in the head and cut his throat as he slept. Seely beat the Negro woman to death with a pistol. The pair then looted Funny's house, stealing a pair of boots, pantaloons, and a dress. They burned the pantaloons, hid the dress in a hollow log in a field back of the house, and traded off the boots before they were arrested.

Fifty-six-year-old James Harris and his twelve-year-old son were crossing the Indian country en route to Texas with a wagon and three horses and the remnants of a stock of goods from a clothing store he had operated at Beatty, Kansas. On October 12, 1875, they camped near the Wichita Agency, twelve miles from Fort Sill. AARON WILSON, a burly Negro twenty years old, stopped at their camp, partook of their evening meal, and was invited to spend the night. At midnight he crept from his blankets and killed Harris with an ax. Harris' death cry awakened his son. The boy begged for his life; Wilson calmly withdrew a double-barreled shotgun from the wagon. The boy fled, but Wilson pursued him and killed him with a charge of buckshot 175 yards from camp. The Negro then took the horses, dressed himself in a new suit of clothes from the wagon, removed the scalps of his victims, and rode off with them wrapped in a handkerchief. Stopping at the Wichita Agency, he exhibited the scalps and told the Indians he had taken them from two white men whom he had killed, supposing from what he had heard of Indian character that these would serve as a recommendation. The chief, however, reported him to the agent. Wilson became frightened and rode away, but was apprehended the next day by a squad of United States troops that had been dispatched from Fort Sill.

For stolid indifference as to the result of his trial, Wilson surpassed anyone ever tried in the Fort Smith court. In passing his sentence, Judge Parker said:

> You have been tried and found guilty of that most revolting and terrible of crimes known to the land as murder. You have been aided and advised by able and experienced counsel, who have done all that could be done by any one under that most conclusive and convincing

set of facts which made up the damning evidence of your guilt. . . . I beg of you not to waste a moment of time, but to at once devote yourself to the preparation of your soul to meet its God. Let me entreat of you by every motive temporal and eternal to reflect upon your past life and present condition and the certain death that awaits you. There is but one who can pardon your offense; there is a Savior who can wash from your soul the stain of murder. I beg of you to fly to him for that mercy which you cannot expect from mortals. When you return to the solitude of your prison, let me entreat you by all that is dear to you in time, by all that is dreadful in the retributions of eternity, that you seriously reflect upon your past conduct and your present situation. Bring to your mind all the aggravated horrors of that dreadful night when you sent two souls without warning into the presence of their God, where you must shortly meet them as accusing spirits. Bring to your mind the mortal struggles and dying agonies of your murdered victims. Recall to your memory the face of that murdered boy. . . .

The sentence was then pronounced. When Wilson was being taken back to the jail, he said to his guards, "By God, that is nothing when you get used to it!"

The other four received their sentences with no manifestations of feelings. All claimed they were victims of vicious conspiracies.

William Leach bore the character of being one of the worst men in the Cherokee Nation. Isham Seely, when remanded to jail and just before his shackles were put on, jumped up, cracked his heels together, and whooped: "Chick-a-mah!"

September 8, 1876—Sinker Wilson
Samuel Peters
Osee Sanders
John Valley

SINKER WILSON murdered Datus Cowan in the Cherokee Nation in 1867. He was arrested and convicted of the crime while the federal court was still at Van Buren, but escaped and remained at large until recaptured by United States marshals. He was taken to Fort Smith and resentenced June 24, 1876.

On June 21, 1876, SAMUEL PETERS, twenty-eight, was convicted of attacking and stabbing to death Charity Hanson at her home on Hiwan prairie in the Choctaw Nation.

OSEE SANDERS, twenty-nine, killed Thomas S. Carlyle, a white man, in a robbery near Tahlequah. About dark on the evening of August 6, 1875, Carlyle and his Cherokee wife were sitting in the passageway that separated the two parts of their double house (a style of architecture frequently seen in the Indian Nations) when Sanders and a stranger rode to the gate and spoke to them. Carlyle recognized Sanders and invited him in, sending his young son to open the gate, which was fastened from the inside. As the men approached the house, Carlyle noticed that both carried pistols in their hands. The stranger seized Carlyle, and Sanders covered the wife with his pistol. The frightened woman grabbed her child and fled, escaping in some tall grass 150 yards away. She heard three shots and saw the two men ride off. When she returned to the house, her husband lay dead in a pool of blood. His pocketbook had been turned inside out, and a trunk containing $1200 in cash and a quantity of Cherokee warrants was missing. Sanders was arrested the next day. He refused to name his confederate, and the latter was never apprehended or identified.

JOHN VALLEY was convicted on May 20, 1876, for the robbery and murder of Eli Hackett in the Cherokee Nation.

December 20, 1878—James Diggs
John Postoak

JAMES DIGGS, a Negro, murdered a cattle-drover, J. C. Gould, in the northern part of the Indian territory near the Kansas line, August 4, 1873. His conviction was the result of the skill and determination of Deputy Marshal James Wilkinson, who took up the case after it had long been abandoned. Gould, with Diggs and another employee, Hiram Mann, a white man, had camped for the night in a deserted cabin. Early the next morning Diggs aroused the people living in the vicinity, reporting that during the night two men had ridden into camp, shot his companions, and chased him into the woods, where he concealed himself under a log until they departed. A posse went to the scene and found Gould and Mann lying side by side in a pool of blood. Gould was dead; Mann was still alive but unconscious, and a doctor was summoned. A search of the premises revealed no evidence of horses having been near, and there was no log where Diggs claimed he had taken cover. Diggs was questioned, and $27 in greenbacks were found concealed in the lining of his coat.

Further evidence showed that Gould had been recently paid this amount in corresponding bills. Diggs was taken to Fort Smith, but in that year Parker was not judge for the Western District of Arkansas. No witnesses appeared against the Negro, and he was released. Wilkinson heard about the case soon after being sworn in under Judge Parker. He located Diggs and placed him under arrest. Meanwhile, the witnesses had scattered to far points of the country. He located some of them in Kansas and Missouri, one in Ohio; and Hiram Mann, who had recovered from his wounds, had migrated to Michigan. All were brought to Fort Smith and testified at the trial, and the jury promptly entered a verdict of guilty.

JOHN POSTOAK was convicted on August 16, 1878, for the murder of John Ingley and his wife in the Creek Nation.

August 29, 1879—William Elliott
Dr. Henri Stewart

WILLIAM ELLIOTT, alias Colorado Bill, already wanted in four states for murder, killed his fifth victim, David J. "Cooke" Brown, in the Choctaw Nation, February 23, 1879. Following his conviction on May 28, 1879, the *Elevator,* listing the charges hanging over him elsewhere, commented: "He will hardly be wanted by any other state after they get through with him here."

DR. HENRI STEWART, a white man, thirty-five years old, had studied medicine at Harvard and Yale and served as a ship's physician in Cuba, South America, and California. In 1877 he ran away from his wife and four children in Ohio and came to the Indian country. He joined Sam Bass and for a time was a member of his notorious gang of Texas train-robbers. In May, 1879, he killed J. B. Jones in an attempted holdup of the Missouri-Kansas-Texas train at Caddo, Choctaw Nation. He was apprehended in Missouri.

September 9, 1881—George W. Padgett
William Brown
Patrick McGowan
Amos Manley
Abler Manley

GEORGE W. PADGETT, a Texas cattle thief, murdered W. H. Stephens on the North Fork of the Canadian River, July 26, 1881, when the latter questioned him about some cattle "bearing a certain Texas brand" that he was driving to the Kansas market.

WILLIAM BROWN killed Ralph Tate near White Bead Hill, Chickasaw Nation, August 19, 1880, through mistaken identity as he waited in ambush for a man named Moore, who had given him a severe beating in a quarrel over a horse race. Brown was captured in Texas.

PATRICK McGOWAN ambushed Sam Latta, July 13, 1880, following an argument over twenty acres of land leased him by Latta in the Chickasaw Nation.

AMOS and ABLER MANLEY's crime was one of the most brutal and unprovoked slayings perpetrated in the Indian country. Ellis McVay, a white farmer, lived with his wife and two children on the line between the Creek and Choctaw Nations. He had a hired man named William Burnett. On the bitter cold night of December 3, 1880, the Manley brothers stopped at his home after the family had retired and asked to come inside and warm. McVay accommodated them, stirring up the fire. They then told McVay they were on their way to take jobs in the Choctaw Nation and asked if they might spend the night. McVay consented. Burnett occupied a cot in one corner of the room, the only other bed available, so a pallet was provided for the visitors by the fire. McVay then returned to bed. About 3:00 A.M. the Manleys arose. Both drew pistols and approached McVay's bed. Amos fired once, striking him in the head; the younger brother, Abler, fired two bullets into his body. Burnett, awakened by the shots, leaped from his cot, and they began firing at him. As he went down he grappled one of them. The other seized a double-bitted ax from beside the fireplace and struck the hired man in the neck, cutting a severe gash. Another blow chopped off Burnett's right hand and sent it flying under the table. While Burnett lay on the floor, bleeding from his wounds, he was struck several additional blows about the back and legs and left for dead. The pair then turned on Mrs. McVay, but a dog started barking, and they went outside, thinking someone was approaching the house. Mrs. McVay grabbed her children, slipped through the back door, and fled half a mile through the frozen night, in nightgown and barefoot, to a neighbor's home.

A doctor was summoned for Burnett, and a posse took the trail of the Manleys. They were apprehended the next day, and Burnett lived to appear in court. The stump of his right arm, the severed hand, and the bloody ax, sent them to the gallows.

June 30, 1882—Edward Fulsom

EDWARD FULSOM had served one term in the penitentiary, and in February, 1881, fled to the Indian country to avoid prosecution on a charge of horse stealing. He beat William Massingill to death with a pistol in a saloon brawl on the Arkansas–Indian Territory line, after the latter had been wounded and lay on the floor, unarmed and helpless. Fulsom was such a slightly built man that his fall on the gallows did not break his neck. His pulse beat for an hour and three minutes before jail physicians pronounced him dead.

April 13, 1883—Robert Massey

ROBERT MASSEY died on the gallows for slaying his business associate, Edmond Clark, in camp on the South Canadian River, two hundred miles west of Fort Smith, the night of December 1, 1881. In the summer of this year the two men had driven a herd of cattle from Dodge City, Kansas, to the Dakota Territory. They had completed the sale and were en route to their homes in Texas when Massey shot Clark in the back of the head as he sat at the fire. He dumped the body in a hole near the camp site and burned his clothing and saddle. He then took the proceeds of the cattle sale, and Clark's horse and six-shooter, and continued to his home in Grayson County, where he was arrested the following April, still in possession of the weapon. He had traded the horse to his brother-in-law.

June 29, 1883—William Finch
Martin Joseph
Tualisto

WILLIAM FINCH, a mulatto, thirty years old, shot and killed two military guards who were returning him to Fort Sill from Decatur, Texas, where he had fled after stealing a horse from an Indian named

Quinette. He was rearrested in Texas by deputy marshals and taken to Fort Smith.

MARTIN JOSEPH. See Chapter IV of text.

TUALISTO, a Creek Indian, needed money to attend a green-corn dance. On July 6, 1881, he ambushed and robbed Emanuel Cochran, a white man traveling through the Choctaw Nation. Deputy Marshal Beck was assigned to the case and gathered enough evidence to obtain a warrant for the renegade's arrest. Meanwhile, Tualisto had been convicted of larceny in the tribal court and sentenced to the whipping post. Beck was on hand for the event. The moment Tualisto had received his punishment, he took him into custody. On the scaffold, the Indian confessed that he had murdered Cochran and bragged that he had killed others. He called the crowd's attention to four buttons sewed on the crown of his hat, then stated that each button represented a man he had slain.

July 11, 1884—Thomas Thompson
John Davis
Jack Woman Killer

THOMAS THOMPSON, a whisky smuggler, was hanged for killing his partner, James O'Holeran, in the Chickasaw Nation, September 20, 1883, and tossing his body into a well.

On June 27, 1883, JOHN DAVIS murdered and robbed William Bullock, who had driven a herd of cattle through the Indian country to Colorado, and buried his body beside the trail.

Nathaniel Hyatt, a white man, farmed in the Cherokee Nation. On May 7, 1883, he left his home on a trip into Arkansas. Two days later his body was found at the roadside pierced by bullets, with the features mutilated beyond recognition. He had been robbed. JACK WOMAN KILLER was arrested and convicted for this crime.

April 17, 1885—William Phillips

WILLIAM PHILLIPS died on the gallows for murdering his father-in-law as the latter slept in bed at his home in the Cherokee Nation in the summer of 1884.

June 26, 1885—James Arcene
William Parchmeal

William Feigel, a Swede, was murdered and robbed near Fort Gibson, November 25, 1872. The perpetrators of this crime might have gone unpunished but for the diligent efforts of Deputy Marshal Andrews, who rode that part of the Indian country. After thirteen years, he was able to piece together enough facts to secure warrants for JAMES ARCENE and WILLIAM PARCHMEAL. The pair confessed in their cells at Fort Smith and were convicted in the February term of court, 1885.

April 23, 1886—James Wasson
Joseph Jackson

JAMES WASSON was a double murderer. He had aided in the slaying of Henry Martin in 1872, but was not captured until he killed Almarine Watkins in 1884 and a large reward was offered for his capture.

JOSEPH JACKSON, a Negro, was hanged for the brutal murder of his wife, Mary Jackson, at Oak Lodge, Choctaw Nation, March 9, 1885.

July 23, 1886—Calvin James
Lincoln Sprole

CALVIN JAMES, a Negro, was leader of a gang of whisky runners. On August 1, 1885, he, Tony Love, Henry Robey, and Albert Kemp went to Texas and each purchased four gallons of whisky. On their return trip, while riding through a secluded section of the Chickasaw Nation, James shot Love in the head to get the whisky he carried. Robey and Kemp were riding some distance ahead. James carried Love's body two hundred yards off the road and concealed it in the brush, then unsaddled his victim's horse and turned it loose. He then told Kemp and Robey he would kill them if they ever mentioned the incident. However, when Love turned up missing, it was ascertained he was last seen with these men, and all three were arrested. Kemp and Robey confessed the whole affair and appeared against James as government witnesses.

LINCOLN SPROLE, a young white man, murdered elderly Ben Clark and his eighteen-year-old son Alex, May 30, 1885, in Paul's Valley, Chickasaw Nation. Sprole and his victims were renters on the Sam Paul farm, and prior to the double slaying, he and Clark had fallen out over the watering of stock at a well on the premises. On the date of the killing, Clark and his son went to White Bead Hill to do some trading, and on their return trip Sprole, concealing himself in a thicket at the side of the road, fired upon them. Clark fell from the wagon seat, shot in the chest. The horses began to run and the boy leaped from the wagon. Another shot from Sprole's Winchester broke his leg at the knee, and as he lay at the roadside, begging for his life, Sprole advanced, raised his weapon again to his face, and shot the helpless, unarmed youth through the right breast and collar bone. Clark died within six hours; his son lived only seventeen days. Sprole left the country, but Deputy Marshal John Williams tracked him down and hauled him to Fort Smith. The *Elevator* of August 9, 1886, speaking of the evidence produced at the trial, commented: "It is only to be regretted that he has not two necks to break instead of one."

August 6, 1886—Kit Ross

KIT ROSS was part Cherokee, twenty-five years old. In 1883, while on a drunken spree, he rode his horse into the home of Jonathan Davis while the latter's wife was seriously ill, and was roughly ejected. He and Davis met frequently afterwards and seemed apparently on good terms, but "revenge lurked in the heart of the treacherous Ross." On December 20, 1885, while Davis was in a store at Choteau, Ross entered in an intoxicated condition. As Davis was leaving, he met Ross at the door and remarked about the weather: "Kit, I believe we will have some snow." Ross replied: "Yes, I believe we will," and as Davis passed outside, stepped behind him and fired two shots into his back. As Ross was being led from the courtroom after the jury had pronounced him guilty, he remarked: "Well, they done it to me."

January 14, 1887—James Lamb
Albert O'Dell

John T. Echols
John Stephens

In the autumn of 1885, Edward Pollard and George Brassfield, who farmed a lease near Lebanon, Chickasaw Nation, hired two young men, JAMES LAMB and ALBERT O'DELL, to help in the harvest. Within a short while Pollard's wife was indulging in "passionate relationships" with Lamb, and Mrs. Brassfield had taken a fancy to O'Dell. Their open conduct became neighborhood scandal. Brassfield finally left his wife, and O'Dell took over. Pollard wasn't so easily dissuaded. He continued "in possession of his chattels, if not his wife" until the night of December 26, when Lamb and O'Dell ambushed him as he returned from a trip to Lebanon and concealed his body on the trail. A few days later a preacher was summoned to the Pollard home to marry Lamb and Mrs. Pollard, who explained that her husband had deserted her and "would not be back." The preacher refused to perform such a ceremony, and the following day the quartet left the community. Pollard's body was found two months later, and the case assigned to Deputy Marshal Mershon. He assembled the facts stated above, arrested the two men and the women at Buck Horn Creek, fifty miles away, and lodged them in jail at Fort Smith. Mrs. Pollard made bond and went to the home of relatives in Missouri, where she gave birth to a child of which Lamb was the father. Mrs. Brassfield gave birth to twins—the "fruits of her debauchery with O'Dell"—which died a few hours after they were born. Lamb and O'Dell, who had stuck together through crime and courtship, now employed separate attorneys. At their trial they prosecuted one another, while the district attorney, using the women as witnesses, prosecuted both.

JOHN T. ECHOLS, a white man, wounded John Pattenridge, February 16, 1886, at White Bead Hill, Chickasaw Nation, in a quarrel over a cattle deal in which Echols felt that he had been cheated; and while his unarmed victim lay on the ground, begging him piteously not to shoot again, fired five more bullets into his body. He then stole Pattenridge's horse and rode away.

On May 28, 1886, JOHN STEPHENS, a mulatto, borrowed a horse from an Indian on the Delaware reservation and rode in the night to the home of Mrs. Annie Kerr, who had appeared as a witness against him in a larceny case. He found Mrs. Kerr and her sixteen-year-old son asleep on a pallet near the door and chopped them to death with an ax. He then rode to the home of Dr. Pyle, also a witness against him, struck Pyle and his wife in the head with an ax, and brutally beat their small child. Dr. Pyle died six days later, but his wife survived to appear in Judge Parker's court and exhibit the ghastly wounds in the back of her head from which fourteen pieces of bone had been removed.

April 8, 1887—Patrick McCarty

PATRICK McCARTY originally had been scheduled to hang on January 14, 1887, with the quartet of Lamb, O'Dell, Echols, and Stephens, but was granted a reprieve until his case could be examined by the President. He was convicted for slaying Thomas Mahoney and his brother in the Cherokee Nation. The Mahoneys farmed near Fort Scott, Kansas. During the slack winter months they had come to the Indian Territory to work with a grading crew on the Atlantic and Pacific railroad, which was under construction, and brought with them two good teams and wagons loaded with plows, shovels, scrapers, and camping equipment. They cleared $200 during the winter, and in the spring, about crop-planting time, began their return trip to Fort Scott, accompanied by McCarty with whom they had made an acquaintance. Several weeks later their bodies were found in a coal bank between Vinita and Coffeyville, and their teams, wagons, and other equipment in possession of a man in Fayetteville, Arkansas, who testified he purchased them from McCarty. McCarty was arrested at Springfield, Missouri, having a high time on the profits and still in possession of a watch taken from Thomas Mahoney. In his confession he related how, on the night of February 17, 1886, after a hard day's journey, the brothers had made camp seven miles south of Coffeyville. He had insisted that they get some rest and allow him to perform the camp chores. When the brothers were asleep he had drawn his revolver and crept to the wagon. He shot one between the eyes; the blood gushing out soaked the feather mattress on which they slept. His second bullet missed, and as the other brother aroused, he had brained him with an ax. He had then buried the bodies and burned the bed and all their clothing to prevent identification. When his attorneys appealed to the President, Judge Parker submitted a lengthy, vigorous statement of facts taken from the testimony at the trial, and the President refused to intercede.

October 7, 1887—Seaborn Kalijah
Silas Hampton

SEABORN KALIJAH was arrested January 17, 1887, by Deputy Marshal Phillips for selling whisky in the Creek Nation, but before he could transfer the prisoner to Fort Smith, the deputy was summoned to Eufaula on another investigation. He left Kalijah in camp in custody of three possemen, Mark Kuykendall, Henry Smith, and William Kelly. When he returned the next morning, he found the three possemen dead. The prisoner had escaped. Smith and Kuykendall had been chopped to death with an ax while they slept and their bodies dragged into the fire and burned from the waists down. Kelly's body lay a dozen yards away, shot and horribly mutilated. Phillips followed Kalijah's trail to the home of relatives and re-arrested him.

SILAS HAMPTON, an eighteen-year-old fullblood Cherokee, killed Abner N. Lloyd, a white farmer living near Tishomingo, December 9, 1886, and robbed his body of $7.50 and a pocketknife. The money he invested in a bright-colored silk handkerchief and some trinkets, which led to his arrest. When told he had murdered a white man, Hampton requested of the marshals: "Don't take me to Fort Smith; kill me right now!"

April 27, 1888—George Moss
Owen Hill
Jackson Crow

On November 26, 1886, GEORGE MOSS, Sandy Smith, Factor Jones, and Dick Butler conspired to steal beef on the range. They entered into an agreement that if any person caught them in the act they would murder whoever it might be. Accordingly they proceeded to the Red River bottoms in the Choctaw Nation and shot a steer belonging to a prominent farmer, George Taff. Taff appeared on the scene shortly after the shot was fired, and Moss promptly killed him. During the shooting, Moss's horse got away and Moss was unable to catch him. Discovery of his horse and the dead body of Taff led to the arrest of all four conspirators. Moss and Smith were taken to Fort Smith by deputy marshals, but Jones and Butler, being citizens of the Choctaw Nation, were released, the Fort Smith court having no jurisdiction. The infuriated citizens, knowing the murderers would probably never be punished in the Choctaw courts, took them to the spot where Taff was murdered, and after hearing their confessions, completely riddled them with bullets, leaving their bodies where they fell on the prairie. Sandy Smith died in jail before the case came to trial, leaving Moss alone to pay the penalty for their crime by due course of law.

OWEN HILL and his wife resided near Gibson Station, Cherokee Nation. They could not get along together, so his wife went to live with her mother. On the night of June 25, 1887, Hill appeared at the home of his mother-in-law with a shotgun. After beating her over the head with the weapon until he supposed her dead, he threw the gun aside and sprang at his wife with a razor. She tried to escape, but he caught her in the yard and cut her throat, nearly severing the head from the body. He was arrested in Kansas City after writing to a friend inquiring if his wife had died of her wounds.

JACKSON CROW assassinated Charles Wilson, a prominent merchant in the Choctaw Nation, August 7, 1884, and while his victim lay dead on the trail near Kully Chaha, bashed his head with the stock of his Winchester. He remained at large until December, 1885, when Deputy Marshal Charles Barnhill and posse trailed him to a house in the Poteau Mountains. Crow refused to surrender until the posse set fire to the building. When taken into custody, he still had Wilson's pistol in his possession.

July 6, 1888—Gus Bogles

GUS BOGLES hanged for the slaying of J. D. Morgan at Blue Tank, a railroad station near McAlester. Morgan's body was discovered the morning of June 28, 1887, near the section house, stripped of coat, hat, shoes, and trousers. Bogles was identified as a man put off the train by the conductor for not having a ticket at the time and place of the murder. When arrested at Denison, Texas, Bogles confessed he had slain Morgan by buckling a strap around his neck and beating him over the head with a pistol. In his testimony at the trial he denied all knowledge of the murder, saying the officers had frightened him into making the confession; that he knew nothing of the crime, had never been in the vicinity, and had never seen Morgan in his life. In pronouncing his sentence, Judge Parker said:

> "In your efforts to escape the consequences [of murder], you have added to your crime that of perjury. This, of course, is not to be wondered at. . . . It is expecting too much of wicked and depraved human nature for us to look for truth from one who has stained his hands with innocent human blood. . . . Sometimes such persons have succeeded, by their falsehoods, in deceiving juries and in cheating justice. You have not succeeded, and you stand before the bar of this court to have announced to you the sentence which the law attaches shall follow. . . ."

Bogles was described as one of the most difficult prisoners ever in the Fort Smith jail. Twice he tried to escape, once by seizing the pistol of a guard who walked too close to his cell, and again by inducing a trusty to smuggle him out in an empty barrel that had been brought into the jail filled with sawdust for filling the spittoons. For several nights preceding his execution, after being locked in his cell, he would whoop and yell like a lunatic for hours, for no other purpose than to annoy the other inmates.

January 25, 1889—Richard Smith

RICHARD SMITH killed Thomas Pringle on March 28, 1888, as the latter walked in the woods with his sweetheart near Wheelock, Choctaw Nation. The ground was soft, and the tracks showed the murderer wore a pair of boots with soles driven full of large round-headed tacks, twenty-one tacks in the right foot and fourteen in the other. Smith tried to hide his trail by wading through a lake, and when arrested the next day was wearing boots corresponding with the tracks except that the heels were missing and the tacks had been removed. But a boy on the premises told deputy marshals that Smith had come home with his gun on the day of the slaying, wet to the waist and complaining that his boots hurt his feet; that afterwards he had knocked off the heels and pulled the tacks from the soles. The heels were found where he had thrown them in the bushes, the tacks were never located, but the holes were still in the shoe soles, plainly visible.

April 19, 1889—James Mills
Malachi Allen

On December 15, 1887, JAMES MILLS and Tom Robin, Negroes, murdered John Windham in the Seminole Nation, shooting him in the back. After he had fallen, they shot him twice in the mouth and body. A group of irate citizens attempted to arrest the killers. In the fight, Robin was wounded and captured and Mills escaped. Robin was taken to Fort Smith, where he died of his wounds. Mills was arrested the following January. They refused to give the motive for their crime.

MALACHI ALLEN hanged for the murder of Shadrach Peters and Cy Love in the Chickasaw Nation, July 15, 1888, in a quarrel over a saddle. In a vicious gun fight with Deputy Marshal McAlester and posse, he was wounded and captured. His gun arm was so badly shattered it had to be amputated before he was taken to Fort Smith.

August 30, 1889—William Walker
Jack Spaniard

WILLIAM WALKER killed Calvin Church at Durant, Choctaw Nation, December 12, 1888, for ten dollars and two quarts of whisky.

JACK SPANIARD'S proper name was Sevier, the name of his grandfather on his father's side. His father and mother died when he was a child, and while living on Spaniard Creek between Muskogee and Webbers Falls, he was given the name of Spaniard. He was a halfblood Cherokee, twenty-eight years old, of fine physique and handsome appearance. He was convicted April 12, 1889, for the murder of Deputy Marshal William Erwin (see Chapter IV). The evidence against him was purely circumstantial but so conclusive that the jury was out only one hour. At the time of his hanging, Fort Smith newspapers described him as "a man of desperate and reckless character, who held human life at a very low estimate."

January 16, 1890—Harris Austin
John Billee
Thomas Willis
Jefferson Jones
Sam Goin
Jimmon Burris

HARRIS AUSTIN shot Thomas Elliott on May 25, 1883, at Tishomingo, Chickasaw Nation, because the latter stole his whisky. As his victim lay wounded, Austin fired a second shot into his body, then walked close to the prostrate form and fired a third time, holding the muzzle of his pistol so close to his forehead that the powder burned his face. Austin fled to the hills, and despite the efforts of United States marshals remained at large until he was shot and captured in a gun battle with Deputy Marshal Carr and posse in April, 1889.

JOHN BILLEE and THOMAS WILLIS hanged for the robbery and slaying of W. P. Williams, April 12, 1888, and burying his body in a shallow ravine in the Kiamichi Mountains.

On March 12, 1889, JEFFERSON JONES murdered sixty-year-old Henry Wilson, who was traveling through the Winding Stair Mountains, Choctaw Nation, robbed the body of $12, and tossed it into a creek, where it was discovered a week later, badly decomposed.

SAM GOIN and JIMMON BURRIS killed Houston Joyce of Franklin, Texas, another traveler in the Indian Territory, as Joyce left their home November 17, 1888, after inadvertently displaying a large roll of money while paying for a meal.

January 30, 1890—George Tobler

GEORGE TOBLER quarreled with Irvin Richmond over a woman, with whom both were infatuated, at a dance in Cache Bottom, Choctaw Nation, the night of April 30, 1889. Later in the evening, when "the revelry was at its height," Tobler placed the muzzle of his pistol to a crack in the wall, and as Richmond danced past less than two feet away fired a bullet into his body.

July 9, 1890—John Stansberry

JOHN STANSBERRY went to the gallows for murdering his wife and infant child in 1889 to be free of his marital ties in order to marry a Creek squaw with whom he had become infatuated.

June 30, 1891—Bood Crumpton

BOOD CRUMPTON was a beardless youth of nineteen. In a drunken and evil mood he shot his companion, Sam Morgan, in the back and dumped his body in a hole near the Pawnee Indian Agency. His was the only execution ordered by Judge Parker for the year 1891, but it had a potent influence on those who witnessed it. As Crumpton stood on the scaffold before the crowd, he said: "To all you who are present, especially you young men—the next time you are about to take a drink of whisky, look closely into the bottom of the glass and see if you cannot observe in there a hangman's noose. There is where I first saw the one which now breaks my neck."

April 27, 1892—Shepard Busby See Chapter IV of text.

June 28, 1892—John Thornton

JOHN THORNTON had committed one of the most revolting crimes recorded on the docket of the Fort Smith court. He was a profligate, a drunkard. Repeatedly he had violated his own daughter, and after she married to escape his horrible abuse, he went to her house in the absence of her husband and emptied a pistol into her head and body. Thornton was a heavily built man. His stay in jail added to his weight. The muscles of his neck were small and flabby and in no condition for the task placed upon them. When he dropped at the end of the rope, blood spurted and the flesh ripped apart. The crowd standing inside the enclosure shuddered with horror as his body dangled before them, swaying slightly, only the tendons of the neck preventing it falling to the ground.

September 24, 1894—Johnny Pointer

JOHNNY POINTER was born at Eureka Springs, Arkansas. His parents were religious, well-to-do, and highly respected people, but apparently had never heard of the old adage, "Spare the rod and spoil the child." What Johnny wanted he got, and if they expressed any opposition, Johnny still had his way. At the age of twelve he set fire to a neighbor boy. He was reprimanded. A year later he stabbed a playmate with a knife and was fined $50 in a Carroll County court. His father paid the fine, and little Johnny boasted: "My old man will never let me go to jail."

Within a month he picked a quarrel with another boy and beat him senseless with a rock. True to little Johnny's prediction, father made a settlement with the parents of the injured child, and Johnny was neither arrested nor punished. By the time he was seventeen, he was so completely out of hand at home that his parents decided what was needed was a change of scene. They sent him to live with relatives in Missouri.

Johnny had grown up to be a bully and a braggart. There were no younger boys here to mistreat. Things were too peaceful, so he decided to go home. He stole a fine riding mare from a man near Springfield and rode back to Eureka Springs. He told his father he had purchased a small pony at an auction and in turn traded it to another man for the mare, agreeing to give him $13 to boot; that this man was in Eureka Springs at the time, and if his father would give him the money he could close the deal.

Foolish father patted his son on the shoulder, told him what a shrewd trader he was, and handed over the amount requested. There being no deal to close, Johnny spent papa's money for a good time about town, and within a few days the owner of the mare and a Missouri sheriff called at the Pointer home with a warrant for Johnny's arrest. Still believing his son's story, certain that the man to whom Johnny had traded his pony was the real thief, father hired a lawyer, put up the price of the mare, and did everything possible to reach a compromise with the man from Missouri.

The owner of the animal could not be swayed, and the sheriff sent to Missouri for requisition papers. Meanwhile father got Johnny

released on bail of $1000, furnished him expense money to leave
the country, and put him on a train for Texas.

No more was heard of the youth until he turned up in jail at
Decatur, due to another misunderstanding over a horse. He wrote
home for money to make his bond, the request was expedited by his
father, and soon Johnny was on his way back to Eureka Springs,
traveling with two men named Ed Vandever and William Bolding.

Vandever and Bolding were also from Arkansas. They had driven
to Texas on a trading expedition, and with a large roll of money and
a good team and wagon to show for their trip, they left Decatur for
their homes. On the night of December 25, 1891, they camped near
the farm of W. G. Baird at Wilburton, Choctaw Nation, where they
purchased hay for their team. Pointer was still with them. The following morning their bodies were found in a creek near the camp,
and Pointer, with the team and wagon and money, was missing. His
description was furnished deputy marshals, who arrested him at Mc-
Alester attempting to dispose of the outfit.

Throughout his trial, conviction, and sentence, Johnny was cocky
and calm and made light of his weeping parents. He even asked
Judge Parker for permission to set the hour of his departure from
earth. Judge Parker consented, and Johnny set half past three in the
afternoon. When the time approached, he weakened. He asked for a
fifteen-minute delay, which was granted. At 3:45 he was brought
from the jail into the gallows enclosure. He began to tremble. On
the scaffold he turned white. His knees buckled so that he was
scarcely able to stand. He died as he had lived—a coward.

November 2, 1894—Lewis Holder

LEWIS HOLDER murdered and robbed his partner, George Bickford,
in the San Bois Mountains, Choctaw Nation, on December 28, 1891,
and dumped his shotgun-riddled body into a gorge. Two exciting
incidents occurred in connection with this case. The first was at the
conclusion of the trial. When Judge Parker pronounced that he "be
hanged by your neck until dead," his words died away and the
courtroom became as quiet as a tomb. Apparently it was more than
the condemned man could bear. His face paled and a tremor shook

his whole body. Suddenly he let out a scream that was heard in the street beyond the walls below, and fell forward on the courtroom floor. Everyone believed the man had cheated the gallows. The room was filled with confusion, and it was with great difficulty that Judge Parker was able to restore order. When the marshals bent over Holder, he was still breathing. They carried him outside into the air, and he recovered. From that moment he was a broken man. Day after day he begged the guards passing his cell not to hang him. When this gained him no consideration, he declared that if he was executed he would return to the spirit and haunt them and Judge Parker and everyone connected with the court. Even this threat failed to stay the hand of justice, and he went to his death as scheduled. On a night in December, a month later, Jailer George Lawson and a half-dozen fellow-officers were sitting in the jail office when an unearthly sound floated from the inky darkness that enveloped the gallows startled them to silence. The tones were so weird and expressive of poignant grief that it was several minutes before the officers ventured into the jail yard. The great death trap stood isolated from the other buildings three hundred feet away. The moaning continued. "No doubt about it," gasped one of the deputies, "it's Lewis Holder's ghost!" Lawson's call for volunteers to investigate met no response, so he went alone. On the floor of the scaffold he found a man in a highly intoxicated condition, and this was the source of the uncanny sounds.

March 17, 1896—Crawford Goldsby
alias *Cherokee Bill*

See Chapter VIII.

April 30, 1896—Webber Isaacs
George Pearce
John Pearce

WEBBER ISAACS ambushed and robbed a peddler, Mike Cushing, smashed his head to a jelly, saturated his clothing with coal oil, and set him on fire. Cushing's identity was established from a tuft of gray whiskers under the chin that had not been consumed by the flames and from bills and letters bearing the name of his concern in

Leavenworth, Kansas, which had been lost from his clothing as his body was dragged into the woods.

The PEARCE brothers murdered William Vandever, their traveling companion, and robbed him of his horses, mules, and a wagon. The crime occurred on November 21, 1894, in the Cherokee Nation.

July 1, 1896—Rufus Buck
Lucky Davis
Lewis Davis
Sam Sampson
Maoma July

Members of the infamous Buck gang, hanged as a quintet for the rape of Rosetta Hassan in the Creek Nation. See Chapter X.

July 30, 1896—George Wilson
(James Casharego)

Last man executed on the Fort Smith gallows. See Chapter XII.

APPENDIX B

Commutations and Pardons

Name	Crime	Date Convicted	Date to be Executed	Final Disposition
George LeFlore	Murder	Dec. 23, 1871	None	Died in jail, Oct. 27, 1872, awaiting sentence.
John Broderick	Murder	Dec. 4, 1872	April 3, 1874	Commuted to five years imprisonment.
Robert T. Barber	Murder	July 2, 1873		Convicted of manslaughter, sentenced to three years in penitentiary at Little Rock.
Frank Butler	Murder	May 27, 1875	Sept. 3, 1875	Killed attempting to escape.
Oscar Snow	Murder	June 7, 1875	Sept. 3, 1875	Commuted to life at Joliet, Illinois. Pardoned.
Black Crow	Murder	Dec. 13, 1876	April 27, 1877	Commuted to life at Moundsville, West Virginia.
Irwing Perkins	Murder	Dec. 16, 1876	April 27, 1877	Commuted to life at Moundsville, West Virginia.
Charles Thomas	Murder	Dec. 27, 1876	April 27, 1877	Commuted to life at Moundsville, West Virginia. Served six years, pardoned.

Name	Crime	Date Convicted	Date to be Executed	Final Disposition
William J. Meadows	Murder	Sept. 18, 1877	Jan. 18, 1878	Commuted to life at Detroit, Michigan.
Joshua Wade	Rape	Sept. 29, 1877	Jan. 18, 1878	Commuted to life at Moundsville, West Virginia.
Thomas Robinson	Murder	Sept. 29, 1877	Jan. 18, 1878	Commuted to life at Detroit, Michigan.
Carolina Grayson	Murder	Dec. 13, 1877	June 21, 1878	Commuted to life at Detroit, Michigan.
Peter Grayson	Murder	Dec. 13, 1877	June 21, 1878	Commuted to life at Detroit, Michigan.
Man Lewis	Murder	Dec. 13, 1877	June 21, 1878	Commuted to life at Detroit, Michigan.
Robert Love	Murder	Dec. 13, 1877	June 21, 1878	Commuted to life at Detroit, Michigan.
Uriah M. Cooper	Murder	Dec. 12, 1879	June 18, 1880	Commuted to life at Detroit, Michigan.
Jackson Marshal	Murder	Dec. 19, 1879	June 18, 1880	Died in jail before execution date.
James N. Heaslet	Murder	Feb. 18, 1880	June 18, 1880	Commuted to life at Detroit, Michigan.
Lum Smith	Murder	Sept. 23, 1880	Dec. 17, 1880	Commuted to life at Detroit, Michigan.

Name	Crime	Date	Date	Disposition
Tulwaharjo	Murder	June 24, 1881	Sept. 9, 1881	Granted new trial; discharged.
Sahquahnee	Murder	Aug. 9, 1881	Oct. 14, 1881	Commuted to life at Detroit, Michigan.
John Jacobs	Murder	Nov. 17, 1882	April 13, 1883	Commuted.
Mat Music	Rape	July 14, 1883	July 11, 1884	Pardoned.
Barua Maha	Murder	March 29, 1883	July 11, 1884	Granted new trial; discharged.
Fanny Echols	Murder	Dec. 18, 1883	July 11, 1884	Commuted to life at Detroit, Michigan.
Dan Jones	Murder	Dec. 22, 1883	July 11, 1884	Commuted.
William Dickson	Murder	Sept. 8, 1884	April 17, 1885	Commuted to life at Detroit, Michigan.
Fred M. Ray	Murder	Nov. 24, 1884	April 17, 1885	Commuted to life at Detroit, Michigan.
William Meadows	Murder	Nov. 24, 1884	April 17, 1885	Commuted to life at Detroit, Michigan.
Mason Holcomb	Murder	Dec. 20, 1884	April 17, 1885	Commuted to life at Detroit, Michigan.
Robert Wolfe	Murder	July 25, 1885	April 23, 1886	Commuted.
Robinson Kemp	Murder	Aug. 12, 1885	April 23, 1886	Commuted to life at Detroit, Michigan.
William Hamilton	Murder	Aug. 14, 1885	None	Died in jail while awaiting sentence.
Meredith Crow	Murder	Oct. 2, 1885	April 23, 1886	Commuted to life at Detroit, Michigan. Served nine years, pardoned.

Name	Crime	Date Convicted	Date to be Executed	Final Disposition
Luce Hammond	Murder	Dec. 4, 1885	April 23, 1886	Commuted to life at Detroit, Michigan.
Hewahnackee	Murder	Dec. 4, 1885	April 23, 1886	Commuted to life at Detroit, Michigan.
Monroe Wiley	Murder	Dec. 4, 1885	April 23, 1886	Commuted to life at Detroit, Michigan.
Blue Duck	Murder	Jan. 30, 1886	July 23, 1886	Commuted to life at Menard, Illinois. Pardoned.
John Parrott	Murder	March 11, 1886	Jan. 14, 1887	Commuted to five years at Menard, Illinois.
Jeff Hilderbrand	Murder	Aug. 2, 1887	April 27, 1888	Died in jail while awaiting execution.
Richard Sutherland	Murder	Sept. 14, 1887	April 27, 1888	Commuted to twenty-one years at Little Rock, Arkansas.
Bill Alexander	Rape	Sept. 16, 1887	April 27, 1888	Commuted to life at Little Rock, Arkansas.
Emanuel Patterson	Murder	Oct. 20, 1887	April 27, 1888	Commuted to life.
Lewis Burrows	Murder	Sept. 15, 1888	Jan. 25, 1889	Commuted to ten years at Little Rock, Arkansas.
Steve Bussel	Murder	Sept. 27, 1888	April 19, 1889	Commuted to life at Little Rock, Arkansas.

Name	Crime			Disposition
William G. Sorder	Murder	Oct. 12, 1888	Jan. 25, 1889	Commuted to life at Little Rock, Arkansas.
George Brashears	Murder	Nov. 2, 1888	April 19, 1889	Commuted to life at Columbus, Ohio.
William Woods	Murder	Nov. 20, 1888	April 19, 1889	Pardoned.
Henry Miller	Murder	Nov. 20, 1888	April 19, 1889	Commuted to life at Columbus, Ohio.
Frank Capel	Murder	March 1, 1889	April 19, 1889	Commuted to life at Columbus, Ohio.
Elsie James	Murder	March 22, 1889	July 17, 1889	Commuted to life at Columbus, Ohio.
Jo Martin	Murder	April 6, 1889	July 17, 1889	Commuted to life at Columbus, Ohio.
Madison James	Murder	Sept. 4, 1889	Jan. 16, 1890	Commuted to fifteen years at Detroit, Michigan.
Charles Bullard	Murder	Oct. 16, 1889	Jan. 16, 1890	Commuted to life at Columbus, Ohio. Served one year; pardoned.

APPENDIX C

Reversals and Acquittals

Name	Crime	Date Convicted	Date to be Executed	Final Disposition
William Alexander	Murder	Jan. 21, 1890	Oct. 1, 1890	Reversed; two mistrials. Nolle prosequi.
John Boyd	Murder	Oct. 29, 1890	April 21, 1891	Reversed on appeal, new trial, convicted of manslaughter, sentenced to ten years.
Eugene Stanley	Murder	Oct. 29, 1890	April 21, 1891	Reversed, new trial. Convicted of manslaughter and sentenced to ten years.
Alexander Lewis	Murder	Oct. 26, 1891	April 27, 1892	Reversed, new trial. Acquitted.
John Brown	Murder	March 22, 1892	June 28, 1892	Reversed, new trial. Again sentenced to hang, reversed, and on third trial sentenced to one year in prison.
Famous Smith	Murder	Jan. 8, 1894	Sept. 28, 1894	Reversed. Nolle prosequi.
John Hicks	Murder	March 7, 1894	Dec. 27, 1894	Reversed, acquitted.
Willie Johnson	Murder	March 7, 1894	July 25, 1894	Reversed; on second trial sentenced to life imprisonment.

Name	Crime	Date Convicted	Date to be Executed	Final Disposition
Marshal Tucker	Murder	March 12, 1894	Dec. 27, 1894	Reversed. Commuted to life at Brooklyn, New York.
John Gourke	Murder	May 22, 1894	Dec. 27, 1894	Reversed; pleaded guilty to manslaughter. Sentenced to four years at Columbus, Ohio.
John Graves	Murder	July 29, 1894	Nov. 2, 1894	Reversed; acquitted on second trial.
Frank Collins	Murder	Aug. 11, 1894	Nov. 2, 1894	Commuted.
Robert M. Hall	Murder	Aug. 17, 1894	Nov. 2, 1894	Reversed; acquitted on second trial.
Sam Hickory	Murder	Aug. 25, 1894	Nov. 2, 1894	Reversed; on new trial sentenced to five years.
Alexander Allen	Murder	Oct. 11, 1894	Dec. 27, 1894	Reversed; on new trial sentenced to life imprisonment.
Henry Starr	Murder	Oct. 20, 1894	Feb. 20, 1895	Reversed, new trial. Reversed, and second new trial ordered. In 1898 allowed to plead guilty to manslaughter and sentenced to five years at Columbus, Ohio.
Dennis Davis	Murder	Nov. 17, 1894	April 2, 1895	Adjudged insane and transferred to asylum.
Thomas Thompson	Murder	Dec. 4, 1894	April 24, 1895	Reversed.

Charles Smith	Murder	Feb. 20, 1895	June 25, 1895	Reversed; on new trial convicted of manslaughter and sentenced to ten years.
John Allison	Murder	May 28, 1895	Oct. 1, 1895	Reversed; on new trial sentenced to seven years.
Mollie King	Murder	Feb. 24, 1896	April 30, 1896	Appealed; on new trial sentenced to life imprisonment.
Eli Lucas	Murder	June 11, 1895	Oct. 1, 1895	Reversed. Released to Choctaw Nation for trial in Indian courts on proof of Choctaw citizenship.
Frank Carver	Murder	June 29, 1895	Oct. 1, 1895	Reversed; on new trial sentenced to life at Columbus, Ohio.
Thomas J. Thornton	Murder	Aug. 14, 1895	Oct. 9, 1895	Sentenced to ten years at Columbus, Ohio.
Buss Luckey	Murder	Aug. 24, 1895	Oct. 20, 1895	Reversed; on new trial was acquitted. Convicted of train robbery and sentenced to fifteen years.
Ed Wilkey	Rape	Sept. 25, 1895	Dec. 19, 1895	Commuted.
Ed Alberty	Murder	Nov. 15, 1895	Jan. 29, 1896	Reversed; acquitted on new trial.
Mary A. Kettenring	Murder	June 24, 1895	Oct. 1, 1895	Reversed; acquitted on new trial.

Name	Crime	Date Convicted	Date to be Executed	Final Disposition
George Frazier	Murder	June 24, 1895	Oct. 1, 1895	Reversed; acquitted on second trial.
Richard Calhoun	Murder	June 24, 1895	Oct. 1, 1895	Reversed; acquitted on second trial.
James Mills	Rape	March 3, 1896	June 23, 1896	Reversed; jury disagreed on second trial; acquitted on third trial.

APPENDIX D

Bond Forfeited

Name	Crime	Date Convicted	Date to be Executed	Final Disposition
Jack Hartgraves	Murder			Never tried. Indicted and arraigned August 8, 1889, released on bond of $5000. Bond forfeited and order rescinded April 30, 1890, upon proof of defendants death.

APPENDIX E

The Famous Grand Jury Charge

On August 5, 1895, a grand jury was called to examine the case of Crawford Goldsby alias Cherokee Bill, charged with the murder of Guard Lawrence Keating. There were, at the time, numerous other cases and such a large variety of crimes to be investigated that the task facing this particular jury was the hardest in the history of the court. To this jury Judge Parker delivered his most notable charge. It is filled with points of law and was considered by the Fort Smith bar, and by himself, the masterpiece of his life in this class of charges.

Gentlemen of the Grand Jury, before proceeding with your deliberations, I desire to address to you a few remarks by way of a reminder of what your duties are under the law. That reminder has already been given to you in the shape of your oath, which is an epitome of the great duties that devolve upon you as the accusing power of the government, in this district, for this term of court, but it is sometimes considered to be more impressive, and we are more apt to understand our duties, when we can converse for a brief time about them, and when we understand them properly we are apt to perform them better than we would if we did not fully comprehend the great responsibilities resting upon us.

I never open a term of court that I am not impressed again and again with the greatness of this government of ours. Its greatness consists of the fact that all of its power is in the hands of those who are to be benefitted or injured by the execution or the neglect to execute that great power—in the hands of the people themselves. There is not a step taken in the execution of these laws enacted by this government that is not taken by the people. In the first place, the laws are made by their agents. They are made for their protection, to secure their rights, and when they do not bring them that protection, and do not secure to them these rights, they are bad laws, they are vicious laws. Every good citizen should never let his partisan opinions or his political views, no matter what party he belongs to, run so high as to forget the great truth of the principle as to what his duty may be as to the government of his country, and its laws. Now, what I have said is based upon the fact that laws are worthless to protect the rights of the people unless they are executed. Society cannot live, it cannot exist, it degenerates into anarchy, into riot, into bloodshed, and into that condition which brings about destruction of all order and of all peace, unless these rules of government called the law are executed promptly and vigorously for the protection of every right that belongs to the citizen. The laws of the United States cannot be executed in this district until you as a grand jury first act in the premises. You occupy such a position as that the government through its officer comes to you and says: "I present this man, or that, or the other, and charge him with a crime." The government is the charging power. The government brings the case before you. Before any action can be taken to ascertain finally the guilt or innocence of a man you must first accuse him in a lawful way by an indictment. That is to say, you must pass upon his case, and see to it by the light of the evidence that the government offers to you, because the government says to you, "I charge this man with crime and here is the evidence supporting that charge." That evidence is presented to you through the district attorney, or some one of the assistants, and you pass upon the question primarily as to whether he shall be called upon in a court of justice to have the question determined as to whether he is guilty or innocent.

We have but to cite this fact to show the great responsibilities that rest upon you, to show you the importance of the position you assume or that is cast upon you, when you are chosen from the body of the people and brought into this court, placed under the sanction of an oath to perform this great duty, to perform it thoroughly, to perform it well, to perform it so that the rights of the citizen which are protected by these laws are really made secure by the proper enforcement of them. That is why you are brought here. It is a principle of law, arising under the Constitution of the United States, that if a man is the accused of a capital, or otherwise infamous offense, he cannot be tried for it, no matter how guilty he may be, no matter how injurious to the community it may be not to try him, unless he is first indicted by a grand jury. That is a matter that is enacted by the law as a safeguard to the liberty of the citizen who may be improperly accused, who might be wrongfully accused, who might be accused in an ex parte way, but the presumption is that if the grand jury investigates his case, and they find facts showing, first, that a crime has been committed, and secondly, that the man accused committed it, then there exists a condition of things that demands the intervention of a petit jury to pass upon that case, and he is accordingly indicted. The grand jury system, in my judgment, is one of the guarantees thrown around the liberty of the citizen, in this country. At the same time it is a method by which it is made easier to determine the guilt or innocence of the party accused when he is put upon trial in a court before a petit jury, because the evidence is sifted out, the facts in some degree are ascertained, and it becomes easier to find out whether he is guilty or innocent than if an indictment was not had, but he was simply tried upon information. When there is an investigation of that kind, the facts are better developed than they would necessarily be if there was no investigation.

The duties of this grand jury are much more onerous than those of a Federal grand jury usually are. Most Federal courts only deal with cases directly affecting their government, but here we have nearly all the Indian Territory attached to this jurisdiction, and the laws of the United States are extended over it to protect that country which for years has been cursed with criminal refugees. They committed some crime back at their homes and fled from justice, taking refuge in the land of the Indians, where, by their acts and their influence, they have made a hotbed of crime. The government, in its treaties with the Indians, obligated itself to keep all these characters out, to remove them as fast as they moved in, but that promise has never been kept except insofar as the court having jurisdiction over that country has brought these criminals out to punish them. For years this court stood alone in the work but of late years the jurisdiction has been divided and now other courts are exercising the same wholesome influence.

Taken as a whole, the juries have done their duties fairly, honestly and impartially, though some grave mistakes have been made and the cause of justice scandalized. By finding a verdict of guilty where guilt exists, you are doing your duty, and also are teaching one of the greatest object lessons. Judging from the vast volume of crime, which has almost submerged us in a sea of blood, we have gone astray, and are almost at the mercy of the man of crime. The greatest question of the hour is, can we properly enforce the law? Crime is gaining strength, especially those crimes affecting human life. This is not caused entirely by the failure of the people to enforce the laws. There are other causes and sources. One of our leading newspapers, in commenting upon the trial of Dr. Buchanan, printed an editorial under the heading of "Laxity of Law." The article went on to say that technical pleas of cunning lawyers often defeat justice; that the appellate courts consider alleged flaws and encourage a system of practice of the law entirely in favor of the criminal and against the cause of right; that they never look to the merits of the case, but seem to be coöperating with the unscrupulous attorneys whose object is to circumvent the law. This is as true as the words of Holy Writ. However honest and fair the trial court may be, it is impossible to bring assassins to merited punishment when appellate courts allow the cases to linger along, and give these murderers an opportunity to take other innocent life in cold blood.

Now, you will understand that you organize as an accusing body. You are organized now as such body, with a foreman to preside over your deliberations—with a foreman as your presiding officer, and who presides over you during these deliberations as he would over any other deliberative body. He puts all questions to a vote that come before you, he determines whether the proposition accusing the man of crime has received the requisite number of votes to authorize the findings of a true bill against a party. He may determine this by counting the votes. He may determine it by calling the roll when there is any question of doubt about it. He has the power, under the law, to swear witnesses, to administer an oath to a witness that is binding upon the witness as though it was administered by the judge of this court, or by the clerk of the court. He leads in the examination of the witnesses, though any gentleman on the jury has a right to ask a witness questions, with his consent. You will bear in mind that the law prescribes the number of votes that shall be cast in favor of indicting a man before you are authorized to return a true bill against him. The law says that at least twelve of your number shall concur in voting the man guilty of the crime charged before an indictment can be returned. You will understand that it takes sixteen of your number to constitute a working quorum. You cannot transact any business unless there are sixteen members of the grand jury present. Now, in this connection, I remark that it is highly important that the whole body should be promptly present at every meeting after recess or adjournment, because you are all interested, of course, in the investigation of these cases. You all want to understand them, and you all want to perform your duties, and prompt attendance is the way to accomplish that, and if this rule is observed strictly it becomes a fact that you are all present, and there could never be any question raised about the quorum.

You will bear in mind that there is a veil of secrecy thrown around your proceedings. There was a much greater necessity for that in the beginning of the grand jury system than there is now, though at times now the rule is necessary in order to secure the independence of the grand jury in their action. The language of your oath is that you are to pass upon these cases without fear, favor or affection; you are not to be controlled by any outside opinion; in fact, you have no right to talk to anybody outside the grand jury room about cases, unless it may be the judge of the court or the district attorney, or some one of the assistants of the district attorney. The matter of passing upon the guilt or innocence of a man is to be determined by you just as it is to be determined by the petit jury, by the law bearing upon the question of which you will be advised by the district attorney or some one of his assistants, and by the evidence that is offered upon that case, and by these, and these alone, are you to be governed. Therefore, you are not to make known what proceedings are transpiring in the grand jury room to anybody on the outside; you are not to inform anyone what you are doing there, whether you have indicted anybody for a crime, or whether anybody has been charged, before you, with a crime. Nor are you permitted to make known how any member of your body votes upon a proposition, or what opinions he expresses upon questions that may be pending before you. Nor are you permitted to make known the testimony of any witness before you, unless you are called upon in a court of justice to make known that evidence and the character of it. You may be called upon, for instance, in a case of perjury, where a party is accused of perjury before you, or in a case where it becomes necessary to impeach the testimony of a witness by proving contradictory statements made before you different from those made in court, and in such cases you may be called upon legally as a witness to disclose the testimony of the witness, but outside of this exception you are to keep that matter a profound secret so that witnesses may act independently. It sometimes is the case—very often is the case—that witnesses are afraid to go before the grand jury and tell the truth if that evidence is to go out before the party is arrested, or the party or his friends might be informed of it, and the witness might, perhaps, be assassinated, or interfered with, or run out of the country. You see there is wisdom in all these rules. Now, of course, this rule I have given you, requiring you to keep these matters a profound secret, is a rule, when properly observed, which secures the administration of justice in the proper way. At the same time it may be taken advantage of unduly—not apt to be, here, because we have safeguards against that, but still you are to see to it that men do not come into the grand jury room and take advantage of this rule of secrecy by falsely accusing other men of crime. We have rules, I say, that prevent that as far as possible. For instance, a party who desires to make complaint, if the case has not been examined by a commissioner, and he has not already given his evidence, is required to go to the district attorney and make his complaint to him, and then the district attorney passes his judgment upon the question as to whether the man is telling the truth or not. If, in the judgment of the district attorney, the man is telling the truth, he is sent to the grand jury. If he is not, if it is a fictitious charge, if it is something that is invented for the purpose of venting spleen or malice or hatred or ill-will against an innocent citizen, the district attorney is apt to detect that, and, consequently, you are not liable to be imposed upon. You are not troubled much by false witnesses, who seek the privacy of your chamber, and who become false accusers. Sometimes men go there who may be mistaken as to whether the act is a crime or not. They may be mistaken as to the identity of the man committing that crime, and they may be mistaken honestly, but it does not often happen. It sometimes occurs, though, that witnesses appear before the grand jury for the purpose of committing downright and deliberate perjury. The perjury is more apt to be committed where the motive is greater. The motive upon the part of the government does not exist to have a man falsely convicted. There is nobody who represents the government who wants a man falsely accused or falsely convicted. It generally occurs that the perjury is upon the other side, where the motive is strongest, where a man is in danger of conviction, where he is likely to pay the forfeit with his life or lose his liberty. The inducement is greater there to invoke this terrible agency of crime, called perjury, which is so often resorted to in this age, than it is upon the part of the government, whose duty it is to see to it that the innocent are protected as well as the guilty punished. No one connected with the court, or with the government, has any interest in that direction, much less have they any desire of that kind; but they have a desire to uncover perjury, to uncover falsehood, and bring to justice false accusers or false witnesses, whenever they can be found, whether they are upon the side of the government or against it.

Now, there is another remark I desire to address to you in regard to the character of evidence you are required to act upon in the grand jury room. You cannot indict a man upon affidavits, or upon ex parte statements that come to you second hand. The general rule is that the witness whose testimony is relied upon must be produced before you. He is to be sworn by the foreman, and you proceed then to examine him. You judge of his credibility and you use exactly the same means that a petit jury may use for that purpose. You look at the very way he gives his evidence, the very consistency, and reasonableness and probability of the story as he gives it, his very manner of testifying. All of these things are passed upon by you. That is the benefit of having the living witness before you. You can see the manner of evidence he is giving sometimes from the way he gives it. There are exceptions, however, to this rule from necessity, and in the interest of public justice. If a witness has once appeared before a man accused of crime in an examining court, for example, and has there given his evidence, and he subsequently dies, that evidence from necessity, and in order that justice may not be defeated, may be relied upon by you, and it may be produced before you properly, more properly by the officer who heard the evidence. He can go before you, or anybody else who heard it may go before you and reproduce it and tell you what that evidence was and you may act upon it just the same as though that witness had stood before you and given that testimony; or, it may be shown from the notes of the officer who takes it down, the commissioner. That is one exception to the rule. The other is, where a witness is permanently sick, and he has given his evidence before an examining court, and his sickness is of that permanent nature that it is hardly probable or reasonable to believe that he will ever recover; his testimony then, I say, may be reproduced in the way I have indicated the same as though he were dead. In that sort of case, before the evidence can be used, it ought to be shown that the sickness of the witness is not merely temporary but is of that permanent and serious character as to disable the party for all time so he could not be able to come and that in all reason and probability he would die before he could be produced before you. Another exception to the rule is where a witness is improperly used by a party accused of crime, or somebody in his interest, where he is induced to leave the district by corrupt means used upon him in the shape of bribery, or by threats or violence, or intimidation, he is induced to absent himself from the district, or to so hide himself away as that the officer cannot serve a subpoena upon him. In a case of that kind, if he has once given his evidence before the commissioner, that testimony may be reproduced before you, and you may act upon it just the same as though the witness were dead. Now, these are exceptions to the rule, but with these exceptions you are required to have the presence of the witness before you, and you are to so examine them as to satisfy yourself, first, of their telling the truth, and then, of course, you are to pass upon the proving power of the story given by them as witnesses to see whether the testimony of any one witness alone, or in conjunction with other testimony, is sufficient to lead you to the belief, first, that a crime has been committed, and, secondly, that the party or parties accused, is the one, or are the ones, who committed it. If the two propositions are then established, your duty calls upon you to say so by presenting your conclusion from that evidence in the character of the charge drawn up by the district attorney's office, and presented by you in the shape of an indictment, signed by Mr. Brooks, as your foreman, and returned into court by you as a body headed by your foreman. That completes your duty as to that case. That case is then in a condition where the court can dispose of it in the way prescribed by law.

Now, it is your duty to pass upon all violations of the laws of the United States where those violations are alleged to have occurred in this district. These violations may be classified. There are violations of laws which affect the operations of the Treasury Department of the United States, for instance. If a party counterfeits the money of the United States, or such counterfeit is found in the possession of a party with guilty knowledge and for fraudulent purpose, that becomes a crime against the operation of the government. This is a matter that you are to look to carefully, because the circulating money of the country which passes into the pockets of the people, and which they receive in exchange for the products of their toil, is required by the law to be kept entirely pure. You cannot keep it pure unless this law against counterfeiting, or passing counterfeit money, and having it in possession for fraudulent purposes, is rigidly enforced. There are always enough bad men who are disposed to violate the law if they can make gain of it, if they can benefit themselves by it, and the only thing that restrains them is the fear of punishment; it is the fear of capture, the certainty of conviction, and the certainty of punishment following that conviction that restrains them. The Treasury Department is, therefore, one of the departments of the government that must be protected by you, and by the petit jury, in all cases where you and it are called upon to enforce the law.

Then there is the Postal Department, one of the great agencies of the government, which is of the highest character because of its great importance to the people of the United States everywhere, so important and so much of a necessity, that we would rather do without one of our meals than to miss our mail one time. We become so anxious about it and so used to it, that it is one of those agencies we depend upon to such an extent that we cannot do without it. And if you wanted to produce a revolution in this country, if you wanted to upset things generally, I think you could do it quicker by suspending the mails of the United States for six months or a year than by any other means. This agency is a matter of great benefit to the people. They are enabled by it to transmit valuables and letters to one another; to transmit letters containing matters that are private between relatives and friends; to transmit packages and things of that character. And they now transmit them as a rule by depositing them in the office with the belief in their minds that they will as certainly arrive at their destination as that they deposit them. Somebody has said, somewhere, that the postal laws of the government, from the way they are executed, make this mail matter just as secure as though each letter was surrounded by a batallion of cavalry to convey it to its destination. And that is true. You take that great system and consider the millions and hundreds of millions in money that is transmitted through it by the people of the United States from one to another, and the millions of letters and the thousands and hundreds of thousands of papers and magazines that pass throughout the country by the means of this great agency, and all with entire safety, and there is the greatest lesson that teaches us what the security of the law means; it teaches us how secure all the rights of men can be made if we look to the proper enforcement of the law. What do I mean by that? This branch of the government is better protected by the agency of the Postal Department, intended to discover, arrest and bring to justice all violators of this law than any other department in it. It is a fact that may be asserted with truth with reference to this department that a robber or an embezzler, or a man who would open a letter wrongfully, or a man who would commit the larceny of a letter or of its contents, has not any possibility of escape, as a rule. Its agents follow him to the uttermost ends of the earth; they arrest him and he is brought to justice before the juries of the country through the means of this great agency of the government. The consequence is that it has this security. How much better would the condition of the country be, how much happier would the people be, if we could only assert this fact with reference to that which is the most sacred thing possessed by any citizen—his life? If the same measure of security, if the same degree of protection, if the same enforcement of the law to protect human life, existed in this country as it does with reference to this department of the government, this tide of bloodshed that is now deluging this land would, in a measure, disappear and human life would have at least the highest possible degree of security thrown around it that could be thrown around it by the power of the law. I say there is an object lesson to be found in the way that the law is enforced as affecting the Postal Department of the government. I ask you to continue to teach that object lesson in this jurisdiction by indicting every man who violates the postal laws in any way. There is another branch of the Postal Department I desire to call your attention to especially. While it is important to protect the property of the citizen, his money in the letter, or his secret in the letter transmitted to his friend, or the transmission of these confidential family matters that exist, and with which the public have no business, it is equally important to protect the morals of the young of this country against the vicious and vile acts of men who would use the mails as a conduit for corruption, for villainy and vice and crime of that character. The law therefore says that the mails cannot be used for the transmission of anything that vitiates the morals, or has that tendency. And this is one of the best laws ever enacted by the Congress of the United States in the interest of good morals. All those who violate this law in the interest of licentiousness, vice and crime are guilty and should be punished. He who makes a threat in an open manner upon a postal card so that it would have a deleterious influence upon the party to whom it is sent, is subject to punishment. The mails paid for by the people are not to be used as a conduit for crime, for the perpetration of crimes, or for the production of bad morals, vice and licentiousness. And I ask you especially if any cases of that kind are discovered by you to indict the parties who may be guilty of having used the mails in this unlawful way.

There is another department of the government, of which I remind you especially, and it is connected with, and grows out of, this department I have called your attention to already, the Treasury

Department. This treasury has to be supplied with funds, with money, and it is necessary that the agencies used to do that should be protected by the courts and juries of the country. There is one system of collecting revenue, growing out of a direct tax on products produced in the country known as liquors, such as whisky, brandy, distilled or fermented liquors, etc., and the law is of that character that unless a man complies with these provisions he is guilty of a crime. If he runs an illicit distillery without complying with the many regulations prescribed by the statutes, he is guilty of crime; he is running what is called a "moonshine" or illicit distillery, and he is subject to punishment. If he carries on the business of a wholesale liquor dealer, without having first paid the tax required by law, he is guilty of crime. If he sells malt or fermented liquors, without having paid the tax, he is guilty of crime. Or if he carries on a retail liquor business, without first having paid the tax, he is guilty of crime. It is highly important that this law should be enforced, for the reason if it is not enforced the government will get but little revenue from that source, and if the government is to recognize this traffic at all, the law should be so administered as to fall equally upon all, and that the man who honestly pays the tax and complies with all the requirements of the law should not be put to a disadvantage, compared with the man who disregards the law and pays no tax. If you do not enforce it, even against the smallest violators, the consequence is that, in a small way, it is evaded, and the traffic is wholly carried on in that way. For instance, you take the business of carrying on a retail liquor dealer's traffic: the law says that if a man sells or offers for sale any foreign or domestic spirits in quantities less than five wine gallons at one time, he is carrying on the business of a retail liquor dealer. He is required by the law to pay twenty-five dollars tax per year, and if he does not pay that tax, the act of entering the business becomes a crime. The law is very comprehensive. It says: "Whoever sells or offers for sale this liquor in any quantity." A man can go out here with a pint cup and he can sell, or offer to sell, a drink of whisky, and if he does he is carrying on the business of a retail liquor dealer. It looks like a trivial thing upon the face of it, but when we look at the consequences arising from it if the law is not enforced, it becomes a serious matter. If the business could be carried on in that way, without paying any tax, of course that is the way it would be carried on. Nobody would put himself in a position where he could be caught up readily by the officers, but he would peddle it around and sell it to single individuals in small quantities. The law is made comprehensive for the purpose of saying to all men: "If you sell it or offer it for sale in any quantity less than five wine gallons, you must pay the tax. If you sell it in quantities more than that, you are a wholesale dealer, and you must pay the tax."

Now, these are the principal departments of the government that may be affected by these violations of the law, that may come before you, and I ask you to see to it that every department of the government that is effected by these violations of the law is sustained. You are emphatically and truly upon the side of the government when you come into a court of justice, not to use that government for the purpose of wrongdoing, but to see that these laws are sustained and the same thing is true with reference to the petit jury —to see to it that no guilty man escapes and that no innocent man is wrongfully accused or punished.

Now, there are other matters that will come before you because of the peculiar jurisdiction of this court. What I have heretofore stated has been stated with reference, more especially, to the established jurisdiction of Federal courts, but in this jurisdiction up to this time, and as it will remain for some time in the future, there is an increased jurisdiction belonging to this tribunal; and this being so, there is cast upon you additional responsibilities. For instance, there comes before you for investigation cases growing out of the taking of human life, or of attempts upon human life in the shape of assaults with intent to kill, and cases growing out of acts affecting the property rights of citizens. And there are cases to be brought before you which grow out of violations of what is called the intercourse law—the law that regulates the intercourse between the people of the United States and the Indian tribes or nations that are rightfully in the Indian country. This does not exist as a part of the jurisdiction of the United States courts generally. Now, in coming to that part of the jurisdiction belonging to us because of this traffic that is carried on in liquor in the Indian country, we approach a subject that is of the gravest importance to the welfare and peace of that country; and while it is impossible to make that country a prohibitory one, we can largely suppress, if we do our duty, this traffic in liquors there, or the taking of them into that country. Of late years there has been much legislation upon that subject. The law as it existed originally is found in that section of the statute which has stood as the law of that country for a great many years. That section is 2139 of the Revised Statutes of the United States, which provided:

> No ardent spirits shall be introduced under any pretense into the Indian country. Every person who sells, exchanges, gives, barters, or disposes of any spirituous liquors or wine, to any Indian under the charge of any Indian superintendent or agent, or introduces or attempts to introduce any spirituous liquor or wine into the Indian country, shall be punishable by imprisonment for not more than two years, and a fine of not more than $300.

That is the law as it has stood ever since Indian reservations were set apart by the laws of the United States. That act was repealed by the act of July 23, 1892, upon the subject of the introduction of liquors of an intoxicating nature. The very gravamen of these statutes is that liquor is prohibited, and liquor of any kind that will intoxicate, or that is spirituous in its nature, is not to be introduced. By the act of July 23, 1892, it was provided:

> Every person who sells, exchanges, gives, barters, or disposes of any ardent spirits, ale, beer, wine, or intoxicating liquors of any kind to any Indian under charge of any Indian superintendent or agent, or introduces or attempts to introduce any ardent spirits, ale, beer, wine, or intoxicating liquor of any kind into the Indian country, shall be punished by imprisonment for not more than two years, and by a fine of not more than $300 for each offense.

That stood as the law repealing the old statute until the last legislation upon the subject, which was upon the first of March, 1895, by an act entitled "an act to provide for the appointment of additional judges of the United States court in the Indian Territory," and for other purposes. I note these different stages of legislation upon this subject because I am coming to the proposition as to whether or not this court has jurisdiction of violations of this law at this time. Section 8 of the act of March 1, 1895, provides:

That any person, whether an Indian or otherwise, who shall, in said Territory, manufacture, sell, give away, or in any manner or by any means, furnish to anyone, either for himself or for another, any vinous malt or fermented liquors, or any other intoxicating drinks of any kind whatsoever, whether medicated or not, or who shall carry, or in any manner have carried, into said Territory, any liquors or drinks, or who shall be interested in such manufacture, sale, giving away, furnishing to anyone or carrying into said Territory, any of such liquors or drinks shall, upon conviction thereof, be punished by a fine not exceeding five hundred dollars and by imprisonment for not less than one month nor more than five years.

This section of the act of March 1, 1895, as this court construes it, as far as such law has reference to acts done in the Indian country, works a repeal of the law passed upon the 23rd of July, 1892. It takes up the whole subject. It legislates fully upon it. It changes the penalty. It embraces, as I have said, the whole subject embraced in the other statutes, and more, too. It is more comprehensive, because it makes it an offense to manufacture in the Territory, or to sell, or to give away to anyone, or in any manner or by any means furnish to anyone, whether he be an Indian or not, either for himself or for another, any vinous, malt or fermented liquors, or any other intoxicating drinks of any kind whatsoever, whether medicated or not, and it prohibits the carrying in, or in any manner having carried into said Territory, any such liquors or drinks. It prohibits parties from being interested in such manufacture and sale or giving away or carrying into the Territory. As I say, it embraces the whole subject embraced in the other statutes, comprehends even more, and it changes the penalty. It is, therefore, new legislation, inconsistent with the other statutes, and they both cannot stand together. That being true, by the rules of law declaring that when one statute repeals an older one, as asserted by the following authorities, the statute of March 1, 1895, manifestly being intended as a substitute for the act of July 23, 1892, repeals the same. In King vs. Cornell, 106 United States, 396, the Supreme Court said:

While repeals by implication are not favored, it is well settled that where two acts are not in all respects repugnant, if the later act covers the whole subject of the earlier, and embraces new provisions which plainly show it is intended as a substitute for the first, it will operate as a repeal. United States v. Tynen, 11 Wall, 88; Redrock vs. Henry, 106 U.S., 596; Wood vs. U.S., 16 Peters, 342, and Murdock vs. City of Mephis, 12 Wall, 590, fully sustain the principle asserted in King vs. Cornell.

Under the subsequent provisions of the statute defining the jurisdiction of the courts in the Indian Territory, which say that the United States courts in the Indian Territory shall have exclusive original jurisdiction of all offenses committed in said Territory, of which the United States court in the Indian Territory now has jurisdiction, if they had jurisdiction of this offense, as prescribed by this statute, they would have, under this legislation, exclusive jurisdiction of it, and this court would have nothing to do with it; but they could not have had jurisdiction of this offense as created by this statute—it being a new offense and punished in a different way—they could not have had jurisdiction of this offense at the time the act passed, when there was no act in existence providing for the offense as it is prescribed here, and the manner of committing it, and the punishment as prescribed by this statute. Therefore, they did not have jurisdiction of this offense as prescribed by Section 8, and consequently they do not have jurisdiction now, but this court has jurisdiction of it, and will continue to have jurisdiction under the provisions of this statute until the first day of September, 1896. Therefore, I say to you, that as to all offenses committed, which are prescribed as offenses by that section, growing out of the manufacture in the Territory, or of the selling, the giving away, or in any manner or by any means furnishing to anyone, either for himself or another, any vinous, malt or fermented liquors, or any other intoxicating drinks of any kind whatsoever, whether medicated or not, or who shall carry or have carried into such Territory any such liquors or drinks, if any of these things are proven before you, your duty is to indict the party. There has never been a Congress yet, except one, where there was an exception made, and that was by a legislative trick, where any of the provisions in any of these laws that I have read were not regarded of the highest importance. They were enacted, in the first place, upon the petition of Indian settlers of that country who looked upon the traffic of intoxicating liquors as a method adopted by vicious, vile and evil-disposed white men to destroy their people and take advantage of their condition and their tribal weakness. And this destruction has been brought about in many instances until whole nations have been wiped from the face of the earth by means of liquor carried to them by white men who were desirous of using them in that way in order that they might get some advantage of them. It is your duty, and I know you will perform it, so see to it, as the people of this goodly state have seen to it for over fifty years, that this provision of the law is enforced.

You will understand that upon the organization of this Indian country, the power to uphold the laws of the United States over that country was put into the hands of the good people of the State of Arkansas, and it has remained there for fifty years and over—ever since 1834. The law at first provided that the court of the United States for the Territory of Arkansas, sitting at Little Rock, was to enforce the laws of the United States over the Indian country. Subsequently, after the territory had been admitted to statehood, when there was a division of the State into two districts and a court was established at Van Buren, the same law prevailed, and the same people of this State were the jurors in whose hands was placed by that law the power to protect these people of that nation, to use all the power that belonged to them to protect them in all the rights which they possessed.

Again, in 1871, when the court was removed from Van Buren to this place, the same power of protecting them remained in the hands of the people of Arkansas. And I want to say that for twenty years, just about now, since the opening of the first court here, as a rule these people have performed that duty faithfully and well. Why a distrust has been entertained of them, or why the jurisdiction was changed, I am not prepared to say, nor is it material that anything should be said upon the subject. All I have to say upon that subject is that the jurisdiction yet remains, and still is in your hands, and as long as it does remain I ask you to vindicate the character established by the people of this State for enforcing the law in that country. Much has been said in that regard. Much has been falsely asserted in regard to it. I can say, in vindication of these jurors and of these people, that the law has been at least as well enforced by them as affecting that country and the rights of its people, as it is enforced in any State of the Union, anywhere. I can say more than that. I can say *even more than that*. I can say that there has not been a band of robbers or highwaymen or assassins in the Indian country that has not been, by the officers of this court and by the juries passing upon their cases and finding them guilty, if they were guilty, more promptly broken up, destroyed and wiped out, than has been the case in the Indian country for twenty years past. This is the truth. More cases of criminals committing high crimes have been tried, a higher percentage of arrests have been made, more convictions have been obtained, although justice has often failed from corrupt influences, as it does everywhere, from improper influences exerted, not always felt, known and understood by the jury when the mistake is made; but, I say, notwithstanding this there has, altogether, been a greater percentage of convictions, more men brought to justice, the law better vindicated, better upheld, and better sustained, and the rights of the people better protected by the people who come to this court as jurors than in any court in the country, I care not whether it is in the old States or in the new States, and when the history of this court comes to be written; when the passions of the hour, prompted by cupidity, avarice and self-interest, and desire for gain shall have all disappeared, those who have been connected with it in upholding the majesty, power and dignity of the law of the United States shall not suffer from that true history. I ask you to keep it up. I ask you to vindicate it still, because when you are doing that you are seeking to protect the people under the protecting agency of the law of the United States, and, as I have already said to you, the only way to protect men in their rights is for the juries of the land to come into the courts with a desire to fearlessly enforce the law, no matter whom it affects. The truth about it is that we are in a peculiar condition in this nation today—in such a condition that, in my judgment, the greatest problem that has ever presented itself to the minds of the people is confronting us now, and that is, whether crime shall be triumphant; whether the man of blood, the man of crime, the man of vicious disposition, the man who destroys human life, who tramples upon the rights of others, shall be the ruler, or the law of the land shall exert its peaceful sway, and by its protecting power, all men made secure under their own vine and their own fig tree, and under their own rooftree. It is a great problem. It is one that is exciting the interest of all good men in the land. You find it in the law journals of the country; you find it in the lectures of judges; you find it as delivered by professors in colleges who are discovering this terrible condition where this wave of blood is about to deluge us and over-power us. Now, what is the reason for that? The reason for it in our jurisdiction is, because we have had to contend with almost the whole earth—the criminals, at least, of all the country. It has been the custom for all these years that when a man committed a crime in an older state, or in any state, and he could get away from the officers, he would run into the Indian country. He became a refugee criminal. And while there are many good men, hundreds and thou-sands of good white men in that country who are properly there, who are there by invitation; there are hundreds and thousands of others who are stained with crime, whose tendencies are corrupted by the crimes that they have committed elsewhere, and it is with this corrupt element assembled from all the States of this Union that this court, and the juries of this court, have had to contend with. That is why the volume has been great. That is why it has been said: "You convict so many men there; you must be cruel, you must be harsh, you must be tyrannical." In fact, that reputation of this court has gone abroad, it has reached the whole land, and it started right here. Often, lawyers who would lose cases, whose client's neck was placed in the halter by the evidence and the law of the case, to vindicate themselves with their clients, would go off and damn the court, and talk about its cruelty, and its inhumanity and wickedness in that direction. There is where it started from; there is the origin of it. Many have acted outrageously in that particular, disgracefully, unprofessionally, and in every other way that ought to be reprimanded. That is the truth about it. There is where it started. But let the record of the court speak for itself and it will vindicate itself. The juries in this court, under the guidance of the court, as a rule have endeavored to uphold the law, to vin-dicate it. Now, then, it is not only your duty to continue to do this for the sake of giving protection of these people under the law, but you, as well as the petit jury, are, for the time being, educators. You are to teach the people everywhere a wholesome lesson, and that is that they must rely upon the law and upon its enforcement, for their protection, and not upon mob violence, not upon that spirit that

causes people to degenerate into a mob and become criminals themselves in an effort to seek protection. There is a prevalance of this
crime everywhere, that men, instead of arresting criminals and bringing them before juries of the country, take them out and put them
to death without judge or jury, and without investigating their cases,
and not being competent to properly investigate them. Every day
they do that. Sometimes you will find that good men are involved in
things of that kind. It is because they have lost confidence in courts
and juries. You say to a community that as sure as a crime is
committed, so sure will the party who has committed it be brought
to merited justice, as the law prescribed that punishment, and you
won't find any mobs in that community. *There are no mobs in the
counties of this state which are in this jurisdiction.* Have you
noticed that? Why is that? It may not be that this court is entitled
to the credit for it, but it is a fact that three or four times a year
sixty or seventy-five men come up here, assist in the enforcement of
the law and go home as educators among their people, and who
are in favor of depending upon the law for the protection of every
right, and the consequence is that mob violence does not exist in
these counties. Everything is peaceable, it is quiet. A man commits
a crime and the people seek to arrest him, as they have a right to
do, and they bring him into the courts that he may be punished.
And it is a rare exception that mob violence exists in the Indian
country. There are cases of it (we have tried in this court three
cases of mob violence since I have been here), but there is not the
amount of it that you would naturally expect from the criminal
condition of that country. And it is because the people have a
belief that we will at least endeavor to enforce the law. Now, when
we are teaching the lesson to all people that we must rely upon
the law of this country to secure peace and good order and the
consequent happiness and prosperity of the people, we are teaching
the greatest lesson that can be taught; and we do that every day
and every hour when we are in the courts of the country seeking
to honestly, impartially and dispassionately uphold and enforce the
law. It may not be inappropriate to give you the opinions of
eminent jurists, of eminent men, showing our condition at this time
in this country, and outlining to us what the duties of every good
citizen are when they go into the courts of the country, and even

when they are outside of the courts. Now, reading from the lecture of Judge Elliot Anthony, President of the Illinois State Bar Association, at its eighteenth annual meeting, held January 24, 1895, at Springfield, Illinois, in which he said, in relation to criminal law:

> There is no subject at the present time before the American people of such transcendent importance as that of the administration of the criminal law.

Much criticism has been indulged in regarding our jury system. The jury of the vicinage is, today, the most complete humbug. It was all right when it was originated five hundred years ago, but the jury system has been reversed since. Then the jury tried the case on their own knowledge of it; now that knowledge of it would disqualify you. The majority of criminals do not want a trial by a jury of the vicinage. They committed crimes at their former homes, and fled because they did not have a good opinion of that law system. All they are entitled to is a fair trial by an impartial jury, and that I am sure they will get here. The truth about it is, for some reason or another, and the reason to my mind is manifest, that the administration of the law affecting the civil rights of the citizen, his property rights growing out of the controversies between man and man, has become to be regarded of much more importance than the enforcement of the law which protects the life of the citizen. Did you ever notice that? The criminal law and its administration has rather fallen into disgrace. That is especially true of the large cities of the country. Now, is it not more important to protect a man's life than it is his property? A man may lose every cent he has on earth and he can earn more; if he cannot, he can depend upon his neighbor, or upon charity. He still has his life. But if his life is destroyed, if the assassin fires into his house and takes his life, robs his family and himself of that which belongs to him, is not that a greater deprivation than to deprive him of his horse, or his cow, or even of all the property which he possesses? Yet I say it is true that the administration of the criminal law has to some extent fallen into disgrace. I apprehend it is because of the corrupt methods resorted to to defeat its administration, and for this reason the people have become so that they look upon it with a kind of contempt. This eminent jurist, continuing, says:

It is as a general rule the least studied and the least understood by our judges of any other branch of the law. Many, up to the time of their accession to the bench, never tried a criminal case in a court of record, and consequently they have no appreciation whatever of the fine points of the law, or what is required by the Supreme Court to sustain a verdict in a case wherein it has once been obtained, and what is worse, they do not study to master the subject. Our methods of criminal procedure are vicious, and our criminal practice still worse. The rights of the defendant are regarded as supreme, while those of the public are almost entirely disregarded and ignored. Those who are charged with a criminal offense in Illinois are privileged characters and dominate the state. They can, under our practice, generally choose their own judges to try them, can fix the time and the season, can select just about such a jury as they see fit, and can then prolong the trial long enough to wear out the patience of the jury and drive the judge to madness. Everything is, as a general thing, ruled against the state, and if they cannot win in the court below, they can in the Supreme Court.

The history of crime is interwoven to a greater or less extent with every government, and will always be the most momentous question with which the human race has to deal. It is the great problem of civilization. He who has not thought upon it, has thought little about humanity, and he who has not paid some attention to the criminal law of his country has not received a liberal education. It ought to be administered with intelligence and enlightenment, but it is not. The great effort seems to be to involve every investigation of crime in a network of subtleties, artificial distinctions, and downright quibbles, shut out all incriminating evidence possible, then decide every case on some technicality. There is dissatisfaction everywhere throughout the country in regard to the methods adopted and the course pursued by our courts in dealing with the violators of the law, and it is but little wonder that the people in some of the oldest portions of the Republic have at times become exasperated at the trifling and juggling which are allowed, to the disgrace of civilization and the age in which we live. Public rights seem to be held in much lower estimation than private rights, and as between the living and the dead there is no equality whatever.

In 1889, David Dudley Field said, in addressing the American Bar Association, of which he was at that time the president:

We are a boastful people; we make no end of saying what great things we have done and are doing; and yet behind these brilliant shows, there stands a spectre of halting justice, such as is to be seen in no other part of Christendom. So far as I am aware, there is no other country calling itself civilized where it is so difficult to convict and punish a criminal and where it takes so many years to get a final decision between man and man. Truly may we say that justice passes through the land on leaden sandals. The judges of the Supreme Court have it in their power to establish by their decisions such a body of criminal law as they see fit. They are hampered very little by statutes and none whatever in regard to the determination of the guilt or innocence of the accused. To build up and establish an arbitrary system of rules and regulations is not the true object and aim of an enlightened judiciary. What society demands and common sense demands, is this: If a man is charged with a crime, then the question should be, is he innocent or guilty; not did the judge err when he told the jury that they must be "satisfied" of the guilt of the accused, instead of "believe" him guilty, after a full consideration of all the evidence.

These are the expressive sentiments of men who are observing men, who are good men, who are skilled in the laws of the country, who are devoted to the true interests of the people everywhere in this land. You cannot pick up the proceedings of a bar meeting, a meeting of lawyers, nor can you scarcely find a lecture delivered on that line in any institution of learning in the country, that does not treat of this subject just as these eminent jurists have spoken of it. It is the solemn truth, and it should be the duty of every good citizen to see to it, in court and out, that no stone is left unturned to undo this condition where the man of crime is in power, where he is practically the ruler, where, if he has things in the shape of money or social power and standing, he breaks through the meshes of the law and makes his trial a mockery, a sham, a delusion, as is manifested in every court in this land, time after time. Juries are deceived; they are humbugged; they are imposed upon by the tricks and artifices resorted to for the purpose of circumventing justice, to cheat the law of its rights and its just demands. I ask you to see to it that nothing of that kind will occur as far as you are concerned, that no effort can be brought forth strong enough or powerful enough to cause you to swerve from the line of duty which is marked out for you by the law, and that is indicated for you by the oath you have taken. See to it that every apparently guilty man accused of crime is properly and promptly indicted so that he may be put upon his trial, and it may be finally ascertained whether he is guilty or innocent. It is the duty of all of us, as citizens and as officers, to see that these great principles of law, enacted for the preservation of the rights of each and every citizen, whether it be the right to life, to liberty or property, shall in every case be enforced, and in every case be vindicated. That no distinction shall be made; or, if any distinction is made, make it against the intelligent and powerful and those who ought to know better, rather than against a man who has less reason and who is ignorant and who may have become criminal from environment, from his surroundings, as is often the case. If any distinction shall be made in the way of punishment, in my judgment, it should be made in favor of a man of that kind, and not in favor of the man with power behind him, who breaks through all of these statutes that have been enacted. And you are to especially see to it if he is a violator of the law that he shall suffer punishment. It is abhorrent, it is disgusting in the extreme, to see this manifestation exhibited all over the land, which has gone so far that there is a sickly sentimentality today in favor of crime. The man who is a criminal is apparently a little better than you who are honest and upright and who have not stained your hands with the blood of a fellow man, or committed some other high crime. There is that sickly sentimentality in favor of crime upon the part of large numbers of people of this land. When you come into this court as jurymen, if you ever had a lingering fragment of such a sentiment, leave it outside the door, because you are here panoplied with the power of your country to uphold the laws of this land, to assist in seeing to it that justice is done in every instance, no matter who may be charged, no matter who the criminal may be, no matter who the innocent person may be. If a man is innocent, protect him in his innocence; if he is guilty, see to it that you assist in bringing him to merited punishment.

I want you to return indictments in every case wherein it is probable that a murder has been committed, and first, I want you to take up the case of Crawford Goldsby, alias Cherokee Bill, who has been regularly convicted in this court of a foul murder, but upon which the sentence was set aside by his appeal to the Supreme Court, which is now pending. He is accused of, while lawfully committed to jail, having secured a pistol and killed Lawrence Keating, one of the guards, as the result of a conspiracy on the part of the prisoners to escape from custody. I want you to especially give that case your attention, and if you think an indictment should be returned, do so speedily, that he may be put on trial to answer for his crime. There are a large number of murderers confined in the jail, and in the interests of good government and humanity, you should act promptly. Something must be done to hold these characters in check.

It is not the severity of punishment but the certainty of it that checks crime nowadays. The criminal always figures on the chance of escape, and if you take that away entirely he stops being criminal. The old adage of the law, "certainty of punishment brings security," is as true today as it ever was.

You will have someone from the district attorney's office, either himself or one of his assistants, who will wait upon you, to give you advice upon questions of law, because you have a right to have information upon these matters to aid you in correctly and properly performing your duties. The district attorney, or one of his assistants, has a right to assist you in the examination of witnesses. Of course, he knows more about these cases than you can possibly know. He has become conversant with them and in that way he can render you very material aid. I desire to say to you in this connection that when you come to vote upon a proposition no one is permitted to be with you when you vote except a member of your body. The district attorney, or whichever one of his assistants may be waiting upon you at that time, will retire at that time. Nobody will be present with you. At all other times the representative of the district attorney's office has a right to be present with you to assist you in the manner I have indicated. There will be a bailiff at your door for the purpose of calling witnesses, and make you as comfortable as is possible in the room we furnish you.

Now, of course, it is your duty to proceed as fast as you can with the business before you, yet at the same time not to proceed so rapidly with it that you would overlook it, or that you would hastily indict a man without fully understanding the case, or that you would hastily ignore the charge against a man without understanding the case. See that you get all the facts in every case. If the witnesses are not all here, examine those who are here, and lay the case over until the others can be produced. You are, of course, to take up the cases first where parties desire to plead guilty before you. It is a rule of law that if a man is brought before you and is informed of the nature of the charge, and you are satisfied he understands its nature, and the consequence of pleading guilty, and the party says, when interrogated by the foreman or any other member of your body, or the representative of the district attorney's office, that he desires to plead guilty to the charge, that you can indict him upon that plea alone. You have a right under the law to do that. I would suggest that you take up these cases first, if there are any. I do not know whether there are any or not. If there are, they will be brought before you, and you will proceed with them as rapidly as you can that they may appear before the court and receive their sentences, whatever they may be. I might outline the order in which you may conduct your business, but of course I do not undertake to make it absolutely binding upon you, it being only directory, because you have necessarily to change it owing to the varying circumstances that will transpire in the course of your deliberations, but dispose first of cases where the parties are in jail—that is, if you can do so, if the witnesses are here. Next, dispose of cases where parties are upon bond. Next, where parties are not in arrest. Now, vary this order of business according to the circumstances. That is to say, if witnesses are here in cases where parties are upon bond, and are not here in cases where parties are in jail, take up the cases first where parties are on bond. If there is a case where it is urgent to get an indictment where the party has not been in arrest, proceed with his case first that he may be arrested upon your indictment returned in his case, if you return one. In other words, vary the order of business according to the circumstances, so you will be enabled to discharge the business before you as rapidly as possible.

You have a right to fix your own hours of meeting and adjournment. The court usually fixes its hour of meeting in the morning at half past eight o'clock, a recess of an hour and a half at noon, and adjourns at six o'clock in the evening. You may conform to that time, or fix other hours, just as you see fit. I say to you, make use of all the time you can in justice to your health to dispose of the business before you as promptly as possible.

In conclusion I say to you that for the time being I put the laws of the United States applicable to this jurisdiction in your hands, and I ask you to sustain them upon your part by a fair, just, impartial, and deliberate investigation in every case that comes before you. If guilt is established, you cannot help it; you must proceed to return your indictment. If guilt is not established, the man who has been charged is vindicated and you ignore the bill and so return it into court. When you proceed in this way, as you have taken your oath to proceed, and as I know you will do, you have performed your duty as good citizens and good jurors, and in such a way as to become an educating influence in the country, and at the same time to give fully the benefit of the law of the land to those who are entitled to its power as a protecting agency.

Gentlemen, you will retire to your room and proceed with your deliberations.

APPENDIX F

The Best Petit Jury Charge

On Wednesday afternoon, December 18, 1895, Judge Parker delivered the following charge to the petit jury that convicted George Wilson (James Casharego), the last man to die on the Fort Smith gallows. It was considered the masterpiece of all his numerous charges to petit juries.

Gentlemen, a moment's reflection satisfies us that in every trial of this character, there is involved one of the gravest propositions upon which depends the social happiness of men, women and children living in a state of civilized society and under a civilized government. That proposition is whether the law of the land, that rule of action which prescribes the conduct of men, when in the hands of the intelligent jurymen of the country, affords a sufficient safeguard for all the rights of the governed, and especially that highest of rights known as belonging to man—the right to life. I say, in every trial of this kind, there is involved that proposition which determines the weal or the woe of the people of this land; that proposition upon which depends the enforcement of the law of the land, the mission of which is the peace and social order and security of all innocent and law-abiding people of the nation. This being a proposition of this magnitude it can be seen at a glance that the responsibility placed upon you by the law as a part of the good people of this land, is the greatest responsibility which you are ever called upon to assume as citizens. Nothing, I say, can ever be done by you, if you perform your duties properly, which will so subserve the true interests of the people of this land. Because of the magnitude of this responsibility, because of the greatness of the issue, you are entitled to the sympathy and honest support of all good men in the faithful discharge of your duty according as you may see the right as God gives you to see it. But notwithstanding you are entitled to this sympathy, when you consider the attributes which you possess, the duty is lightened. When we but reflect for a moment that you are possessed with memories, with judgment, with reason, with the power of observation, with the knowledge of right and wrong, with a high sense of justice, a strong desire to see the right prevail, an inherent love of equal and exact justice to all under all circumstances, a reverence for the truth, and high regard for the law of the land— when you have all of these things as attributes of your nature, and as a part of the qualifications which enable you to perform rightfully, honestly and well this high duty cast upon you by the laws of your land; I say the consideration of sympathy is lessened, because when you can apply, in the discharge of this great duty, these great attributes of your nature, the duty is easier of solution, easier of performance than it would be if you did not possess them. Besides these attributes you have all Nature to aid you in your search for the truth in this case. It has been truthfully said, it has been well said, that Providence always throws a protecting shield around the innocent, and it may be as truthfully said as a corollary to that proposition, that Providence always points to the guilty as unerringly as it protects the innocent. There may be exceptions, but Nature, when properly studied by her subjects, never lies to them. They may sometimes misinterpret her on abstract questions, it may take long to understand her rightly, but when once properly understood the Almighty never lies, and Nature is but His revealed will. When He has forged a chain of circumstances around an individual, He has done it for the wisest of purposes—to protect human life, to teach those who think they have a safeguard in the secrecy which is to accompany the commission of a crime that detection is all around them, and justice is certain to overtake them. For centuries, yes, for ages, if geology be true, the lightnings had played in the heavens and men were awed and terrified from their sight. Morse came with the capacity to read their laws, and he chained them, and taught them to carry our messages of affection, our messages of fortune and misfortune, to friends thousands of miles away. When Nature is correctly read she never deceives. For centuries the blood had gone to the heart and returned again to the extremeties. For centuries physicians had dissected the human frame and had failed to discover the great law of life, that the lungs received the oxygen from the air we breathe and transmit it to the blood; that the blood thus provided with new life was sent out to feed the most remote organ, it may be said by a mechanism more delicate than human genius has ever been able to construct. Harvey came, read Nature's law aright, made the discovery, and it was no longer a mystery. And so it is with Nature everywhere. We look out of that window and see the leaves falling from the trees. The unthinking say the frost has come and killed the leaf, and so it falls. Pick it up, and examine it. At the end of the stem you find a little cavity which covered a bud that had been gradually growing and growing and crowding the little leaf off until it fell, and next spring that little bud, which will remain torpid through the cold winter, will expand with the increased heat and grow into a green leaf. These are Nature's laws which always tell the truth. These are Nature's laws which are a part of the great system of Nature, designed by its God—Nature's laws to govern the workings of Nature in their innocence, and that they may serve the purposes of man. Nature has a set of laws which apply to the criminal acts of men as well as to their innocent acts. And let us read what one of the greatest American thinkers says upon that subject:

The league between virtue and Nature engages all things to assume a hostile front to vice. The beautiful laws and substances of the world prosecute and whip the criminal. He finds that things are arranged for truth and benefit, and that there is no den in the wide world to hide a rogue. Commit a crime, and the world is made of glass. Commit a crime, and it seems as if a coat of snow fell on the ground such as revealed in the woods the track of every partridge and fox and squirrel and mole. *You cannot recall the spoken word. You cannot wipe out the foot track.* You cannot draw up the ladder so as to leave no inlet or clew. *Some damning circumstance always transpires.* The laws and substances of nature, water, snow, wind, gravitation, *become penalties to the thief.*

So I say it is true that you have Nature in her honesty, in her great purpose to subserve men, and especially to protect innocent life, to aid you in the solution of this problem, if you will but read her aright, and you can apply to her, and to her laws, these great attributes which belong to you, and which I have named, and when that application is properly made the solution of the problem of ascertaining the truth or falsity of the charge preferred against this defendant becomes, in my judgment, comparatively easy, one which is easy to solve one way or the other. You will find that by Nature's law these things which are invariably left around human action, human conduct, called circumstances, if read aright by the true law of Nature, will either always point towards innocence, and therefore it is truthfully said in the language of the book I read from that "Nature reveals innocence," or if guilt exists they will invariably point, if read aright, towards guilt. And therefore, while Nature, will all her mighty power protects innocence, she at the same time, in the interest of man, in the interest of the enforcement of the law, in the interest of the upholding of the dignity and power and supremacy of government that it may be reverenced by men and its laws obeyed by them, is equally all-powerful in uncovering guilt. Then it is that we are to solve these problems by these tracks which Nature has left around the occurrence, and which Nature permits us to read. And I say to you, in this connection, that it is but these natural things which make up what we call in the law that volume of testimony so often resorted to in the courts, called circumstantial evidence. When true, when forming a connected chain, when properly produced to the jury, it is all-powerful in its proving power as though a human agent in the shape of a living being had applied to the transaction at the time of its occurrence some one of his five senses in order that he might come here as a positive eye-witness before you and tell you of the occurrence. You see and understand that in this case, as in a large proportion of cases where human life has been taken, there is no human eye which witnessed the destruction of that life, except the eye of the author of the crime. The eye of the man who has been murdered, if murder exists, is closed in death. His tongue is silent. No one of his five senses can be used to reproduce the occurrence before you. It is true that he can be brought here with all of his gaping wounds, from which there was streaming his heart's blood, with his mangled clothing, with the bloody garments which were found near him—they can all be produced before you as inanimate circumstances upon which no influence can be exerted to induce them to tell that which is false. They are motiveless, they are inanimate, and therefore no motive can cause them to be influenced, and yet, though they be inanimate, in the language of the great poet, Shakespeare, they are made upon occasions like this to speak with wondrous power to enable you to see the truth of this case.

Now, gentlemen, it is necessary that we should proceed in detail to see what this crime as charged is, then see whether or not it exists as charged, then whether or not this defendant is the author of that crime. These are the several general propositions which make up the one asserted here by the government in this indictment. It is stated in the first count of this indictment that this defendant took the life of the man who is alleged to have been murdered, named Zachariah W. Thatch, and that he did it willfully and with malice aforethought; that he did it with a blunt instrument, a more particular description of such blunt instrument being to the grand jurors unknown; that he used that blunt instrument in such a way as to willfully and with malice aforethought destroy the life of Zachariah W. Thatch. That is the charge in the first count of the indictment. The charge in the second count of the indictment pertains to the killing of the same man, of the same name, by the same party, the defendant, George W. Wilson. It is alleged in that count of the indictment that the means used by the defendant in taking the life of Zachariah W. Thatch were unknown to the grand jury, but that he used these unknown means in such a way as to willfully and with malice aforethought destroy his life. Now, if you believe this charge to be true, as I have named it to you, then you are to designate the count in the indictment which is appropriate as the one upon which you will find your verdict. If you find, from the circumstances of this case, that it was a blunt instrument used, and its nature was unknown to the grand jury, judging from the character of the evidence here, then your appropriate finding would be upon the first count of the indictment. If you are unable, as was the grand jury, in your judgment, from the testimony here, to find beyond a reasonable doubt the nature of the instrument used, then the appropriate finding would be upon the second count of the indictment, where the instrument is alleged to have been unknown to them.

We now proceed, I say, in detail, to ascertain what propositions are necessary to be found. First, we are required to find that Zachariah W. Thatch is dead. That is the very initial point in this case. It is the point from which we start, because, if it should turn out in an investigation that a man was not dead, that stops the inquiry. We need not go any further. And by proceeding in this way there might be cases where the work could be shortened. I take up these propositions in detail because it makes it easier for you. If I were to tell you in a general way, by so many sentences, that certain things must be found, and stop there, you might overlook them when you came to make the application of the law. So we must enter into this charge in detail in order that you may the better recall the testimony bearing upon each proposition as we go along and have it fixed in your mind as to whether or not that proposition is established and established to the extent required by the law.

In ascertaining the proposition that he is dead, that inquiry necessarily involves the identity of the body found, with the dead body of Zachariah W. Thatch. Then it becomes, right at this point, a question of identity, because the government does not produce the body; the government claims that was the body of Mr. Thatch, and it is to the identity of that body that we are to confine our investigation here. Now we are to proceed to ascertain how his identity may be established, and in doing that we cannot do better than to read from the charge of the court here, delivered to the jury which tried the case of the United States versus Graves, a man tried in this court some time ago, and you will ascertain from the principles of law laid down in that charge exactly how you may ascertain that this was the body of Mr. Thatch; but you will bear in mind all the time that all these propositions I will enumerate to you in detail—the fact of the death of Thatch, involving his identity; the fact that he died by violence of the kind described in the indictment; the fact that violence was criminal, and the concluding fact that the defendant was the author of that violence, may all be established by these things called circumstances, which are a part of Nature.

This is a case like hundreds of others which occur in the administration of justice in this country where you may not be able to look upon the face of a dead man, or look into it and see that it is the face of a certain man, because the face may have been destroyed. The decaying finger of time may have touched it. It may no longer exist, and the question then becomes pertinent right here: how we are to establish the identity in this case of Thatch, how we are to ascertain that proposition. You see a man alive, with whom you are acquainted—your friend, a man you have met often; you can look into his face and from the nature of that face, its form or appearance, and its very cast, its features, its lineaments, made up of a number of things combined, you can swear, from an observation of these, to the identity of the person, from that face and from this combination of things which produces a certain appearance, and this combination, as it is illuminated by the light which comes through the windows of the soul, his expression and intelligence which exists in the human mind and which beams out over the face, you are able to know it. You can look into the face of a friend or an acquaintance and name him as a man whom you know. When a man is dead this illuminating power which is connected with the human mind, and which comes from the mind, disappears, and, necessarily, the human face, while it is preserved, until it is destroyed, only presents the general outline which it had when the person was alive. There was something about it in life which is gone forever, it is destroyed, and you will have a little more difficulty in recognizing the face of a man, although he may be an acquaintance, yet, as a general rule, you can recognize him by his face. But suppose his face is gone, the body is partially, or it may be entirely, destroyed; what then are you to do? When a man has been murdered the rights of society and the rights of its members have been thus wickedly trampled upon by a brutal assassination; are you to make no effort to discover the crime and punish the criminal because the identity of the remains of the person, by the means I have named, cannot be ascertained? Not at all. You can go to the means extraneous to the body of the person. You can, in other words, fall back upon that evidence which is so often and so generally and usually relied upon, called "circumstantial evidence," to ascertain that fact. Now, the fact to be proven under this proposition is the identity of Zachariah W. Thatch, the man alleged by the government to have been murdered. That is a proposition which, if a man would come before you and say he had looked at the dead body, he saw it, and from its face, its form, its appearance he knew it, then you could take the statements of a witness of that character as the positive statements of an eye-witness to that fact. As I have already told you, in regard to a live person, we can recognize it from a combination of things, such as the character of the nose, the appearance of the eyes, the shape of the mouth, and the general appearance and outline of the face of the party, and all these things which are illuminated by that light which comes from the soul, from the mind. When there is no opportunity of that kind, identity may be made in that way by a person having looked at and observed the man, and being able to tell what he observed at that time and to tell it to a jury. Now, in the absence of both of these opportunities, the man being dead, and thus one of the means of recognition gone, or if the face is so far decayed as that persons cannot look into that face, the inquiry naturally arises whether there are other means of identification. Mr. Burrill, an eminent writer upon the subject of circumstantial evidence, says:

> Where the body is found, shortly after the commission of the crime, and the face has not been disfigured by the violence employed, or by accident, or in the natural course of decay, the identification is made in the form of direct and positive proof of the fact by those to whom the deceased is known. But where the features have been destroyed the body may be identified by circumstances, as by the dress, articles found on the person, and by natural marks upon the person. In Colt's case, where a considerable portion of the face had been beaten in by blows—Colt was the brother of the inventor of Colt's pistols, and he murdered a man in the city of New York, mutilated him by

cutting him up, put him in a barrel, started to ship him to Charleston, or New Orleans, or some other place, and was discovered—and the progress of decay had otherwise rendered direct recognition impossible, the body was identified in this way. In McCann's case, where the face of the deceased had been eaten away by the hogs, identification was effected in a similar manner. Even where nothing but a skeleton has been found, it may sometimes be identified by peculiar marks, and by objects discovered near it. In the case of Rex versus Clews (4 Carrington & Payne, 221) the body of a man, after the lapse of twenty-three years, was identified by his widow from some peculiarity about his teeth, and by a carpenter's rule and a pair of shoes found with the remains, and also identified. But in examining skeletons, great attention should be paid to their anatomical characteristics, upon which the important fact of the age and sex of the person depends, as these may be decisive of the whole case in favor of the accused. Where the body has been purposely mutilated, and especially where it has been dismembered, with a view to its destruction, by fire or otherwise, its identification becomes a matter of greater difficulty, the head being usually destroyed first, for the very purpose of preventing recognition, but it occasionally happens that even the agency of fire, which is generally selected as the readiest and most effectual means of destruction, proves inadequate to the purpose contemplated.

Sometimes it may happen that it will not even dry up and destroy his blood.

In Webster's case, the head of the deceased had been placed in a furnace, and exposed to a strong heat for a considerable time, but some blocks of mineral teeth resisted the action of the fire so effectively that they were identified by a dentist as part of a set of artificial teeth which had been made for the deceased, and which the latter wore at the time of his disappearance. Some other portions of the body, which had not been subjected to the action of the fire, were also identified by peculiar appearances. A case is mentioned by Mr. Wills, in which the remains of a female, consisting merely of the trunk of the body, from which the other parts had been cut, were identified by a curious train of circumstantial evidence, embracing several facts of conduct on the part of the prisoner.

Mr. Wills, on circumstantial evidence, further says:

It is not necessary that the remains should be identified by direct and positive evidence, where such proof is impracticable, and especially if it has been rendered so by the action of the person accused. A man was convicted of the murder of a creditor, who had called for the payment of a debt, and whose body he cut in pieces, and attempted to dispose of by burning. The effluvium and other circumstances alarmed the neighbors, and a portion of the body remained unconsumed, sufficient to prove that it was that of a male adult, and various articles which had belonged to the deceased were found on the person of the prisoner, who was apprehended putting off from Black Rock, at Liverpool, after having ineffectually attempted to elude justice by drowning himself. The identification of human remains has been facilitated by the preservation of the head and other parts in spirits; by the anti-putrescent action of the substances used to destroy life; by the similarity of the undigested remains of food found in the stomach with the food which it has been known that the victim has eaten; by means of clothing or other articles of the deceased traced to the possession of the prisoner, and unexplained by any evidence, that he became innocently possessed of them; by means of artificial teeth and by means of other mechanical coincidences.

Mr. Wills further says upon the subject of identification:

Identification is often satisfactorily inferred from the correspondence of fragments of garments, or of written or printed papers, or of other articles belonging to or found in the possession of persons charged with crime, with other portions or fragments discovered at or near the scene of crime, or otherwise relating to the corpus delicti, or by means of wounds or marks inflicted upon the person of the offender.

I think that is sufficient upon that proposition. You are told by these cases I have referred to (and they are simply the declarations of the law which are recognized everywhere as being the law) that the identity of the remains may be proven purely by circumstances, may be proven by circumstances extraneous to the body—that is, that there are garments found which belonged to him, found upon him, or identified as his, and garments found near where the body was found, or garments or property of his, proven to be his, found in the possession of a defendant and not satisfactorily accounted for upon the theory that his possession is an innocent one. All these means, then, in this case may be used for the purpose of enabling you to come to the conclusion as to whether the body of the man found in Rock Creek, at the place described by the witnesses, was the body of Zachariah W. Thatch. If so, if these circumstances all combined, whether connected immediately with the body or extraneous of it, in your judgment, as honest, as intelligent and as just men, are sufficient to establish this proposition beyond a reasonable doubt, then you have proven the fact that Zachariah W. Thatch is dead, because that body was dead; there can be no controversy over that proposition. If that was his body, then he is dead. That is the first proposition to be established.

The next proposition to be established is, did he die by violence, either of the kind named in the first count of the indictment, or by violence exercised in such a way as that the means by which it was exercised—that is, the weapon with which death was produced—was unknown to the grand jury, and is not known to you, beyond a reasonable doubt. That is the second proposition to be established. Now, how are you to get at that? By the same method by which you may find the other one. You are to see in what condition that body was; whether or not it presented any evidence of violence. You go to the evidence and see what the condition of the skull was; whether the testimony shows to you that it was crushed or that it was broken. If so, that is a fact which would ordinarily satisfy reasonable men that that act was one which might produce the death of Thatch, that it might cause his death, and you would be justified, in the opinion of the court, in so finding. But, of course, as to what the evidence is, and as to its weight, you are to finally determine, and any suggestions which may be made by the court upon the weight of testimony are made to you with the distinct reservation to you that you are the ultimate arbiters, not only as to what the testimony is, but as to what its proving power amounts to. While the Federal courts, under the practice prevailing in them, may take up the testimony of each witness, even, and detail it to the jury, tell them in the judgment of the court what it proves, I do not do that, but if I were to do it, it is always done by leaving to you the ultimate right of passing upon that very proposition and solving it for yourselves. Then, upon this point, you look to the testimony and see from it whether or not the second requisite of this charge is established beyond a reasonable doubt.

The third proposition is, was he killed willfully, and with malice aforethought. These are the attributes of murder. In addition to the physical fact that he is dead, he must be killed in a certain way so that we are able to say, under the law, that he was murdered, that his life was taken in that wicked and wanton way defined by the laws of the United States to be murder. These attributes—that is, that it was done willfully and done with malice aforethought— are the things which go to characterize an act so that it may be named as murder. They have a legal meaning attached to them. Each expression has a legal meaning attached to it. For that reason we must stop here long enough to get that meaning, to ascertain what it is. We will inquire first, whether that killing was done willfully; we will see what is meant by that. We will then go to the method that may be adopted by you in finding that proposition. What is meant by "willful" as used in this connection? The law says it means intentional, and not accidental. That is a definition of "willful" which is remarkable for its brevity, and also for its power. It is the most powerful definition which could be given when we get in mind the strong contrast existing between a death produced by an accident and one where there has operated to produce the act which results in death the agency called the human mind. In the law a thing which is called an "accident" is something which transpires after a man has used the care exacted of him by the law to prevent its occurrence. When he does that, although human life may be destroyed, it is called an accident; it is called misadventure; it is not a crime. Whenever he uses that care which the law says he ought to use under the circumstances, considering the character of the weapon handled or being used, and the dangerous consequences which may be produced by it, you have a condition which is not willful, a condition which is outside of the domain of willfulness, and it is called a case of misadventure. Now, the opposite of that is this expression which enters into the crime of murder, known as an intentional act. It means this: If the evidence in a case shows that the act which produced death was intentionally done, because of the intimate connection between an act which will produce death known as a deadly or dangerous act and death, the law says you are authorized to find not only that the act was done intentionally but that the death was intentional, because of that connection between cause and effect, between action and result, between the deadly act and the death. Then in this case, if, from the circumstances of it, from the character of the wounds, from the fact that the skull was crushed, from the concealment of the remains, from the effort to cover up all traces of the fact of the killing, and of the manner of the killing, and from all these facts and circumstances combined which have gone to you as evidence in this case, you are able to conclude as rational men, as just men and as men loving truth, beyond a reasonable doubt that that killing was done willfully, then you may take that proposition as established, you may take it as proven in the case. You can only know it, when a murder is alleged to have been done, in secret as this is alleged to have been done, by the means of these circumstances, by these means which Nature by her great law presents to you as proven facts either to show the truth or falsity of the proposition alleged. You can only know it that way, as you can only know all the elements which enter into any and every secret crime committed as this was committed, if it was committed, in the hour of night, when no human eye except the eye of the author of the crime beheld it. You can only know it by the light of these things left around it, and which can be seen through Nature and by Nature's laws to enable you to fathom this mystery, to know the truth of this case. Then, look at the evidence. You must understand the meaning of this expression, not only because it is necessary for you to understand it as an element which enters into the crime of murder, but because if you find this to be a case where the killing was done without provocation, and therefore outside of a state of case where the law of self-defense would be applicable, or a killing in the absence of mitigating facts and therefore outside of a state of case where the law of manslaughter would be applicable, and you have a set of facts and circumstances which show that it was done willfully, done wrongfully, done illegally, you have that which establishes the other element of the crime known as "malice aforethought," which is the distinguishing characteristic of the crime of murder, that which stamps it as murder and gives it a character different from any other homicide, or from any other crime which results in death.

Let us now see how "malice aforethought" is defined. The law says that this characteristic of murder means the doing of a wrongful and illegal act in a way which is not justified or mitigated, and which act results in the taking of a human life causelessly and wickedly in such a way as to show premeditation, to show that it was thought of beforehand, to show that it was planned by its perpetrator, by its author, and that it was executed by him in pursuance of a previous purpose to take that human life. We cannot entertain a purpose to wrongfully destroy human life. We can entertain a purpose to defend ourselves and be justified in entertaining it, and we can deliberate upon it, we can premeditate upon it, but if it be a case of killing where there is nothing of that kind in it, and the killing is shown to have been wrongfully and illegally done, and the facts and circumstances show, under such a state of case, premeditation and deliberation, these are evidences of malice aforethought, because they show the existence of a state of case where human life has been destroyed in such a way as to show that it was wrongfully and illegally destroyed, without just cause, or in the absence of mitigating facts. Mr. Wharton, in Section 35 of his work upon Homicide, says:

Malice is implied from any deliberate, cruel act committed by one person against another, however sudden, as where a man kills another suddenly without any, or without considerable, provocation, and with a deadly weapon, it being a maxim based on ordinary experience that no person unless under the influence of malice would be guilty of such an act upon slight or upon no apparent cause.

Again upon this subject:

Where there is a deliberate intent to kill, unless it be in the discharge of a duty imposed by the public authorities, or in self-defense or in necessity, the offense must be murder at common law, as evidenced by the execution of the deliberate intent, wrongfully and improperly.

Further, upon the definition of malice aforethought—and I want you to observe in this connection that there is a proposition referred to which will be a little more elaborately given after a while, and which has reference to the fact that you are not required in the investigation of these cases, before you can come to a conclusion of guilt, to find the existence of a motive for the crime, or the adequacy of that motive, for if you were to stop, to hesitate and to fail to enforce the law and thus stop the wheels of justice until you could find an adequate motive for a deliberate and wicked and unprovoked killing, you never would, in the judgment of honest men and of men with pure hearts and proper minds, find a motive which was adequate, because all this world, with its riches, if it be a case where lucre was the cause, was the motive, is not a motive sufficient in the judgment of a good man to destroy an innocent human life, and therefore we never do find motives which are adequate, and if we are to wait until we do that is the end of all enforcement of the law, that is the end of all the protecting power arising from the enforcement of the law; but we are not required to do that, as you will learn further on. I read to you now from the case of Lander versus The State, upon the subject of malice aforethought:

> When the law makes use of the term "malice aforethought" as descriptive of the crime of murder, it is not to be understood merely in the sense of a principle of malevolence to particulars, but as meaning that the fact has been attended with such circumstances as are the ordinary symptoms of a wicked and malignant spirit.

It is not necessary to show that a man had special spite or hatred or ill will against the man whom he may have killed, because it very often happens that men kill when there is nothing of this kind existing. But there is another motive which prompts them. There is always a motive to cause the hand of the murderer to strike its victim. There always does exist a motive for that, but sometimes we lose it because of its inadequacy in our judgment—we overlook it sometimes. It is not necessary that that should be proven. It is not necessary that it should be shown that there was any special spite or hatred or ill will against the party slain. That sometimes exists as a motive, as a cause, and sometimes it does not; sometimes there are other reasons for the killing. A man may kill for revenge, he may kill from jealously, he may kill from a great many things from which spring special spite, or a grudge, or a state of ill will which he desires to satisfy, but there are many other reasons for a killing which are equally as wicked, and even perhaps more so, because it often happens when a man kills from ill will that he has considerable provocation. He goes too far, he exceeds his authority and takes human life. But still, when we look at the uniformity and the wickedness of the mind of men there are many things which are highly provocative in the law which are not justifiable, nor can they be mitigated, and that is a case where the man who takes human life is entitled to the greatest sympathy, if he is otherwise a good man. It often happens that this is true. But when we come to a case where a man kills for gain, for lucre, to get that which does not belong to him, we must all agree in the truthfulness of the proposition that that is a motive of the basest character, that that is a motive of the most degrading nature, showing a heart void of social duty and a mind fatally bent upon mischief. Further, upon this line:

Malice, in its legal sense, denotes a wrongful act done intentionally, without just cause or excuse. The legal import of the term, it has been said, differs from its acceptation in common conversation. It is not, as in ordinary speech, only an expression of hatred or ill will to an individual, but means any wicked or mischievous intent of the mind. Thus, in the crime of murder, which is always stated in the indictment to be committed with malice aforethought, it is neither necessary in support of such indictment to show that the person had any enmity to the deceased, nor would proof of the absence of ill will furnish the accused with any defense when it is proved that the act of killing was intentional and done without justifiable cause. Malice in law is a mere inference of law which results simply from a willful transgression of the law. It imports simply the perverse disposition of one who does an act which is unlawful without sufficient legal excuse therefor. And the precise and particular intention with which he did the act, whether he was moved by anger, hatred or a desire for gain, is immaterial. He acts maliciously in willfully transgressing the law.

Now, the other expression which denotes the meaning of malice aforethought is: The killing of a human being done in such a way as to show that he who did it had a heart void of social duty and a mind fatally bent upon mischief. That implies that the man who thus kills has forgotten the great obligation which we all owe to each other not to destroy innocent human life but to protect it. And when we do destroy it without just cause, when we do destroy it for gain, in order that we may get property, or from a spirit of vengeance, or from any other motive which stamps the killing as a crime of a high degree, and which is of a character that may be taken into account by those who pass in judgment upon the case as evidence of a malignant spirit, as evidence of a heart which is void of this duty, when the circumstances, from their wickedness, from their unprovoked character, from the fact that there is nothing shown to mitigate the act or to justify it, are in existence as evinced by the testimony, the very fact that such an act is proven shows that he who did it had a heart fatally bent upon mischief. There are degrees of crime by the law of morals, and there are degrees of crime by the laws of the land. If a crime which results in the taking of a human life is committed by lying in wait, by watching an opportunity in the darkness of the night, by taking action when the party is off his guard, such a crime is known to the law of the land as assassination, as the highest crime which can be committed which destroys human life, because it is done by taking advantage of the unsuspecting victim; the party who commits it awaits his opportunity, he takes advantage of the helpless condition of the innocent and murdered man; and it is known, I say, as assassination; it is known as a killing by lying in wait, and it is denounced by the legislatures in every State and in every civilized country as a killing which alone is murder—a killing by lying in wait, a killing by assassination.

I told you a while ago that to enable you to find the existence of malice aforethought, or that the act was done willfully, you need not stop to hunt for motive. If the motive exists, if it is proven, it becomes evidentiary in the case and you may use it. You may use it not only to enable you to characterize the killing, to show what manner of killing it was, but you have the right to use it also to bring that killing home to a particular individual charged with it, because if you can trace the connection between the motive existing in the breast or mind of a particular party as the cause which produces the deadly act, you have a fact which brings the crime home to the party who possessed that motive, and, I say, if it is manifested in a case, you are not required to look after it, you are not required to pass upon its adequacy, you may still use it as evidence in the case for the purposes I have named. Now, Mr. Wharton, that eminent author upon the subject of criminal law, in his work upon Homicide, Section 670–A, says:

> It is sometimes urged, is it likely that one man should kill another for so small an article? Are we not to infer when there is a homicide

which is followed by the stealing of a mere trifle that the homicide was the result of sudden passion rather than *lucre causa?* Or for some prejudice or spite is it likely that one man would assassinate another, and thus expose himself to the gallows? No doubt, when a tender mother kills her child or a friend kills a friend, and nothing more than the fact of killing is proved, we may be led to infer misadventure or insanity from the motivelessness of the act. But we have no right to make such an inference because the motive is disproportionate. We are all of us apt to act upon very inadequate motives, and the history of crime shows that murders are generally committed from motives comparatively trivial. A man unaccustomed to control his passions, and unregulated by religious or moral sense, exaggerates an affront or nourishes a suspicion until he determines that only the blood of the supposed offender can relieve the pang. Crime is rarely logical. Under a government where the laws are executed with ordinary certainty, all crime is a blunder, as well as a wrong. If we should hold that no crime is to be punished except such as is rational, then there would be no crime to be punished, *for no crime can be found that is rational.* The motive is never correlative to the crime, never accurately proportioned to it. Nor does this apply solely to the very poor. Very rich men have been known to defraud others even of trifles, to forge wills, to kidnap and kill, so that an inheritance might be theirs. When a powerful passion seeks gratification it is no extenuation that the act is illogical, for when passion is once allowed to operate reason loosens its restraints.

There is the germ from which springs this bloody crime which results in the death of innocent human beings—unbridled passion— a desire for gain—a mind which has never been regulated by that high moral sense which governs honest men, a mind which is not prompted by that spirit of amity and good fellowship which causes a good man to love another as his brother. That is all out of the mind. He may be shrewd, he may be quick-witted, in some respects, he may be sagacious, but when he becomes a criminal by assassination, by killing another in an unprovoked way, in the darkness of night, he does it because he is entirely void of moral nature; he has not that principle of right imbedded in his mind which teaches him the difference between right and wrong, and that is the secret of the commission of a crime committed in that way. A little further upon the subject of "motive," reading from the charge of Judge

Landon in the Billings trial, a noted case in the State of New York, where he said:

> I speak first of motive. No man commits a crime without some motive leading him to commit it. That motive may seem to be strong or weak. You are not to inquire whether the motive is one that would ordinarily lead to the commission of the crime charged. It is difficult for the mind that is fortified by the consciousness of its own rectitude to conceive of an adequate motive for any crime. No motive will lead an entirely just man to the commission of any crime. You could not be moved to take the life of your fellow-man except in the just defense of your own lives and rights, or the just defense of the lives and rights of those whom it is your duty to defend. But just defense is no crime. You may, however, properly inquire what motives usually lead men to the commission of crimes, and you will find where mens' consciences and morals are depraved they are often led into the gravest of crimes by the simplest of motives. A small sum of money, a word spoken in anger or insult, wrongs real or imaginary, revenge, jealousy, hatred, envy and malice often lead to the crime of murder.

We find that any one of these may become the mainspring of high crimes of this nature.

A word or two further as to how you may find this distinguishing trait of murder known as "malice aforethought." I have already told you that you may find it, as well as other propositions in the case, from the circumstances surrounding that case. I will add to that by saying that you must find it in that way if you are to find it at all, because it is a condition of the mind, just like "willfully." You cannot know a mental condition except by the light of circumstances. No human power has ever devised any scheme by which we can apply to the working of the human mind directly or immediately any one of the five senses. You cannot touch it, you cannot taste it, you cannot feel it, you cannot hear it, you cannot smell it; therefore, there is no direct method of understanding the movements of the mind, but we are to bear in mind all the time that by law and by logic it is a legitimate method to reason from effect to cause, or from cause to effect, and when you have an effect produced, when you have a dead body presenting marks of deadly violence, you are to gather up all the circumstances connected with that death, if you find that to be the condition as an effect, and to reason back to the

cause of it. If it is an act which evidences that it was done deliberately, done because the mind dictated it should be done, and not
done accidentally, then we have that which shows the existence of
premeditation, of thought of beforehand, and consequently that
which shows malice aforethought. We may take into consideration all
the facts showing the time of the killing, the manner of the killing,
the concealment of the fact of death, or the attempt to conceal it by
placing the body under water and putting logs upon it, the attempt
to obliterate evidences of the death—all these things are pertinent
facts, pertinent circumstances surrounding the transaction to show,
first, that a killing occurred, and to show it was a crime, and to show
that it had connected with it this attribute of murder known as
"malice aforethought." We may resort to all these circumstances
for that purpose as means which we must use if we are to get at
the proposition as to whether the killing was one which was murder
or not, because, as I have already told you, you cannot know it in
any other way.

There are but few more things to be said by the court in this case.
You are to bear in mind that there are just two general propositions
entering into your verdict, the truth of the case and the principle
of the law applicable to that truth. I have given to you the language
of the law defining this crime of murder charged in this indictment.
Then the question becomes pertinent upon my part to ask you
whether or not, in your judgment, the proposition asserted in this
indictment has been so proven, as under the principles of the law
which I will give you in a moment, the crime of murder has been
established. If that is the truth of the case, then the principle of
the law applicable to that truth is that which defines the crime which
tells you what is murder. In that way you get at a rational result;
in that way you arrive at what is called your true speech, your very
dictum—your verdict. Every proclamation which you make here in
the shape of a verdict has involved in it and interwoven with it, I
say, the law of the case which is applicable to the truth of it as you
find it by your judgment and by your consciences.

Now we come to the point where I am to remind you, as I have
already, but I remind you again, that your certain duty is to find
out what the truth of the case is as ascertained by you from the
evidence which has been offered before you. As we so often remark,

it is impossible to reproduce actually and really this occurrence, or to reproduce it as it would be reproduced upon a stage. It is a drama which cannot be presented to a jury in that way. The bloody drama can only be seen by the light of the testimony which illuminates it, which lights it up, so you are able, as honest, conscientious, and intelligent men, of judgment and reason and memory, having a desire to arrive at the truth, to see to it by the light of these circumstances which are brought here as witnesses and offered before you in this case. Then let us go over again the general propositions necessary to be found. First, you are to find whether the man alleged to have been killed is dead, and in passing upon that you are to take into consideration all of these circumstances surrounding it, and whether he was killed in such a way as to make the crime murder. Then when we come to the proposition as to the guilt or innocence of the defendant you are to ascertain whether by the light of this testimony he had the means at hand to produce this deadly result, and, secondly, whether he had the opportunity to produce it. Then what are the circumstances in the case pointing to the guilt or innocence of the defendant. All these facts and circumstances you have a right to take into consideration; you have a right to have them all pass in review again and again, if necessary, when you come to consider the case in your jury room, in order that you may the better see whether guilt or innocence exists here. Every item of testimony is to be considered, not by itself alone, because some of it may be very insignificant when considered alone, but when considered in conjunction with other facts, when considered as a link going to make up the chain of evidence, it may have great proving power, it may have great weight as a fact in the case. Then it is your duty to see what presumptions you can legitimately draw from the facts and circumstances in this case. The law says that if a man has been killed, and killed in such a way as to show it was done murderously under the law I have given you defining the crime of murder, then you are to look to see whether the party accused of the killing was found in possession of any of the property of the man killed. If so, that is the foundation of presumption; it is not conclusive in the beginning, but it is a presumption which you are to look at just as you would look at it as reasonable men outside of the jury box. The party so found in possession of such property, recently after the crime, is required to account for it, to show that as far as he was concerned that possession was innocent, and was honest. If it is accounted for in that way, then it ceases to be the foundation for a presumption. If it is not accounted for in that satisfactory, straightforward and truthful way that would stamp it as an honest accounting, then it is the foundation for a presumption of guilt against the defendant in this case, just upon the same principle as if a certain man is charged with robbery or larceny, and is found in the possession of the property stolen or robbed, recently after the crime, he is called upon to explain that possession. If his explanation of it is truthful, if it is consistent, if it is apparently honest, if it is not contradictory, if it is the same at all times, if it has the *indicia* of truth connected with it, that may cause to pass out of the case the consideration of the presumption arising from the possession of the property, but if it is not explained in that way it becomes the foundation of a presumption against the party who is thus found in possession of that property. Now, that is not the only foundation for a presumption, but you take into consideration the very appearance of this property, whether there were bloodstains upon it indicating that there was blood of some kind there, and if so whether that fact has been satisfactorily explained by the defendant in this case. If not, whether in your judgment there is that in these numerous bloodstains upon these clothes, bedclothing and found upon the straw in that bed, whether or not that fact, if it has not been satisfactorily explained, is a fact upon which you may base a presumption that there was an act of deadly violence perpetrated while the party was upon these bedclothes, or while he was connected with them in such a way as that the blood was the blood of the murdered man, or the missing man. Now, another foundation of a presumption is the fact of his false statements. You understand that Nature, in her bountiful provision, has given to man a set of rules by which he may know the truth above all other things that rule, which underlies all nature, and which comes from the same source that this state of nature comes, which has its abiding place in the very breast of God Himself, because God is truth—the truth. *The truth is the same yesterday, today, tomorrow and forever.* If a man makes a statement to you today about a transaction which is one thing, and details to you another one tomorrow which is something else, and another again which is something else, you necessarily call upon him to explain why he has made these contradictory statements, because you know they are not the attributes of truth, you know they do not belong to the truth, because the highest attribute which it possesses is harmony, its consistency, and it possesses these attributes at all times, whether it is spoken in the stillest and smallest voice with which it can be uttered, or whether it is heard in the thunders of the clouds, or in the roar of the waters of the ocean, or in the voice of the mighty earthquake, it is still the voice of truth and the voice of Nature, *and it speaks the same at all times,* and it has always attending it that which stamps it as true. Therefore, if statements in this case before you which are false were made by the defendant, or upon his side of the case, if they were made by his instigation, and knowingly instigated by him, you have a right to take into consideration the falsehoods of the defendant, to see whether they are falsehoods. Then you are to look at them to see whether he satisfactorily explains to you the making of those false statements, and if he does not they are the foundation of a presumption against him for the reasons I have given you, because they are not in harmony with Nature, they are not in harmony with truth, they do not speak the voice of truth, they speak the voice of falsehood, they speak the voice of fraud, they speak the voice of crime, they are not in harmony with that great law which in all of its parts is consistent and harmonious. Then look to these statements and view them, not alone, but in connection with the other circumstances in the case, all the other circumstances which have gone before you as evidence, to see whether or not the conduct which is urged by the government as accusatory, as inculpatory, has been satisfactorily explained by the defendant upon the theory of his innocence. If so, then that conduct passes away as proving facts in the case; it is no longer the foundation as proving facts; but if these explanations are not satisfactory, if they are not in harmony with the truth, the presumption must remain in the case and you have a right to draw that inference from these circumstances I have named.

In passing upon the credibility of the evidence you consider the relation the witnesses bear to the case, their interest in it—not because they exhibit zeal in hunting up the evidence as to whether a crime had been committed or not, for that is commendable, that is the duty of every citizen, and if all of us performed it in all circumstances as we ought to, crime would virtually disappear in the country; and when witnesses exhibit zeal, when they exhibit energy, when they exhibit enterprise in gathering up all the circumstances and *minutiae* which surrounds a case, they are entitled to the commendation of all. That does not show an interest which would create any undue bias in the judgment of the law against any man who might testify. If a man is related to the case, however, so as to be affected by the result of it directly or immediately, that is a condition which you are to necessarily look at, because we are all largely creatures of self-interest. If that self-interest is great, if it involves the result which may deprive us of life, it is the greatest which can ever confront us. If that is the condition, in passing upon the testimony of such a witness we are to view that evidence in the light of that condition, not that we are to necessarily exclude the testimony because of that condition, but we are to apply this self-evident principle which is applicable to all of us, that when we are so situated we are more apt to testify so as to benefit ourselves than to testify against ourselves, or even to keep along the strict line of truth. We are more apt to wander from that line when there is that condition confronting us than if we are entirely disinterested. Such testimony is to be looked at in the face of that condition, and above all things in the face of the other facts and circumstances. The defendant goes upon the witness stand in this case, and you are to view his evidence in the light of his relation to the case in the way I have named, and in addition thereto you are to look at all the other facts and circumstances in the case as bearing upon his evidence to see whether it contradicts what he says, and therefore weakens it; whether it is so as to be contradictory and inconsistent from statements made by him at other times; whether it is shown to lack these elements of truthfulness known as rationality, consistency, naturalness; whether these things are all absent from it, and whether, in your judgment, it seems to be consistent and probable in itself when you come to look at the story and listen to it and weigh it by your judgment. If it has these attributes they are evidences of its being true; if it hasn't them, but has the opposite, this opposite condition made up of these circumstances is an evidence of its being false.

The law says it is your duty in the investigation of these cases to gather up all the accusatory facts, see what their combined proving power is, and if it is equal to the testimony of one positive, credible, uncontradicted eye-witness, then you proceed further in the case to see whether that condition is destroyed or broken down or eliminated from the case by the testimony which is exonerating in its nature, which goes to show innocence. If it is not, then the condition remains as one that sufficiently proves the case. That does not mean that you have to have a witness of that kind before you can convict a man, that you have to have a man who stood by and saw this act of deadly violence committed. That is impossible in a majority of cases. But it means that the facts and circumstances left around that occurrence, under Nature's laws, are equal in proving power to what would be the testimony of one such witness. When there is that amount of evidence in the case the law says the case is established beyond reasonable doubt, and when it is proven in that way guilt is established, and conviction of that guilt is a matter of solemn and imperative duty under your consciences and your oaths.

Now, what is meant by that proposition? When we have given that to you we are done; we have submitted the case to you, we have passed it to your judgments, we have placed it in your hands that you may deliberate upon it, that you may discharge this great and solemn duty which I told you in the beginning, rests upon you as the highest duty, the greatest responsibility ever cast upon any citizen of this proud government. I say, it is to be proven beyond a reasonable doubt. Not absolutely demonstrated, because the law recognizes that you cannot demonstrate a proposition growing out of human conduct. It is impossible to do that. The law does not exact of you, in the performance of this great duty, impossibilities. It does not command you with one voice to uphold the dignity and power and supremacy of this mighty protecting agency called the law of the land, and at the same time make it impossible for you to do so. It permits you to do it in a possible and reasonable way. Now, to what degree of certainty, then, must the several propositions making up this crime be established? First, the proposition of the law, which is an axiom, supposes that all men, when they enter upon the trial of a case are clothed with the presumption of innocence, which presumption surrounds all of us, just as does the presumption of sanity. The law, from public policy, for the encouragement of the good and the discouragement of vice, holds out to all mankind that men are innocent. It does not always hold that out, because if it did there would be no crimes existing, no matter what the conduct of men might be, but it declares when a man is charged with a crime that he is panoplied by this presumption of innocence, and it further declares that that presumption remains with him until the proof in the case drives it out of the case. The proof in the case does destroy it, does drive it out, when it carries the propositions making up the crime to a point where you are able to say, as reasonable men, that you have an abiding conviction to a moral certainty of the truth of the charge, or so it is established that there is no longer confronting the conclusion a doubt for which a good reason can be given. In other words, if all doubts are driven out of the case for which good reasons can be given, no other doubts are to be paid any attention to, we are not to consider them for a moment, because they exist as confronting every human proposition. Men doubt the existence of the Deity. They sometimes are so skeptical that they doubt their own existence. There are so many doubting Thomases in the world that they will not even believe a proposition when it is proven absolutely. Well, of course, that is not the deliberate mind, that is not the reasonable mind. The reasonable mind is the one which takes into consideration deliberately and dispassionately and coolly all the proving facts and all the disproving facts, and whenever that mind is brought to a condition that its possessor is able to say he is satisfied with the truth of the charge, that it is proven to that degree of certainty that he willingly and readily believes it, and will take whatever action upon that belief that duty calls upon him to take, it is then established as such propositions are usually required to be established by reasonable men, and that is the test, that is the source of the rule. I will read to you, briefly, the opinion of the Supreme Court upon this proposition, commenting upon the charge of the court in the case of Haupt versus Utah, where a man was upon trial for murder, and where the court below gave this charge to the jury:

The court charges you that the law presumes the defendant innocent until proven guilty beyond a reasonable doubt; that if you can reconcile the evidence before you upon any reasonable hypothesis consistent with the defendant's innocence you should do so, and in that case find him not guilty. You are further instructed that you cannot find the defendant guilty unless from all the evidence you believe him guilty beyond a reasonable doubt. The court further charges you that a reasonable doubt is a doubt based on reason, and which is reasonable in view of all the evidence, and if from an impartial consideration of all the evidence you can candidly say you are not satisfied of the defendant's guilt, you have a reasonable doubt. But if after such impartial comparison and consideration of all the evidence you can truthfully say that you have an abiding conviction of the defendant's guilt, *such as you would be willing to act upon in the more weighty and important matters relating to your own affairs,* you have no reasonable doubt. It is difficult to conceive what amount of conviction would leave the mind of a juror free from a reasonable doubt if it be not one which is so settled and fixed as to control his action in the more weighty and important matters relating to his own affairs. Out of the domain of the exact sciences and actual observation there is no absolute certainty. The guilt of the accused in a majority of criminal cases must necessarily be deducted from a variety of circumstances leading to proof of the fact. Persons of speculative minds may in almost every such case suggest possibilities of the truth being different from that established by the most convincing proof. The jurors are not to be led away by speculative notions as to such possibilities. In the case of the Commonwealth versus Webster, the Supreme Judicial Court of Massachusetts said in its charge, that it was not sufficient to establish a probability, though a strong one, arising from the doctrine of chances, that the fact charged against the prisoner was more likely to be true than the contrary, and said:

"The evidence must establish the truth of the fact to a reasonable and moral certainty, a certainty that convinces and directs the understanding and satisfies the reason and judgment of those who are bound to act conscientiously upon it. This we take to be proof beyond reasonable doubt. It is simple, and as a rule to guide the jury is as intelligible to them generally as any that could be given with reference to the conviction they should have of the defendant's guilt to justify a verdict against him. In many cases, especially where the case is at all complicated, some explanation or illustration of the rule may aid in its full and just comprehension. As a matter of fact, it has been the general practice in this country of courts holding criminal trials to give such explanation or illustration. The rule may be, and often is, rendered obscure by attempts at definition which serve to create doubts instead of removing them, but an illustration like the one given in this case by reference to the conviction upon which the jurors would act in the weighty and important concerns of life, would be likely to aid them to a right conclusion when an attempted definition might fail. If the evidence produced be of such a convincing character that they would unhesitatingly be governed by it in such weighty and important matters they may be said to have no reasonable doubt respecting the guilt or innocence of the accused, notwithstanding the uncertainty that attends all human evidence."

The instruction in the case before us is as just a guide to practical men as can well be given, and if it were open to criticism it could not have misled the jury when considered in connection with the further charge, that if they could reconcile the evidence with any reasonable hypothesis consistent with the defendant's innocence they should do so, and in that case find him not guilty. The evidence must satisfy the judgment of the jurors as to the guilt of the defendant so as to exclude any other reasonable conclusion. The instruction is not materially different from that given by Lord Tenterden as repeated and adopted by Chief Baron Pollock in the case of Rex versus Muller. "I have heard," said the Chief Baron, addressing the jury, "the late Lord Tenterden frequently lay down a rule which I will pronounce to you in his own language:

"It is not necessary that you should have a certainty which does not belong to any human transaction whatever. *It is only necessary that you should have that certainty with which you would transact your own most important concerns in life.* No doubt the question before you today, involving, as it does, the life of the prisoner at the bar, must be admitted to be of the highest importance, but you are only required to have that degree of certainty with which you decide upon and conclude your own most important transactions in life. To require more would be really to prevent the repression of crime, which is the object of criminal courts to effect."

Gentlemen, that is the definition of the degree of certainty you are to arrive at in this case before you find the defendant guilty. When you have arrived at it, as sensible men, as just men, I say to you, under the law it is your duty to find the defendant guilty, and to specify in your verdict under which count you find him guilty. If you do not arrive at that conclusion to that degree of certainty, it is equally your duty to pronounce him not guilty. I say to you, in conclusion, as I said to you in the beginning, that the very power and majesty of this government and this law is in your hands in every case as a part of the people of this land. You represent them, and you represent the whole of them, to see to it that the maxim, (while it is not there in burning letters, it has been pronounced as existing in this court, and as engraven over its doors) that *no guilty man shall escape and no innocent man shall be punished,* shall be verified in this case, as it should be in every case. You will find forms upon the back of the indictment. I submit the case to you. I ask you to pronounce your solemn, your just, and your impartial judgment, as good men and good citizens and good jurors, upon this case.

You will retire to make up your verdict.

NOTES

NOTES

CHAPTER I
1. *U.S. Statutes at Large*, XVI, 47.
2. *Records of Disposition of Cases*, 1872–1873, United States Court for the Western District of Arkansas.
3. S. W. Harman, *Hell on the Border; He Hanged Eighty-Eight Men*, 195.

CHAPTER II
1. *Laws of the U.S.*, IX, 128–129.
2. *Ibid.*, Sec. 1.
3. *Ibid.*, Sec. 24.
4. *Ibid.*, Sec. 25.
5. *U.S. Statutes at Large*, V, 379.
6. *Ibid.*
7. *Ibid.*, VI, 594.
8. J. Fred Patton, *The History of Fort Smith, Arkansas,* publication of Fort Smith Chamber of Commerce.
9. The promontory stood thirty feet about the water and completely commanded both rivers. It was about one hundred yards west of the present Arkansas-Oklahoma boundary. It had been named by French hunters and traders, who made it a favorite stopping place as they

journeyed up the Arkansas in the early days, trading jackknives, glass beads, and other trinkets to the Indians for furs. (William Brown Morrison, *Military Posts and Camps in Oklahoma*, pp. 15–16.)

10. This fort consisted of a stockade formed of heavy square timbers driven closely together in the ground, with wooden blockhouses and a sufficient number of outer buildings for barracks and officers' quarters. The buildings were arranged to form a hollow square and the blockhouses set at opposite angles, facing the river. (John H. Reynolds, *Municipal Offices*, publication of Arkansas Historical Association, Vol. I.)

11. Patton, *op. cit.*

12. *Laws of the U.S.*, IX, 337.

13. *Ibid.*, 838.

14. Harman, *op. cit.*, pp. 26–28.

15. *Ibid.*

16. Dallas T. Herndon, *The High Lights of Arkansas History*, pp. 86–87.

17. John C. VanTramp, *Prairie and Rocky Mountain Adventures, or, Life in the West*, p. 510.

18. Patton, *op. cit.*

19. *U.S. Statutes at Large*, IX, 594.

20. *Ibid.*, X, 269.

21. *Official Records of the Rebellion*, I, Sec. 1, 682.

22. Herndon, *op. cit.*, p. 102.

23. Morrison, *op. cit.*, p. 24.

24. *Ibid.*

25. *Arkansas Gazette*, January 20, 1860.

26. *U.S. Statutes at Large*, XVI, 47.

27. Harman, *op. cit.*, pp. 70–71.

28. *Common Law Records of the United States Court for the Western District of Arkansas*, IV, 1–117.

29. Letter from Attorney General George H. Williams, dated June 27, 1874. (Filed November 9, 1874, Book of Records IV, 1874, 426.)

30. On September 8, 1865, commissioners of the United States government met delegations from the several tribes at Fort Smith. The Indians were informed that all their rights under previous treaties had been forfeited and advised the terms under which they could be restored to proper relations with the federal government. In the spring of 1866, at Washington, commissioners of the United States government negotiated treaties with delegates of the Five Civilized Tribes. The Seminole treaty was ratified July 19, 1866; the Treaty of Chickasaws and Choctaws ratified June 28, 1866; Creek treaty ratified July 19, 1866; and the Cherokee treaty July 19, 1866. (*U.S. Statutes at Large*, XIV, 755–785.)

31. Edward Everett Dale, *Cow Country*, p. 32.

32. J. H. Beadle, *Western Wilds and The Men Who Redeem Them*, pp. 194–211.

33. Under the Intercourse Law no person was permitted to reside or trade in the Indian country without a license from the Superintendent

of Indian Affairs, or his agents. To secure a license the applicant was required to post a penal bond not to exceed $5000, to be secured by one or more sureties, and a new license was required every three years. Only citizens of the United States could secure a license, and foreigners were required to secure a permit from the President of the United States. Any person attempting to reside in the Indian country and trade without a license was to be fined $500 and forfeit his merchandise to the government. (*Laws of the United States*, IX, 129.)

34. Dallas T. Herndon, *Centennial History of Arkansas*, I, 924.
35. May 3, 1873.
36. May 17, 1873.
37. February 11, 1875.
38. *Ibid.*
39. August 21, 1873.
40. August 28, 1873.

CHAPTER III

1. Fay Hempstead, *History of Arkansas*, I, 29.
2. *Ibid.*, p. 28.
3. Married December 12, 1861.
4. William S. Speer mg. ed., *The Encyclopedia of the New West*, pp. 28–29.
5. Hempstead, *op. cit.*, p. 461.
6. *Ibid.*
7. Speer, *op. cit.*
8. James A. Garfield was chairman of this committee. He later became President of the United States; William Wheeler, Vice-President; William Hale, of Maine, declined the appointment as Postmaster General under President Grant; James N. Tyner accepted the position and later became assistant Attorney General for the Post Office Department; and Isaac C. Parker became known throughout the world as "The Hanging Judge" of Fort Smith, Arkansas.
9. Speer, *op. cit.*
10. *Cherokee Advocate*, December 21, 1872.
11. *Ibid.*
12. Harry P. Daily, *Judge Isaac C. Parker*, address at the thirty-fifth annual meeting of the Bar Association of Arkansas, 1932.
13. Hempstead, *op. cit.*, p. 460.
14. Dallas T. Herndon, *Centennial History of Fort Smith*, p. 898.
15. R. H. Mohler, *City of Fort Smith*, p. 108.
16. The Fort Smith *Herald*, founded in 1852 and purchased by Frank Parks in 1870; the *Independent;* the *Thirty-Eighth Parallel*, edited by George M. Turner; the *New Era*, edited by Valentine Dell, later to become United States Marshal. And there were others that existed for only short periods. The *Elevator* was established in 1878, and the *Times* founded in 1882. The most prominent during Judge Parker's term was the

Elevator, and in the latter years this newspaper carried rather full and detailed accounts of the court's work, of the condemned's crimes, and of the hangings.

17. Daily, *op. cit.*

18. *Western Independent,* April 8, 1875.

19. *Oklahoma Star,* November 23, 1874.

20. *Rev. St., Chap. I, Sec. 533,* forty-third Congress, 1873–74.

21. Benton, Washington, Crawford, Scott, Polk, Franklin, Johnson, Madison, Carroll, Sevier, Sebastian, Fulton and Boone.

22. Phillips, Crittenden, Mississippi, Craighead, Greene, Randolph, Cross, St. Francis, Monroe, Woodruff, Jackson, Independence, Izard, Poinsett, Marion, Sharp, and Lawrence.

23. Harman, *op. cit.,* p. 44.

24. Wheeler was described by Fort Smith newspapers as "a man of few words, who made very little outward show of whatever he saw, felt or did, but a kinder, more generous heart never beat in a human bosom." He was a native of New York. He had gone west in 1858 and settled in southern Michigan, where he enlisted in the Federal Army, September 1, 1861. He had served as a private, sergeant, first lieutenant, and captain in the engineers, infantry, and cavalry branches of the service, and fought in the battles of Pea Ridge, Prairie Grove, and Newtonia, Arkansas, and in Missouri and Louisiana, under Generals Frémont, Blunt, and Steel. After the war he had settled at Powhatan, Arkansas, where he was appointed assistant assessor of internal revenue, assessor, and later collector. He had edited a newspaper at DeVall's Bluff in 1869, but resigned to become quartermaster general of militia with the rank of brigadier general. At the state Republican convention in 1872 he received the nomination for senator from Arkansas and Prairie counties but declined to run. Instead he ran for the office of state auditor and was elected. When his term expired in 1875, he moved to Fort Smith and was appointed clerk of the Fort Smith Federal Circuit Court for the Eighth Judicial Circuit and clerk of the United States Criminal Court for the Western District of Arkansas.

25. *Records of the United States District Court for the Western District of Arkansas,* 1875–1897.

26. List of United States Marshals for the Western District of Arkansas succeeding Marshal Sarber, giving their names, the President by whom appointed, and date of commissions:

James F. Fagan	Grant	July 2, 1874
D. P. Upham	Grant	July 10, 1876
Valentine Dell	Hayes	June 15, 1880
Thomas Boles	Arthur	Feb. 20, 1882
John Carroll	Cleveland	May 21, 1886
Jacob Yoes	Harrison	Jan. 29, 1890
George J. Crump	Cleveland	May 29, 1893 to
		June 1, 1897

27. At one term of court he prosecuted eighteen men for murder and convicted fifteen of them. "His success," Judge Parker said of him when he left office in 1893, "is attributable to close application, indomitable energy and tireless perserverance. As a lawyer, he was a very close, shrewd and prudent examiner of witnesses." His record was surpassed by no other prosecutor of his day and time.

28. Harman, *op. cit.,* pp. 71–72; also Anna L. Dawes, *Lend A Hand,* pp. 1–4.

29. See Appendix A, "Chronology of Hangings."

30. See Appendix A, "Chronology of Hangings."

CHAPTER IV

1. *Fort Smith Elevator,* May 8, 1896.

2. *Attorney General Report,* 1885, p. 14.

3. Harry P. Daily, *op. cit.*

4. Angie Debo, *Tulsa: from Creek Town to Oil Capital,* p. 74.

5. Emmett Dalton, *When the Daltons Rode,* p. 59.

6. Harry P. Daily, *op. cit.*

7. Tulsa *World,* February 3, 1936, article "Lookout Tower on Bald Hill"; Tulsa *World,* August 20, 1933, article "A Hill Perpetuates Belle Starr's Memory"; also Harman, *op. cit.,* pp. 304–305.

8. *Indian Champion,* July 5, 1884.

9. *Indian Champion,* June 21, 1884.

10. *Elevator,* August 3, 1888.

11. *Ibid.,* October 26, 1888.

12. *Elevator,* January 18, 1889.

13. *Indian Chieftain,* May 26, 1892.

14. *Elevator,* August 4, 1893.

15. *Indian Champion,* June 21, 1884.

16. *Elevator,* November 26, 1886.

17. *Ibid.,* August 3, 1888.

18. *Ibid.,* March 25, 1887.

19. *Ibid.,* April 6, 1888.

20. August 15, 1879.

21. November 30, 1875.

22. See Note 26, Chapter III.

23. John Carroll had been a resident of Arkansas since 1865. He was born in Virginia, spent the early years of his life in the old Cherokee Nation east of the Mississippi, came west with the Cherokees, and settled at Fort Gibson, where he married a fullblood Cherokee woman in 1858. In that year he moved to Missouri. When the war broke out, he joined the Confederate Army. He served throughout the war, participating in numerous battles, and was discharged with the rank of colonel. He had served in the Arkansas legislature and in the constitutional convention of 1874 before becoming United States Marshal.

24. *Tucker v United States,* 151 U.S. 164, 14 Sup. Ct. 299.

310—NOTES

25. Harry P. Daily, *op. cit.*
26. Orpheus McGee, Aaron Wilson, William Leach, Isham Seely, Gibson Ishtonnubbee. (See Appendix A, "Chronology of Hangings.")
27. *Western Independent.*
28. John Valley, Osee Sanders, Sinker Wilson, Samuel Peters. (See Appendix A, "Chronology of Hangings.")
29. John Postoak, James Diggs. (See Appendix A, "Chronology of Hangings.")
30. William Elliott alias Colorado Bill, Henri Stewart. (See Appendix A, "Chronology of Hangings.")
31. George W. Padgett, William Brown, Patrick McGowan, Amos and Abler Manley. (See Appendix A, "Chronology of Hangings.")
32. Edward Fulsom, Robert Massey. (See Appendix A, "Chronology of Hangings.")
33. Martin Joseph, William Finch, Tualisto. (See Appendix A, "Chronology of Hangings.")
34. Thomas Thompson, John Davis, Jack Woman Killer. (See Appendix A, "Chronology of Hangings.")
35. William Phillips. (See Appendix A, "Chronology of Hangings.")
36. James Arcene, William Parchmeal. (See Appendix A, "Chronology of Hangings.")
37. *Records of the United States District Court for the Western District of Arkansas,* 1875–1885.
38. *Attorney General Report,* 1889, p. 22.
39. *Laws of the U.S.,* XIX, 230.
40. Harman, *op. cit.,* p. 45.
41. Harry P. Daily, *op. cit.*
42. Harman, *op. cit.,* pp. 72–74.
43. *Attorney General Report,* 1884, p. 150.
44. December 25, 1885.
45. *Attorney General Report,* 1885, p. 30.
46. *Ibid.,* 1886, p. 20.

CHAPTER V.

1. Wayne Gard, *Frontier Justice,* p. 288.
2. *Ibid.,* p. 285.
3. *Indian Chieftain,* January 8, 1877.
4. *Elevator,* July 29, 1887.
5. Harry P. Daily, *op. cit.*
6. *Cherokee Advocate,* March 6, 1895.
7. *Cherokee Advocate,* June 2, 1882.
8. *U.S. Statutes at Large,* XIV, 236.
9. *Indian Journal,* March 1, 1888; also *Federal Reporter,* "Cherokee Nation v. Southern Pacific," XXII, 900. (Reversed on a procedural matter, 135 U.S. 641, 34 L. ed. 295, 10 S. Ct. 965, but affirmed by the Supreme Court on the main principle involved.)

10. Carl Coke Rister, *Land Hunger: David L. Payne and His Oklahoma Boomers,* pp. 90–91.

11. *Indian Journal,* March 3, 1881; also *Federal Reporter,* "United States v. David L. Payne," VIII, 883–96.

Payne was arrested again in 1883 (*Indian Chieftain,* September 21, 1883) and brought to trial before Judge C. G. Foster in the district court at Topeka, Kansas, on four charges of "conspiracy against the Government in attempt to settle the Oklahoma country." See *Federal Reporter,* "United States v. Payne et al," XXII, 426–27.

12. Parker said so again in 1885, when Connell Rogers, clerk in the Union Agency at Muskogee, accompanied the military in the summer of 1884, arrested Payne, and burned his Rock Falls settlement in the Outlet. Rogers was indicted in the United States Court at Wichita for arson. He was placed under arrest by Marshal Boles of the Western District of Arkansas, and the United States Attorney in Kansas applied for a writ of removal in order to try him in Wichita. Judge Parker issued a writ of habeas corpus, held Rogers for investigation as to the jurisdiction of the Kansas court, placed him under bond of $1000, and sent him home. (*Indian Journal,* January 8, 1885.)

13. *Indian Chieftain,* November 19, 1896.

14. *Ibid.*

15. *Elevator,* February 25, 1887.

16. Document, Office of the Secretary of State, signed S. P. Hughes, Governor of Arkansas, January 29, 1887.

17. *Elevator,* March 18, 1887.

18. *Ibid.,* November 26, 1886.

19. Harry P. Daily, *op. cit.*

20. *Ibid.*

21. Address of President John Rogers in the published report of the Fort Smith School Board, 1896–1897.

22. Harman, *op. cit.,* p. 90.

23. For example, from the Congressional Record we get the following statement of the work done in the United States Court for the Western District of Arkansas for one year, November 1, 1882, to November 1, 1883:

> The grand total (all crimes) foots up 588, of which 388 were convicted, 55 acquitted, 18 in which nolle prosequi was entered, 47 ignored and 20 forfeited their bond.
>
> Mistrials by jury during the year. 7
>
> Number of applications for witness in behalf of defendant at U.S. expenses and acted on. 143
>
> Number of witnesses recognized in open court. 575
>
> Number of murder cases tried by jury. 20
>
> Number convicted of murder, 9; manslaughter, 4. Total 13
>
> Number of days consumed in trial of murder cases. 116

Number of accounts examined and allowed for actual expenses. 26
Number of orders to pay witnesses. 1,996
Number of marshal's accounts currents examined and approved. 45
Number of other accounts, commissioners', etc., examined and approved. 30
Number of sentences passed upon defendants convicted. 388
Number of civil cases on docket November 1, 1882. 70
Number of cases commenced during the year. 158
Number of civil cases pending between November 1, 1882, and November 1, 1883. 228
Number of civil cases disposed of between November 1, 1882, and November 1, 1883. 92
Number of other orders made during said period in relation to jury, jury commissioners, etc., and entered on record. 3,060
Number of pages of record written and made up during said time. 1,520
Number of days of court held during said year. 291

24. Emmett Dalton, *op. cit.*, p. 54.

25. James Wasson, Joseph Jackson. (See Appendix A, "Chronology of Hangings.")

26. Calvin James, Lincoln Sprole. (See Appendix A, "Chronology of Hangings.")

27. Kit Ross. (See Appendix A, "Chronology of Hangings.")

28. James Lamb, Albert O'Dell, John T. Echols, John Stephens. (See Appendix A, "Chronology of Hangings.")

29. Patrick McCarty. (See Appendix A, "Chronology of Hangings.")

30. Silas Hampton, Seaborn Kalijah. (See Appendix A, "Chronology of Hangings.")

31. Jackson Crow, George Moss, Owen Hill. (See Appendix A, "Chronology of Hangings.")

32. Gus Bogles. (See Appendix A, "Chronology of Hangings.")

33. Richard Smith. (See Appendix A, "Chronology of Hangings.")

34. James Mills, Malachi Allen. (See Appendix A, "Chronology of Hangings.")

35. William Walker, Jack Spaniard. (See Appendix A, "Chronology of Hangings.")

36. Harris Austin, John Billee, Thomas Willis, Jefferson Jones, Sam Goin, Jimmon Burris. (See Appendix A, "Chronology of Hangings.")

37. "The big knot is the secret of a good execution," Maledon once said. "The right way and the humane way to hang a man is to break his neck, not to strangle him to death. It takes a long time to strangle a man to death, and it isn't pretty to look at, for he kicks a good deal. But if you break his neck there are no contortions. He is unconscious the instant the neck breaks, and he hangs motionless. It is a painless death, and as instantaneous as any death can be. . . .

"You put the rope around the neck . . . draw it up just tight enough to touch the skin all around without choking or interfering with the circulation of the blood, and put the big knot right under the left ear . . . so it lies in the hollow back of the jawbone. Then, here's a little secret the most of them don't know: to keep the knot from slipping out of position below the ear, you bring the rope up . . . over the top of the head and let it hang down in a curve on the other side. That holds the knot steady under the ear, and when you spring the trap the man drops through, and when the rope snaps taut that big knot throws his head sidewise and cracks his neck in a jiffy. It always works that way for me. That's why they call me the 'Prince of Hangmen.' " (A. B. MacDonald, *Hands Up!*, pp. 155–156.)

38. Dalton, *op. cit.*, p. 54.

39. Twelve of the seventy-nine executions were performed by Deputy Marshal George Lawson and the remaining seven by various officers attached to the court.

40. Harman, *op. cit.*, p. 44.

41. *Records of the United States District Court for the Western District of Arkansas, 1875–1890.*

CHAPTER VI

1. *Elevator*, January 22, 1886; *ibid.*, June 25, 1886; MacDonald, *op. cit.*, p. 231; Harman, *op. cit.*, pp. 259–260.

2. The popular belief is that after he had spent one year in prison Belle Starr had him pardoned. (MacDonald, *op. cit.*, p. 234; Harman, *op. cit.*, pp. 260–261. Burton Rascoe in his important volume *Belle Starr, The Bandit Queen*, p. 195, claims he was killed in the Indian Territory by an unknown party in July, 1886.) The facts are: Blue Duck served eight and a half years in prison, during which time he developed consumption. Doctors gave him only one month to live, and President Cleveland, in March, 1895, issued a pardon "to permit him to die among friends."

3. Harman, *op. cit.*, p. 558.

4. Rascoe, *op. cit.*, pp. 45–71; Duncan Aikman, *Calamity Jane and the Lady Wildcats*, pp. 158–165; Cameron Rogers, *Gallant Ladies*, pp. 117–144.

5. Rascoe, *op. cit.*, pp. 76–77.

6. Harman, *op. cit.*, p. 559.

7. *Ibid.*, p. 559–562.

8. *Elevator*, February 15, 1889; Rascoe, *op. cit.*, pp. 115–119. Cole Younger always denied his part in the Liberty, Missouri, robbery and claimed that during this year he was in Louisiana and California, as was also Jesse James. (Augustus C. Appler, *The Life, Character and Daring Exploits of the Younger Brothers*, p. 24; William Ward, *The Younger Brothers, the Border Outlaws*, p. 116; Robertus Love, *The Rise and Fall of Jesse James*, pp. 88–92.

9. Appler, *op. cit.*, pp. 273–287.

10. Rascoe, *op. cit.*, pp. 153–154.

11. *Democratic Statesman* (Dallas), April 17, 1874; Rascoe, *op. cit.,* p. 117.

12. Rascoe, *op. cit.,* pp. 156–157; Aikman, *op. cit.,* pp. 178–179.

13. Rascoe, *op. cit.,* pp. 166–167; Aikman, *op. cit.,* p. 181.

14. Owen P. White, *Lead and Likker,* p. 183.

15. Old Tom's brother-in-law was Bill West, the most powerful man in his day in the Cherokee Nation. A blow from his fist was as deadly as a Winchester bullet. With this formidable weapon he killed several men, and a law was passed declaring Bill's fist a deadly weapon. Old Tom and Bill had been close companions, but one day they quarreled over the division of the spoils of a plundering expedition. West struck at Tom, but the wily savage dodged the blow and at the same time deftly placed a long, keen knife blade between the former's ribs. This was the tragic end of Bill West. At this time there was a reward of $2000 offered for West's head, and $5000 for that of Starr. Old Tom was in need of ready cash, and determined to run the risk of losing his own head by trying to collect the reward on that of his brother-in-law. He cut off West's head, put it in a gunny bag, and proceeded to Tahlequah, the capital, where he presented his gory charge to the chief, with the proof that it was the right head, and demanded the reward. The chief and the treasurer both knew Tom's reputation. They also knew that the reward on West's head was only $2000, while that on Tom's was $5000. But Starr was there himself and meant business. At the muzzle of a six-shooter the treasurer forked over the $2000, and old Tom departed with the money to the delight and astonishment of the people of Tahlequah without killing a single person. (*Elevator,* February 27, 1891.)

16. A member of the first sextet hanged by Judge Parker, September 3, 1875. Before he fell through the trap for the murder of William Seabolt, Evans confessed his part in the Grayson robbery.

17. Dallas *Democratic Statesman,* April 7, 1874.

18. Austin *Weekly Democratic Statesman,* April 9, 1874.

19. Dallas *Democratic Statesman,* April 7, 1874.

20. Dallas *Daily Herald,* August 7, 1874.

21. Rascoe, *op. cit.,* pp. 195–198.

22. Lon R. Stansbery, "Cowtown Catoosa, Dark and Bloody Ground of Indian Territory" Tulsa *World,* June 25, 1937.

23. Homer S. Chambers, "Catoosa—Indian Territory Cattle Capital" Tulsa *World,* April 10, 1938.

24. Rascoe, *op. cit.,* pp. 116–117.

25. *New Era,* February 22, 1883; *Indian Journal,* March 22, 1883; *Cherokee Advocate,* March 23, 1883.

26. See Chapter IV.

27. Rascoe, *op. cit.,* pp. 224–229.

28. *Indian Journal,* March 11, 1886.

29. *Indian Chieftain,* February 14, 1889.

30. *Elevator,* February 8, 1889.

31. *Indian Chieftain,* February 14, 1889.
32. *Ibid.*
33. *Elevator,* February 22, 1889.
34. *Indian Chieftain,* March 7, 1889.
35. Affidavit of J. R. Hutchins, Ardmore, Oklahoma, 1950; *Indian Chieftain,* January 30, 1890.

CHAPTER VII
1. *Elevator,* June 10, 1892.
2. *Ibid.*
3. Harman, *op. cit.,* p. 636; Dalton, *op. cit.,* pp. 94–97; Emerson Hough, *The Story of the Outlaw,* pp. 378–379.
4. *Elevator,* May 15, 1891.
5. *Elevator,* September 18, 1891 (This robbery is admitted in Dalton, *op. cit.,* pp. 131–134.)
6. Stillwater *Gazette,* July 22, 1892; Harman, *op. cit.,* p. 637; Hough, *op. cit.,* p. 379; J. A. Newsom, *Life and Practice of the Wild and Modern Indian,* Ch. X, "Going Out of the Outlaws," p. 173.
7. Stillwater *Gazette,* June 10, 1891.
8. Hough, *op. cit.,* p. 380.
Although the identity of raiders was never established, and it has always been the general, though perhaps erroneous, opinion that the Daltons tried their hands bank-robbing at the expense of this little Oklahoma community, in his book p. 102 Dalton states: "Until toward the very end, when we held up some banks, our activities were directed at the express company and its allies. . . ."
9. *Elevator,* May 15, 1891; Harman, *op. cit.,* pp. 633–635; Glenn Shirley, *Six-Gun and Silver Star,* pp. 25–27; Dalton, *op. cit.,* pp. 13–14, 24–25; Hough, *op. cit.,* pp. 475–476; Newsom, *op. cit.,* pp. 157–158; William MacLeod Raine, *Famous Sheriffs and Western Outlaws,* p. 207.
10. Harman, *op. cit.,* p. 635; Dalton, *op. cit.,* p. 41.
11. *Elevator,* May 8, 1891; *Ibid.,* September 18, 1891; Harman, *op. cit.,* pp. 635–636; Hough, *op. cit.,* p. 378.
12. Dalton, *op. cit.,* pp. 69–72.
13. Evett Dumas Nix, *Oklahombres,* p. 44; Harman, *op. cit.,* p. 637; Raine, *op. cit.,* p. 208.
14. *Coffeyville Journal,* October 6, 1892; David Stewart Elliott, *The Last Raid of the Daltons,* pp. 16–42; Harman, *op. cit.,* pp. 637–643; Hough, *op. cit.,* pp. 381–390; Nix, *op. cit.,* pp. 47–51; Newsom, *op. cit.,* pp. 164–167.
15. *Indian Chieftain,* November 10, 1892.
16. Harman, *op. cit.,* p. 664.
17. *Ibid.; Daily Oklahoma State Capital,* January 24, 1894.
18. *Indian Chieftain,* January 11, 1894.
19. *Daily Oklahoma State Capital,* January 24, 1894; *Indian Chieftain,* January 25, 1894.

20. *Indian Journal*, March 22, 1895.

A picturesque account of the siege of the Rogers home is given by Harman, *op. cit.*, pp. 667–673.

CHAPTER VIII

1. *Indian Chieftain*, November 1, 1894.
2. *Ibid.*, January 24, 1895.
3. Harman, *op. cit.*, p. 643.
4. Letter from Bill Cook, U.S. Jail, Fort Smith, Arkansas, March 19, 1895.
5. *Eagle-Gazette*, June 28, 1894.
6. Letter from Cook, *op. cit.;* Harman, *op. cit.*, p. 389.
7. *Eagle-Gazette*, June 28, 1894; Harman, *op. cit.*, pp. 390–391.

Jim Cook was tried in the tribal courts for the slaying of Houston, found guilty of manslaughter, and sentenced to eight years in the Cherokee National Prison. He escaped prison in December, 1896, was recaptured at Muskogee, and was returned to the penitentiary April 6, 1897. *Eagle-Gazette*, November 8, 1894; *Ibid.*, November 29, 1894; El Reno *News*, January 22, 1897; *Indian Chieftain*, April 18, 1897.

8. *Daily Oklahoma*, October 23, 1894.
9. Harman, *op. cit.*, p. 647.
10. *Indian Chieftain*, November 1, 1894; *Daily Oklahoma State Capital*, October 26, 1894; Atoka *Citizen*, November 22, 1894.
11. *Indian Chieftain*, February 28, 1895.
12. *Indian Chieftain*, November 15, 1894.
13. *Eagle-Gazette*, November 22, 1894.
14. *Ibid.*, November 29, 1894; Albert Bigelow Paine, *Captain Bill McDonald, Texas Ranger: A Story of Frontier Reform*, pp. 123–125; Harman, *op. cit.*, p. 648.
15. *Daily Oklahoma State Capital*, January 15, 1895; *ibid.*, January 19, 1895; *Indian Chieftain*, January 17, 1895; Harman, *op. cit.*, pp. 650–652.
16. *Daily Oklahoma*, February 9 and March 29, 1895; *Cherokee Advocate*, February 13, 1895; *Indian Chieftain*, February 14 and April 4, 1895; *Indian Journal*, April 5, 1895; Stansbery, *op. cit.*
17. *Indian Chieftain*, February 14, 1895.
18. *Daily Oklahoman*, March 29, 1895; *Indian Chieftain*, April 4, 1895; *Indian Journal*, April 5, 1895.
19. Harman, *op. cit.*, pp. 387–389; *Eagle-Gazette*, November 29, 1894; *Elevator*, March 20, 1896; Glenn Shirley, *Toughest of Them All*, pp. 131–134.
20. February 1, 1895.
21. *Ibid.*
22. *Indian Journal*, March 1, 1895; *Cherokee Advocate*, March 6, 1895; *Indian Chieftain*, March 7, 1895; Goldsby v United States, 159 U.S. 70.
23. Harman, *op. cit.*, p. 400.
24. *Indian Chieftain*, April 25, 1895.

25. *Ibid.*, May 9, 1895.

26. *Ibid.*, April 25, 1895.

27. *Elevator*, October 21, 1887; March 23, 1888; March 30, 1888; August 3, 1888; August 24, 1888; July 25, 1890.

28. *Indian Journal*, December 5, 1889.

29. Cherokee Bill was the tool to be used in overcoming the guards. The other members of the plot indicted by the grand jury investigating the case were Frank, Ed, and Lou Shelly, George and John Pearce, and Lou Shelly's wife. The Shellys were sent to prison on other charges; the Pearce brothers hanged with Webber Isaacs, April 30, 1896; Andy Critten-den, an important witness, went to the penitentiary; and Mrs. Shelly was released on bond. Finally the government abandoned the case. *Indian Chieftain*, July 18, 1895; September 5, 1895; April 23, 1896.

30. "This 'gobble' was first brought to the attention of Judge Parker's court and the people of Fort Smith when a white man, who was under indictment for assault with intent to kill, was asked why he wished to kill the prosecuting witness, who was an Indian. The prisoner replied that he did not wish to kill, only wanted to disable him, so shot him in the right arm. The court, curious to know the object of the assault, questioned more closely, and was told that he shot because the Indian had 'gobbled at him,' and that meant 'death,' hence when he shot it was self-defense. Judge Parker took sudden interest in what he half suspected was a falsehood, patched up for the occasion, and a dozen more witnesses were brought in who proved conclusively that the Indian's 'gobble' meant sure death to someone within hearing of the uncanny sound; that it was as much a threat to kill as if spoke in so many words." From footnote, 406, Harman, *op. cit.*

31. *Ibid.*, pp. 407–408.

32. The foregoing details of the slaying of Keating and surrender of Cherokee Bill are taken from accounts in the *Indian Chieftain*, August 1, 1895; Stillwater *Gazette*, August 1, 1895; *Elevator*, August 2, 1895; Oklahoma City *Times-Journal*, August 2, 1895; and Harman, *op. cit.*, pp. 404–406.

33. *Indian Chieftain*, August 8, 1895.

34. For the foregoing account of the trial and sentence of Cherokee Bill, I have relied on the following sources: *Indian Chieftain*, August 15 and August 29, 1895; Rogers (Arkansas) *Democrat*, August 10, 1895; *Elevator*, August 16, 1895; Harman, *op. cit.*, pp. 418–430; *Goldsby v United States*, 163 U.S. 688, 16 Sup. Ct. Rep. 1201.

35. Oklahoma City *Times-Journal*, December 4, 1895; *Indian Chieftain*, December 5, 1895; January 16, 1896; *Elevator*, March 20, 1896.

36. March 20, 1896.

37. 163 U.S. 688, 16 Sup. Ct. Rep. 1201.

CHAPTER IX

1. *Op. cit.*

2. Atoka *Independent*, January 25, 1878.

3. *Ibid.*, March 15, 1878.
4. *Indian Chieftain,* October 26, 1883.
5. *U.S. Statutes at Large,* XXII, 383–390.
6. June 5, 1884.
7. *U.S. Statutes at Large,* XXIII, 69–72.
8. Harman, *op. cit.*, p. 50.
9. *U.S. Statutes at Large,* XXIII, 482.
10. Harman, *op. cit.*, p. 50.
11. *Attorney General Report,* 1885, pp. 36–43.
12. *Ibid.*, 1889, p. 10.
13. *Elevator,* July 29, 1887.
Congress had done very little to assist the marshals in performing their duties in the Indian country. Not until more than twoscore of these officers had been killed did "congressional conscience" move this august body to pass an act providing that any person "who shall, in any manner, obstruct, by threats or violence," any agent or police or other officer engaged in the service of the United States in the discharge of his lawful duty within the Indian territory, or "who shall commit . . . murder, manslaughter, assault with intent to murder, assault, or assault and battery . . . against any person who at the time, or at any time previous belonged to either of the classes of officials noted, shall be subject to the laws of the United States relating to such crimes, and . . . to the same penalties as all other persons in said cases." *U.S. Statutes at Large,* XV, 583, an act approved June 9, 1888.
14. Reports from the *Missouri Republican. (Indian Chieftain,* October 26, 1883.)
15. *Congressional Record,* August 16, 1888; also *H.R. Report* 3613, 1888.
16. *U.S. Statutes at Large,* XXV, 655–666.
This act was given to the President for his signature January 25, 1889. Not being returned within the time required under the Constitution, it became a law, February 6, without his approval.
17. Harman, *op. cit.*, pp. 158–159.
18. *Alexander v United States,* 138 U.S. 153, 11 Sup. Ct. Rep. 350; *Elevator,* February 6, 1891.
19. *Lewis v United States,* 146 U.S. 370.
20. *Elevator,* June 1 and 8, 1891.
21. *Hickory v United States,* 151 U.S. 303.
22. *Ibid.*
23. *Hickory v United States,* 160 U.S. 408.
24. *Ibid.*
25. During the seven years from 1889 through November, 1896, a total of fifty criminal appeals were taken to the Supreme Court. Forty-eight were appeals from death sentences taken on writs of error and two were appeals taken by demurrer. Of these forty-eight cases, which held the fate of fifty-two men, thirty-seven were reversed. Before final disposition was made of these thirty-seven, all had been arraigned and come to trial

twice, and four had been tried three times. Out of the original fifty-two sentenced to death, only fifteen were executed. U.S. Reports, 138 to 165.)

CHAPTER X

1. Webber Isaacs, George Pearce, John Pearce. (See Appendix A, "Chronology of Hangings.")

2. *Indian Chieftain*, September 26, 1895; *Elevator*, July 3, 1896.

3. Harman, *op. cit.*, pp. 499–500.

4. *Indian Chieftain*, August 15, 1895; *Daily Oklahoman*, August 31, 1895.

5. Harman, *op. cit.*, p. 503.

6. *Ibid.*, pp. 505–511.

7. *Ibid.*, p. 511.

8. *Ibid.*

9. *Indian Chieftain*, October 3, 1895; *Elevator*, July 3, 1896.

10. *Buck et al. vs United States*, 163 U.S. 678.

CHAPTER XI

1. Glenn Shirley, "He Outrobbed Them All," *True West*, December, 1955; *Indian Chieftain*, December 22, 1892; Harman, *op. cit.*, p. 367; Shawnee *Herald*, March, 1908.

2. *Ibid.*; Zoe A. Tilghman, *Outlaw Days*, p. 124.

3. Shawnee *Herald*, *op. cit.*

4. *Indian Chieftain*, December 15, 1892.

5. *Ibid.*

6. Harman, *op. cit.*, p. 371.

7. *Indian Chieftain*, December 15, 1892.

8. *Starr v United States*, 153 U.S. 614, 14 Sup. Ct. 919.

9. Shawnee *Herald*, March 18, 1908.

10. *Elevator*, January 27, 1893.

11. Other members were Lin Cumplin, Happy Jack, Bud Tyler, and Frank Cheney. Cumplin went to Alaska, where he attempted to hold up an express messenger and was slain. Happy Jack was killed a few months after the Bentonville robbery and Frank Cheney shot a year later by marshals in the Indian Territory. Bud Tyler died in bed from his wounds "with his boots off."

12. *Elevator*, July 7, 1893. (See also *Indian Chieftain*, July 6, 1893; Harman, *op. cit.*, pp. 365–366.)

13. *Indian Chieftain*, July 27, 1893.

14. *Starr v. United States*, 153 U.S. 614, 14 Sup. Ct. 919.

15. *Ibid.*

16. *Elevator*, November 10, 1893.

17. *Starr v United States*, 153 U.S. 614, 14 Sup. Ct. 919.

18. *Indian Chieftain*, September 19, 1895.

19. *Starr v United States*, 164 U.S. 627, 17 Sup. Ct. 223.

20. *Ibid.*

21. U.S. Reports, 138–165; especially *Smith v United States,* 151 U.S. 50, 14 Sup. Ct. 234; *Alberty v United States,* 162 U.S. 499, 16 Sup. Ct. 864; *Lucas v United States,* 163 U.S. 612, 16 Sup. Ct. 1168; *Indian Chieftain,* February 20, 1896.

22. *Ibid.* (U.S. Reports).

23. 150 U.S. 442, 14 Sup. Ct. 144.

24. 146 U.S. 370.

25. 162 U.S. 625, 16 Sup. Ct. 952.

26. *Brown v United States,* 164 U.S. 221, 17 Sup. Ct. 33.

27. 159 U.S. 489, 16 Sup. Ct. 51.

28. 232 U.S. 642.

29. In Oklahoma today flight is a circumstance tending to prove guilt, and it has been so held in many cases. *Quinn v. State,* 55 Okla. Cri. 116, 25 P. 2d 711; *Pittman v State,* 8 Okla. Cri. 58, 126 P. 696; *Wettengel v State,* 30 Okla. Cri. 388, 236 P. 626.

30. Harry P. Daily, *op. cit.*

31. William F. Semple, "Isaac C. Parker, Judge of the United States Court," *The Journal,* Oklahoma Bar Association, August 25, 1951.

32. In March, 1898, Henry Starr pleaded guilty to manslaughter and was sentenced to five years in prison at Columbus. Pending his third trial, he was also convicted of three robberies, receiving an additional ten years. Through the influence of his mother, and on his promise to reform, he was pardoned by President Theodore Roosevelt. He married, entered the real estate business in Tulsa, and prospered five years. On the morning of March 27, 1915, he led a gang of men he had recruited in an attempt to rob two banks at Stroud, Oklahoma. The gang was routed and later captured, and Starr himself badly wounded and captured by a fourteen-year-old youth, Paul Curry. Starr pleaded guilty and was sentenced to the Oklahoma State Penitentiary for twenty-five years. He was paroled again in 1919 and managed to keep at liberty until 1921. On February 22 he was shot and killed while robbing the People's National Bank in the little Ozark village of Harrison, Arkansas. *Daily Oklahoman,* March 29–31, 1915; *Ibid.,* February 23, 1921; Records of the Oklahoma State Penitentiary, McAlester, Oklahoma; also Harman, *op. cit.,* p. 365; Tilghman, *op. cit.,* pp. 126–127.

33. *Elevator,* February 21, 1896.

34. *Ibid.,* May 8, 1896.

35. *Davenport v United States,* 163 U.S. 682, 16 Sup. Ct. 1200; *Luckey v United States,* 163 U.S. 692, 16 Sup. Ct. 1203; *Thornton v United States,* 163 U.S. 707, 16 Sup. Ct. 1207; *King et al. v United States,* 164 U.S. 701, 17 Sup. Ct. 995; *Dyer v United States,* 164 U.S. 704, 17 Sup. Ct. 993.

36. One old man followed the murderer of his son for months from the Indian Territory to the Rocky Mountains; and when he finally overtook the killer, he arrested him, securely fastened him to his own body with rivets and chains, and brought him back to Judge Parker's court, where he listened to the trial and witnessed the execution.

37. In March, 1896, the women of northern Texas sent a signed petition to President Cleveland, Secretary Hoke Smith, and Congress, calling attention to robberies and crimes committed by outlaws from the Indian territory.

38. Harman, *op. cit.*, p. 60.

39. *U.S. Statutes at Large*, XXV, chap. 333, Sec. I.

40. *Ibid.*, XXVI, p. 720.

41. *Ibid.*, XXVII, p. 12.

42. Harman, *op. cit.*, p. 60.

43. *U.S. Statutes at Large*, XXVIII, 693.

By an act approved June 7, 1897, Indian courts were abolished, and after January 1, 1898, the United States courts in the Indian Territory had original, exclusive jurisdiction over all civil and criminal cases and all persons irrespective of race. *U.S. Statutes at Large*, XXX, 83.)

44. See Appendix D, "The Famous Grand Jury Charge."

45. *Elevator*, May 8, 1896.

46. *Ibid.*, February 8, 1895.

CHAPTER XII

1. *Wilson v United States*, 162 U.S. 613, 16 Sup. Ct. 895; *Elevator*, December 20, 1895; *ibid.*, July 31, 1896.

2. *Records of the United States District Court for the Western District of Arkansas*, 1875–1896.

3. Harry P. Daily, *op. cit.*

4. "A Word for Judge Parker," *Elevator*, May 29, 1896.

5. *Ibid.*, March 2, 1894.

6. *Ibid.*, May 29, 1896.

7. Helen Hunt Jackson, *A Century of Dishonor*, p. 30.

8. Harry P. Daily, *op. cit.*

9. *Elevator*, September 18, 1896; Jackson, *op. cit.*, p. 296.

10. Attorney General Report, 1893, pp. 20–21.

11. *Eagle-Gazette*, November 28, 1894.

12. *Oklahoma Star*, November 2, 1876; Atoka *Independent*, January 25, 1878.

13. *Elevator*, May 11, 1894.

14. Parker's family Bible (in possession of Mrs. Kate Bailey Parker, Fort Smith, Arkansas).

15. Harman, *op. cit.*, pp. 100–101.

BIBLIOGRAPHY

BIBLIOGRAPHY

Aikman, Duncan. *Calamity Jane and the Lady Wildcats.* Henry Holt and Company, New York, 1927.

Allsopp, Fred W. *Folklore of Romantic Arkansas,* Vol. I. The Grolier Society, 1931.

Anderson, LaVere Schoenfelt. "A Hill Perpetuates Belle Starr's Memory," Tulsa *World,* August 20, 1933.

Appler, Augustus C. *The Life, Character and Daring Exploits of the Younger Brothers.* G. E. Wilson, Chicago, 1875.

Arkansas Gazette, January, 1860; November, 1896.

Atoka *Independent,* 1877; 1878.

Atoka *Indian Champion,* 1884; 1885.

Atoka *Indian Citizen,* 1889; 1899.

Atoka *Vindicator,* 1872–1876.

Attorney General Reports, 1877–1896.

Barde, Frederick S. "The Story of Belle Starr." *Sturm's Oklahoma Magazine,* Vol. XI, No. 1, September, 1910.

Beadle, J. H. *The Undeveloped West; or, Five Years in the Territories.* National Publishing Company, Philadelphia, 1873.

————. *Western Wilds and the Men Who Redeem Them.* Jones Brothers and Company, Cincinnati, 1877.

Benson, Henry C. *Life Among the Choctaw Indians and Sketches of the Southwest.* Cincinnati, 1860.

Biscup, Walter. "Dashing Belle Starr Was Called 'Lily of the Cimarron.' " *The American Indian,* Vol. 1, No. 4, January, 1927.

————. "The Notorious Belle Starr Died With Her Boots On." *The American Indian,* Vol. 1, No. 5, February, 1927.

Boder, Bartlett. "Belle Starr and Her Times." *Museum Graphic,* Vol. V, No. II. Spring, 1953.

Booker, Anton S. *Wildcats in Petticoats.* E. Haldeman-Julius Girard, Kansas, 1945.

Botkin, B. A. (editor). *A Treasury of Western Folklore.* Crown Publishers, Inc., New York, 1951.

Buel, J. W. *The Border Outlaws.* Sun Publishing Company, St. Louis, 1882.

Cantonwine, Alexander. *Star Forty-Six, Oklahoma.* Pythian Times Publishing Company, Oklahoma City, 1911.

Chambers, Homer S. "Catoosa—Indian Territory Cattle Capital." Tulsa *World,* April 10, 1938.

Chandler, Robert P. "Last Man to Die by Creek Law." Tulsa *World,* February 10, 1946.

Cherokee Advocate, 1874; 1876; 1877–1883; 1894.

Coffeyville *Journal,* October, 1892.

Common Law Records, United States District Court for the Western District of Arkansas.

Congressional Record, Vol. 19, August 16, 1888.

Conkling, Roscoe P. and Conkling, Margaret B. *The Butterfield Overland Mail,* 1857–1869, Vol. I. The Arthur H. Clark Company, Glendale, California, 1947.

Cox, James. *My Native Land.* Blair Publishing Company, Philadelphia, 1903.

Croy, Homer. *He Hanged Them High.* Duell, Sloan & Pearce, Inc.–Little, Brown & Co., New York and Boston, 1952.

Dacus, Hon. J. A. *Life and Adventures of Frank and Jesse James, the Noted Western Outlaws.* N. D. Thompson and Company, St. Louis, 1880.

Daily, Harry P. "Judge Isaac C. Parker." An address at the thirty-fifth annual meeting (1932) of the Bar Association of Arkansas. *The Chronicles of Oklahoma,* Vol. XI, No. 1, March, 1933.

Daily Oklahoma State Capital, Guthrie, Okla., 1894; January–March, 1895.

Daily Oklahoman, Okla. City, Okla., October, 1894; January–March, 1903; March, 1906; March, 1915; June, 1918; March, 1920; February–August, 1921; June–October, 1928.

Dale, Edward Everett. *Cow Country.* University of Oklahoma Press, Norman, 1945.

——— and Lytton, Gaston. *Cherokee Cavaliers.* University of Oklahoma Press, Norman, 1939.

Dallas *Daily Herald,* August, 1874.

Dalton, Emmett. "Beyond the Law. First True Account of the Exploits of the World's Most Noted Outlaws." *The Wide World Magazine,* May–September, 1918.

Dalton, Emmett (in collaboration with Jack Jungmeyer). *When The Daltons Rode.* Doubleday, Doran & Company, Inc., Garden City & New York, 1931.

"The Dalton Gang of Outlaws." *Frontier Times,* Vol. 28, No. 8, May, 1951.

Davis, Clyde Brion. *The Arkansas.* Farrar & Rinehart, Inc., New York, 1940.

Dawes, Anna L. *Lend a Hand.* Indian Rights Association, Philadelphia, 1886.

Debo, Angie. *And Still the Waters Run.* Princeton University Press, Princeton, 1940.

———. *The Rise and Fall of the Choctaw Republic.* University of Oklahoma Press, Norman, 1934.

———. *Tulsa: From Creek Town to Oil Capital.* University of Oklahoma Press, Norman, 1943.

Democratic Statesman, April, 1874.

Documents in re Indian Territory in the United States Court at Fort Smith, Arkansas, Vols. 1–2. Phillips Collection, University Library, Norman, Oklahoma.

Donald, Jay. *Outlaws of the Border.* Forsee and McMakin, Cincinnati, 1882.

Douglas, Clarence B. *History of Tulsa, Oklahoma,* Vol. I. The S. J. Clarke Publishing Company, Chicago, 1921.

Draper, Wm. R. *A Cub Reporter in the Old Indian Territory.* E. Haldeman-Julius Girard, Kansas, 1946.

Duke, Thomas S. *Celebrated Criminal Cases of America.* The James H. Barry Company, San Francisco, 1910.

Eagle-Gazette, January–November, 1894; February, 1895.

Eaton, Frank. *Pistol Pete, Veteran of the Old West.* Little, Brown & Co., Boston, 1952.

El Reno *News,* January, 1897.

Elliott, David Stewart. *Last Raid of the Daltons.* Coffeyville *Daily Journal,* Coffeyville, Kansas, October 22, 1892.

Fanning, Pete. *Crimes of the Great West.* Privately printed, San Francisco, 1929.

Foreman, Carolyn Thomas. "Mashalltown, Creek Nation." *The Chronicles of Oklahoma,* Vol. XXXII, No. 1, Spring, 1954.

Foreman, Grant. "A Century of Prohibition." *The Chronicles of Oklahoma,* Vol. XII, No. 2, June, 1934.

————. *Advancing the Frontier.* University of Oklahoma Press, Norman, 1933.

————. *The Five Civilized Tribes.* University of Oklahoma Press, Norman, 1934.

————. *Fort Gibson.* ("Historic Oklahoma Series," Number 1.) University of Oklahoma Press, Norman, 1936.

————. *A History of Oklahoma.* University of Oklahoma Press, Norman, 1942.

————. *Muskogee: The Biography of an Oklahoma Town.* University of Oklahoma Press, Norman, 1943.

————. "Oklahoma's First Court." *The Chronicles of Oklahoma,* Vol. XIII, No. 4, December, 1935.

Fort Smith *Elevator,* 1878, and complete issues January, 1885–June, 1900.

The Fort Smith National Cemetery. History of the United States National Cemetery and Military Occupation of Fort Smith, Arkansas, n. p., n. d. Prepared under the direction of the Quartermaster General, U. S. Army.

Fort Smith *New Era,* May, 1873; 1875; February, 1883.

Fort Smith *Western Independent,* August, 1873; April, 1875; April, 1876; 1878; 1888.

Gard, Wayne. *Frontier Justice.* University of Oklahoma Press, Norman, 1949.

Gish, Anthony. *American Bandits.* E. Haldeman-Julius Girard, Kansas, 1938.

Gittinger, Roy. *The Formation of the State of Oklahoma.* University of Oklahoma Press, Norman, 1939.

Glasscock, C. B. *Bandits of the Southern Pacific.* Frederick A. Stokes Company, New York, 1929.

Graves, Richard S. *Oklahoma Outlaws*. State Printing and Publishing Company, Oklahoma City, 1915.

Gray, James R. "Last Choctaw Execution." Tulsa *World,* September 17, 1950.

Handbook of Fort Smith and Sebastian County, Arkansas. C. S. Burch Publishing Company, Chicago, 1887.

Harlow, Victor E. *Oklahoma*. Harlow Publishing Co., Oklahoma City, 1934.

Harrington, Fred Harvey. *Hanging Judge*. The Caxton Printers, Ltd., Caldwell, Idaho, 1951.

Harman, S. W. *Hell on the Border*. Phoenix Publishing Company, Fort Smith, Arkansas, 1898.

Hempstead, Fay. *Historical Review of Arkansas*. Lewis Publishing Company, Chicago, 1911.

———. *Pictorial History of Arkansas*. N. B. Thompson Publishing Company, St. Louis, 1890.

Hendricks, George D. *The Bad-Man of the West*. Naylor Co., San Antonio, 1941.

Herndon, Dallas T. *Centennial History of Arkansas,* Vol. I. The S. J. Clarke Publishing Company, Chicago, 1922.

———. *The High Lights of Arkansas History*. Arkansas History Commission, Little Rock, 1922.

Hough, Emerson. *The Story of the Outlaw*. The Outing Publishing Company, New York, 1907.

House of Representatives Report 3613, Fiftieth Congress, 1888.

Hunter, J. Marvin and Rose, N. H. *The Album of Gunfighters*. Hunter and Rose, Publishers, San Antonio, 1951.

Indian Journal, 1876–1883; 1886–1895.

Indian-Pioneer History (Grant Foreman Papers), Vols. 1–113.

Indian Progress, February, 1875.

Jackson, H. H. *A Century of Dishonor*. Harper & Brothers, New York, 1881.

Jones, W. F. *The Experiences of a Deputy U. S. Marshal of the Indian Territory,* n. p., Tulsa, 1937.

Lamb, Arthur H. *Tragedies of the Osage Hills*. Osage Printery, Pawhuska, Oklahoma, n. d.

Laws of the United States, Vols. IX, XIX.

Lawson, W. B. *The Indian Outlaw, or Hank Starr, the Log Cabin Bandit*. Frank T. Fries, Orville, Ohio, n.d.

Lester, D. C. "Belle Starr, Oklahoma's Woman Outlaw." *Daily Oklahoman,* August 21, 1921.

The Life of Texas Jack (Nathaniel Reed) By Himself. Tulsa Printing Company, (c. 1936).

"Lookout Tower on Bald Hill." Tulsa *World,* February 3, 1936.

Love, Robertus. *The Rise and Fall of Jesse James.* G. P. Putnam's Sons, New York, 1926.

MacDonald, A. B. "Fill Your Hand." *The Saturday Evening Post,* Vol. 198, No. 41, April 10, 1926.

————. *Hands Up! Stories of Six-Gun Fighters of the Old West.* The Bobbs-Merrill Company, Inc., Indianapolis, 1927.

Meserve, John Bartlett. "From Parker to Poe, Being a Brief Sketch of the Early Judiciary of Tulsa County." *The Chronicles of Oklahoma,* Vol. XVI, No. 1, March, 1938.

Morris, Lerona Rosamond. *Oklahoma—Yesterday, Today, Tomorrow.* Co-Operative Publishing Company, Guthrie, Oklahoma, 1930.

Morrison, James D. "Problems in the Industrial Progress and Development of the Choctaw Nation, 1865–1907." *The Chronicles of Oklahoma,* Vol. XXXII, No. 1, Spring, 1954.

Morrison, William Brown. *Military Posts and Camps in Oklahoma.* Harlow Publishing Corp., Oklahoma City, 1936.

Mumey, Nolie. "Belle of the Ozarks—1846–1889." *Frontier Times,* Vol. 29, No. 8, May, 1952.

"The Murder on Turkey Creek." *The Chronicles of Oklahoma,* Vol. XII, No. 3, September, 1934.

Murphy, James Oakley. "The Work of Judge Parker in the United States District Court for the Western District of Arkansas—1875–1896." Unpublished thesis, Phillips Collection, University Library, Norman, Oklahoma.

Neville, A. W. *The Red River Valley, Then and Now.* North Texas Publishing Company, Paris, Texas, 1948.

Newson, J. A. *Life and Practice of the Wild and Modern Indian: The Early Days of Oklahoma.* Harlow Publishing Co., Oklahoma City, 1923.

Nix, Evett Dumas. *Oklahombres.* Eden Publishing House, St. Louis and Chicago, 1929.

Nye, Captain W. S. *Carbine and Lance.* University of Oklahoma Press, Norman, 1937.

Oklahoma City *Times-Journal,* August–December, 1895.

Oklahoma Criminal Reports, Vols. 8, 30, 55.

Oklahoma Star, November, 1874; November, 1875; November, 1876.

Otis, Elwell S. *The Indian Question.* Sheldon and Company, New York, 1878.

Paine, Albert Bigelow. *Captain Bill McDonald, Texas Ranger.* J. J. Little & Ives Company, Inc., New York, 1909.

Patton, Fred J. *History of Fort Smith, Arkansas.* Chamber of Commerce, Fort Smith, n.d.

Payne, Ransom. *The Dalton Brothers and Their Astounding Career of Crime.* Laird and Lee, Chicago, 1892.

Preece, Harold. *Living Pioneers.* The World Publishing Company, Cleveland and New York, 1952.

Raine, William MacLeod. *Famous Sheriffs and Western Outlaws.* Doubleday, Doran & Company, Inc. Garden City & New York, 1929.

Rascoe, Burton. *Belle Starr, the Bandit Queen.* Random House, New York, 1941.

Records of the United States District Court for the Western District of Arkansas, 1872–1896.

Reports of the Commissioner of Indian Affairs, 1865; 1867; 1868; 1869.

Revised Statutes, Forty-third Congress, 1873–1874.

Reynolds, John H. "Municipal Offices." Arkansas Historical Association, I.

Rister, Carl Coke. *Land Hunger.* University of Oklahoma Press, Norman, 1942.

Rogers *Democrat,* August, 1895; March–September, 1896.

Rogers, Cameron. *Gallant Ladies.* Harcourt, Brace & Co., New York, 1928.

Rogers, John William. *The Lusty Texans of Dallas.* E. P. Dutton & Co., Inc., New York, 1951.

Rucker, Alvin. "When Banditry Was in Flower." *Daily Oklahoman,* February 11, 1932.

Russell, James Lewis. *Behind These Ozark Hills.* The Hobson Book Press, New York, 1947.

Semple, William F. "Isaac C. Parker, Judge of the United States Court." *The Journal* (publication of the Oklahoma Bar Association), Vol. 22, No. 30, August 25, 1951.

Shackleford, William Yancey. *Belle Starr, the Bandit Queen.* E. Haldeman-Julius Girard, Kansas, 1943.

Shawnee *Herald,* March, 1908.

Shirley, Glenn. "He Outrobbed Them All." *True West,* December, 1955.

———. "Outlaw Queen." *True West,* Vol. 1, No. 2, Fall, 1953.

———. *Six-Gun and Silver Star.* University of New Mexico Press, Albuquerque, 1955.

332— BIBLIOGRAPHY

———. *Toughest of Them All*. University of New Mexico Press, Albuquerque, 1953.

Smith, Wallace. *Prodigal Sons*. The Christopher Publishing House, Boston, 1951.

Speer, William S. (editor). *The Encyclopedia of the New West*. United States Biographical Publishing Company, Marshall, Texas, 1881.

Stansbery, Lon R. "Cowtown Catoosa, Dark and Bloody Ground of Indian Territory." Tulsa *World*, June 25, 1937.

Starkey, Marion L. *The Cherokee Nation*. Alfred A. Knopf, Inc., New York, 1946.

St. Louis *Globe-Democrat*, 1896.

St. Louis *Republic*, 1896.

Stillwater *Gazette*, June, 1891; July, 1892; August, 1895.

Supreme Court Reports, Vols. 8, 10, 11, 16, 17.

Thoburn, Joseph B. and Wright, Muriel H. *Oklahoma: A History of the State and Its People*, Vols. I–II. Lewis Historical Publishing Company, New York, 1929.

———. *A Standard History of Oklahoma*, Vols. I–II. The American Historical Society, Chicago and New York, 1916.

Thompson, William P. "Courts of the Cherokee Nation." *The Chronicles of Oklahoma*, Vol. II, No. 1, March, 1923.

Thrilling Events, Life of Henry Starr. Written in the Colorado Penitentiary by Himself. "Published July, 1914, and sold by R. D. Gordon, Tulsa, Oklahoma."

Tilghman, Zoe A. *Outlaw Days*. Harlow Publishing Corp., Oklahoma City, 1926.

United States Reports, Vols. 135, 138, 142, 146, 150, 151, 153, 157, 158, 159, 160, 161, 162, 163, 164, 165.

U. S. Statutes at Large, Vols. V, VI, IX, X, XIV, XV, XVI, XXII, XXIII, XXV, XXVI, XXVII, XXVIII, XXX.

VanTramp, John C. *Prairie and Rocky Mountain Adventures*. Segner and Condit, Columbus, 1867.

Vinita *Indian Chieftain*, January, 1877, and complete issues January, 1884–December, 1892; November, 1896; 1897.

Ward, William. *The Dalton Gang, the Bandits of the Far West*. Westbrook, Cleveland, n.d.

Weekly Democratic Statesman, April, 1874.

"When There Was No God West of Fort Smith: Judge Isaac Parker's Court, Its Rise and Fall." (3 Parts) *Daily Oklahoman*, October 21, 28, and November 4, 1928.

White, Owen P. *Lead and Likker*. Minton, Balch and Company, New York, 1932.

Wilson, Neill C. and Taylor, Frank J. *Southern Pacific*. McGraw-Hill Book Company, Inc., New York, London, and Toronto, 1952.

Wright, Muriel H. *The Story of Oklahoma*. Webb Publishing Company, Oklahoma City, 1930.